The Shell
and
the Kernel

The Shell

Renewals of

and

Psychoanalysis

the Kernel

Volume I

Nicolas Abraham
and
Maria Torok

Edited, Translated, and with
an Introduction by
Nicholas T. Rand

The University of Chicago Press/Chicago & London

The University of Chicago Press, Chicago 60637
The University of Chicago Press, Ltd., London
© 1994 by The University of Chicago
All rights reserved. Published 1994
Printed in the United States of America
03 02 01 00 99 98 97 96 95 94   1 2 3 4 5

ISBN: 0-226-00087-7 (cloth)
        0-226-00088-5 (paper)

Much of this book originally appeared in *L'écorce et le noyau,*
© Flammarion 1987. This translation has been published with the
support of the Ministère Français de la Culture et de la Communication.

Library of Congress Cataloging-in-Publication Data

Abraham, Nicolas.
    [Ecorce et le noyau. English]
    The shell and the kernel: renewals of psychoanalysis / Nicolas
Abraham and Maria Torok; edited, translated, and with an
introduction by Nicholas T. Rand.
        p.   cm.
    Includes bibliographical references and index.
    1. Psychoanalysis.   2. Freud, Sigmund 1856–1939.   I. Torok, Maria.
II. Rand, Nicholas T. (Nicholas Thomas) III. Title.
BF173.A3313   1994
150.19'5—dc20   93-47621
                                                                      CIP

⊗ The paper used in this publication meets the minimum requirements of the American
National Standard for Information Sciences—Permanence of Paper for Printed Library
Materials, ANSI Z39.48-1984.

Contents

VII PSYCHOANALYTIC COMMUNION

Acknowledgments

First and foremost, I want to thank Alan G. Thomas, my editor at the University of Chicago Press, whose sagacity and clear vision of the importance as well as the mechanics of this project have helped steer it toward completion. In addition, the high standards of the entire staff of the University of Chicago Press have been inspiring. Professor Françoise Meltzer of the University of Chicago receives my warmest acknowledgment for her instrumental support of this American edition of *The Shell and the Kernel.*

Truly special thanks are due my friend Professor Marian Rothstein of Carthage College, who has read—and reread—every translation and Editor's Note, and the General Introduction, improving the quality of my work at every turn. Many other friends and colleagues, among them Andrew Bush, Gail Dreyfuss, Douglas Kelly, Mathew Kramer, Elaine Marks, Yvonne Ozzello, Esther Rashkin, and Ivan Soll, have to various degrees contributed to the success of this work. Without the able assistance of typists Sue Grass-Richards and Amy F. Scarr, and especially the warm competence of Sandra Ellis, this book would not have seen the light of day. My gratitude goes to the Graduate School of the University of Wisconsin–Madison for its generous and repeated financial support of the project.

Nicholas Rand

Note on the Translation

All translations either have been expressly prepared for this volume or are revisions of my previously published versions. Chapters 2 and 5 had been translated by unidentified hands; those versions were not used but have been acknowledged. Minor changes have been introduced in the text at Maria Torok's request, including changes in wording and the addition or removal of paragraph breaks. Whenever the changes are substantial enough to warrant the reader's notice, they are footnoted. Except for chapter 2, bracketed information in the text and footnotes has been added by the editor.

Introduction: Renewals of Psychoanalysis

Nicholas T. Rand

In *The Shell and the Kernel* Nicolas Abraham and Maria Torok outline a form of psychoanalysis that insists on the particularity of any individual's life story, the specificity of texts, and the singularity of historical situations. A cohesive collection of essays written over two decades, and ranging from psychoanalysis to literary criticism and philosophy, the work presents not a doctrine but rather a cluster of insights open to further development and discovery on the part of readers. A first approximation of the book's spirit would be to picture two people in unceasing intellectual and emotional exchange, intent on illuminating yet more aspects of human suffering, on exploring ever more avenues of sympathetic understanding, even as they struggle, sometimes unwittingly, to shake off the various theories handed down to them. The crux of the book's philosophy may be formulated simply. Theories need to be abandoned or revamped if inconsistent with the actual life experience of patients or the facts of a text. In Abraham and Torok's view, attempting to analyze a person in the light of predetermined ideas (such as theories of repressed incestuous wishes or fear of the castrating father) runs the risk of condemning the person's genuine suffering to eternal silence.

The authors of this book emigrated separately from Hungary to

France in the late 1930s and 1940s respectively. Nicolas Abraham (1919–75) took a degree at the Sorbonne in philosophy, and Maria Torok (b. 1925) studied psychology. As a guest member of the Centre National de la Recherche Scientifique in the 1950s, Abraham undertook projects in the phenomenology of poetics and the theory of translation while completing his training as an analyst.[1] Torok worked as a psychologist in Family and Children's Service agencies before becoming an analyst. Both gained membership in the Paris Psychoanalytic Society (a chapter of the International Psychoanalytic Association) and practiced clinical psychoanalysis from 1956 on. Upon Abraham's death in 1975, Torok assumed general editorship of their common writings and continues to work as an analyst and as a consultant to other analysts throughout Europe.

To date, the works of Abraham and Torok collected in French are *Cryptonymie: Le Verbier de l'Homme aux Loups* (Paris: Aubier-Flammarion, 1976), with an introduction, "Fors," by Jacques Derrida; *L'Ecorce et le noyau* (Paris: Aubier-Flammarion, 1978, 1987); *Jonas* (Paris: Aubier-Flammarion, 1981); and *Rythmes: De l'oeuvre, de la traduction et de la psychanalyse* (Paris: Flammarion, 1985), with an afterword, "Paradictique," by Rand and Torok. *Cryptonymie* has been translated into English as *The Wolf Man's Magic Word: A Cryptonymy* (Minneapolis: University of Minnesota Press, 1986); excerpts from *L'Ecorce* and *Rythmes* have appeared in several English-language journals; and a complete translation of *Rythmes* is forthcoming from Stanford University Press. The bulk of *Jonas* will appear in volume 2 of the present edition of *The Shell and the Kernel*. An additional French volume of Abraham's unpublished papers, case studies, and notes is planned. This English edition of *The Shell and the Kernel* departs from the French edition in several ways. An explanatory subtitle, *Renewals of Psychoanalysis,* has been added, and the work has been divided into two volumes because of its length. Four uncollected essays by Torok have been added to volume 1, and similar additions of recent essays by Torok will be made to volume 2. In the spirit of the French edition, the essays appear in thematic groupings, though also following a roughly chronological order. Each part carries a theoretically oriented Editor's Note explaining the essays' conceptual place in Abraham and Torok's work.

Most of the essays in volume 1 are based directly on the authors' clinical findings. Part 1 presents Torok's previously unpublished essay on

1. Some of the essays Abraham completed during this period are either included in the posthumous collection *Rythmes*, edited by N. Rand and M. Torok (Paris: Flammarion, 1985), or discussed in the editors' "Afterword" to that volume; in English see N. Rand and M. Torok, "Paradeictic: Translation, Psychoanalysis, and the Work of Art in the Writings of Nicolas Abraham," *Diacritics* 16, no. 3 (1986): 16–25.

fantasy, an essay which characteristically bridges the methodologies of Husserlian phenomenology and Freudian psychoanalysis. Part 2 features Torok's classic essay on the meaning of penis envy in women, proposing fundamental methodological revisions for the clinician as well as the feminist scholar in literature and the social sciences. Part 3 contains Abraham's assessment of the scope and originality of Freudian psychoanalysis as he develops his concept of anasemia; the methodological centrality of this concept determined Torok's choice of the essay's title, "The Shell and the Kernel," for the entire collection. The essays in part 3, all of which are devoted to Abraham and Torok's theory of secrets and multiple secret "identities," offer insight into the nature of melancholia, manic-depressive psychosis, the neurosis of failure, and psychosomatic illness as well as into the mechanisms of concealment in language and texts. Part 5 presents one of Abraham and Torok's most original concepts, the idea of transgenerational haunting. This theory of the phantom, as the authors call it, advances the clinical understanding of phobia and obsessional behavior while providing a perspective from which to analyze political motives, social movements, and ideological currents as well as enigmas in literature (explored through Abraham's simultaneously literary and psychoanalytic sequel to Shakespeare's *Hamlet*). Parts 6 and 7 comprise work on the issues and methods involved in studying psychoanalytic discourse and Torok's argument for the necessity of psychoanalyzing Freud. The volume concludes with Torok's conception of the psychoanalytic dialogue.

While most of the essays in volume 1 develop psychoanalytic theory on the basis of clinical discoveries, volume 2 delineates the underlying conceptual framework. Part 1 of volume 2 presents Abraham's theory of disasters or trauma, a methodological blueprint for conducting fundamental interdisciplinary research in philosophy, biology, sociology, and clinical psychoanalysis. The concepts of symbol and symbolic operation, developed through a combination of Husserlian phenomenology and Freudianism, implicitly guide all of Abraham and Torok's investigations. Part 2 outlines the project of a psychoanalytic esthetics, and part 3 studies the problem of self-making and sexuality in both the clinical and literary realms. There a commentary on the story of the prophet Jonah extends Abraham's vision of a psychoanalytic esthetics. Part 4 features essays on the concept of dual unity, providing a vantage from which to consider mother-child relationships, child analysis, family therapy, and the interaction of characters in fiction. This part outlines a unified theory of human development, social organization, and language. Part 5 shows the authors' approach to the history of psychoanalysis, with particular reference to the Freud-Ferenczi letters and the work of Melanie Klein.

Abraham and Torok did not write *The Shell and the Kernel* as a book; it represents their work as it evolved over fifteen years (or, counting the addition of Torok's more recent essays, nearly a quarter of a century). In the headnotes to each part, I point out relationships among essays that only become manifest when set in the larger context of the authors' *oeuvre* as it stands today. Later in this Introduction, I will take up at length one general area of thought that is of central importance in appreciating the shape, motives, and contexts of the psychoanalytic renewal before us. (Readers should know that I am not a neutral observer. For the past fifteen years I have been collaborating with Maria Torok on projects ranging from the posthumous edition in French of Abraham's works to the critical study of Freudian psychoanalysis, the latter inspired in part by the perspectives developed in *The Shell and the Kernel*.[2] In addition, I have investigated and attempted to further the relevance of Abraham and Torok's ideas for the analysis of literature and philosophy.[3] By now I see myself as a continuer rather than as a student and disseminator of their work.) The editorial apparatus thus allows the reader to choose among several points of entry to Abraham and Torok's work. The Editor's Notes stay close to the stuff of individual essays, while the Introduction is intended to create the broad vision of a hypothetical unity and to show the fundamental lines of coherence that Abraham and Torok's essays implicitly harbor, which the authors would undoubtedly have conveyed explicitly had the work been projected from the start as a continuous whole.

The broadest aim of *The Shell and the Kernel* is to restore the lines of communication with those intimate recesses of the mind that have for one reason or another been denied expression. As this aim implies, Abraham and Torok ardently advocate the methods of psychoanalysis even as they resist the universalist tendencies of some psychoanalytic theory. Their position is therefore paradoxical. They undertake a highly effective if

2. See our most recent articles, "Questions to Freudian Psychoanalysis: Dream Interpretation, Reality, Fantasy," *Critical Inquiry* 19, no. 3 (1993): 567–94; and *"The Sandman Looks at The Uncanny,"* in *Speculations after Freud: Psychoanalysis, Philosophy, Culture,* edited by Michael Münchow and Sonu Samdashani (London: Routledge, 1994). See also our coedited special issues of the interdisciplinary journal *Cahiers Confrontation,* nos. 8, 12, 14 (1982, 1984, 1987). Other aspects of my collaboration with Torok become manifest in the Editor's Notes to each part.

3. See N. Rand, *Le cryptage et la vie des oeuvres: Du secret dans les textes de Flaubert, Stendhal, Walter Benjamin, Baudelaire, Stefan George, Edgar Poe, Francis Ponge, Heidegger et Freud* (Paris: Aubier, 1989); idem, "Family Romance or Family History? Psychoanalysis and Dramatic Invention in Nicholas Abraham's *The Phantom of Hamlet,*" *Diacritics* 18, no. 4 (1988): 20–30; and idem, "Translator's Introduction: Toward a Cryptonymy of Literature," in N. Abraham and M. Torok, *The Wolf Man's Magic Word: A Cryptonymy* (Minneapolis: University of Minnesota Press, 1986), pp. li–lxix.

piecemeal critique of a number of Freudian tenets and case studies—without disputing the ultimate validity of the psychoanalytic enterprise. Abraham and Torok's version of psychoanalysis is a set of changes brought to Freudianism, divested for the most part of the Oedipus complex, the death drive, penis envy, the primal scene, and yet imbued with the problem of infantile sexuality, the unconscious, dream interpretation, and the importance of transference in the psychoanalytic situation.

A theory of being as symbol forms the early basis of Abraham and Torok's investigation and definitions of psychoanalysis. The treatise "Symbol or Beyond Phenomena" (1961; to be published in volume 2 of this work) reveals the principal motives and intellectual contexts of *The Shell and the Kernel*. In the preamble, Abraham defers to Freud, Husserl, and Ferenczi (in that order), stating that he owes them everything, "even the courage to reach beyond their thought." Abraham's synthesis of Husserlian phenomenology and Freudian psychoanalysis in this essay is unique, and the results achieved through this combination help to explain *The Shell and the Kernel*'s unorthodox brand of Freudianism. Abraham's theory is neither an application of phenomenological methods to psychoanalysis nor a study of parallelisms between the two. "Symbol or Beyond Phenomena" is the combined result of Abraham's dissatisfaction with phenomenology and of his conviction that, nevertheless, the philosophical interrogations of phenomenology, if adjusted, could transform Freudian psychoanalysis into an investigative and interpretive theory of being.

I now offer a distillation of Abraham's ideas, seen through the lens of both authors' subsequent work. Briefly put, Husserlian phenomenology seeks to provide a fresh methodological perspective on the nature of being by proposing to view the world in its relation to the apprehending consciousness and, vice versa, by seeing consciousness in its relation to the world appearing before it. The systematic investigation of the world's presence for consciousness and consciousness's presence to itself defines the field of phenomenology. For Abraham's theory of symbol, the crucial contention is the irrelevance of the world's reality without consciousness, which alone attributes sense or meaning. In this contention Abraham also discovers the shortcomings of phenomenology. If the definition of being as signification generated by acts of consciousness does represent a genuine methodological renewal—because it thrusts the processes of sense-giving to the forefront of philosophical inquiry—Husserl's assumption that consciousness is directly transparent to itself curtails further inquiry into the nature and genesis of consciousness. In Abraham's view, Freudian psychoanalysis stands ready to resolve this problem since it advances the unconscious as the entity capable of giving sense to the acts of consciousness. With the Freudian unconscious, however, phenomenological transparency vanishes because consciousness cannot fully control or grasp the meaning of its acts. To understand this shift, consider the neurotic symptom, characterized by the patient's inability to recognize the submerged or repressed reasons that brought it about. Abraham's methodological combination of phenomenology and psychoanalysis occurs at this juncture. If, for the phenomenologist, the world exists only in relation to a sense-giving consciousness, for Abraham the psychoanalyst the sense of both the world and consciousness itself resides in a transphenomenological realm, beyond the reach of direct apprehension—in the unconscious, for example. Leaving behind the Freudian domain of psychopathology and the description of unconscious mental processes, Abraham effectively generalizes the idea of symptom, positing beyond all phenomena an analyzable sphere that motivates their individual existence, giving them their specific underlying sense. Abraham makes this methodological leap because he sees the most productive conceptual originality of Freudian psychoanalysis in the structure of the symptom as a telltale memory trace of latent or unavailable promptings and traumas. In keeping with this principle, Abraham suggests further that the world and the psyche are the result of catastrophes whose fragmented remnants survive in the phenomena they engender; hence his treatise on symbol is also a theory of disasters. While phenomenology contributes the idea of the world's fundamental link to a sense-giving agent, the scope of Freudian psychoanalysis is enlarged. It is now called upon to investigate apparently inaccessible sources of meaning and thereby, ultimately to read in all areas of animate and inanimate existence the symptomlike or symbolic genesis of being.[4]

In summary, Abraham defines psychoanalysis as an investigative theory of the readable sources of meaning. This definition indicates a threefold program of research and foreshadows the future methodological course of Abraham and Torok's work: (1) Psychoanalysis investigates the domain and configuration of incoherence, discontinuity, disruption, and disintegration; in short, it uncovers obstacles to harmonious functioning. (2) At the same time, psychoanalysis identifies the ways (symbolizations and introjection) in which avenues of functioning are created and traumas or obstacles to functioning can be (and have been) surmounted. (3) Psychoanalysis studies the failure of the human capacity to transcend trauma; it searches for means to restore that ability. The second and third areas of research—the domain of clinical psychoanalysis and of the general theory of mental processes—are concerned with language as a system of

---

4. See the additional discussion of Abraham's theory of "transphenomenology" and its relationship to the concept of "anasemia" in the Editor's Note to part 3 of this volume.

expressive traces (consider in this light Freud's rhetoric of the dreamwork and the linguistic mechanism of jokes) and with pinpointing the dysfunctions of the expressiveness of language (see Abraham and Torok's concept of cryptonymy, discussed below). Abraham and Torok's ultimate aim, then, is to intensify the telltale aspects of language, that is, to increase the eloquence and readability of symptoms even in the face of the most resistent of pathologies: the blocked expression of a memory trace which cannot tell the submerged history of its own (traumatic) origins.

All of Abraham and Torok's writings elaborate components of this vast and cohesive research program. I turn now to two of this program's fundamental concerns: the process of introjection, posited by Abraham and Torok as the basic principle of mental organization; and the obstacles to introjection, or the enemies of the creation, expansion, and renewal of psychic life—in other words, the forces of mental disorganization.

LIFE AND PSYCHOANALYSIS: THE ROLE AND SCOPE OF INTROJECTION

Abraham and Torok have a characteristic way of being at once systematic and unsystematic. In their choice and discussion of the clinical problems they discovered over many years of practice, they are methodical; but as they refine and widen their understanding of people, they do not always clarify the theoretical ramifications of their work. They are committed throughout to expressing their insights as rooted in the lives of the people who led them to their discoveries. Abraham and Torok expend little rhetorical energy in promoting the novelty of an idea or explaining how an approach departs from standard modes of thinking.[5] Hence, readers are ushered into a world that is presented as familiar, as a place where they have somehow always been; yet they emerge with the certainty of having encountered something genuinely new. The disparity in *The Shell and the Kernel* between the substance of the ideas and their style of presentation may leave the reader with the paradoxical feeling of having been won over and mystified at the same time. Abraham and Torok's work often

---

5. In fact, Abraham and Torok attribute several of their original discoveries and elaborations to theoretical forebears. This tendency—a result both of modesty and of the desire to make new ideas palatable in a restrictive institutional framework—is especially noticeable with respect to the concepts of introjection and anasemia (see Torok's "The Illness of Mourning and the Fantasy of the Exquisite Corpse" and Abraham's "The Shell and the Kernel" in this volume).

requires rereading; it rewards serious concentration on sets of interrelated essays. Seeing beyond the deceptively simple style and unassuming tone of the essays to the richness and exacting difficulty of their conceptual content, readers will ultimately recognize the work as a fundamental renewal of psychoanalytic thought.

The characteristic features of Abraham and Torok's work—the open-ended quality of individual essays, the points of contact among them, and their ability to initiate a process of intellectual and emotional growth in the reader—can be seen as enacting, on the level of textual performance, the most fundamental of the psychoanalytic principles to emerge from *The Shell and the Kernel:* introjection. The authors discuss introjection throughout the book (and imply it frequently), but the centrality of this concept only appears in retrospect. Abraham and Torok give no systematic account of their distinctive view that mental life consists of the vicissitudes of introjection. The synthesis of this overarching principle is left to the reader.

At first glance, Abraham and Torok's concept of introjection may resemble Breuer and Freud's early therapeutic principle of abreaction, the releasing of pent-up emotions, and Freud's mature theory of working-through, according to which the patient is led to recognize and overcome unconscious repressions. Certainly, the combination of abreaction and working-through can be considered the basis of Abraham and Torok's concept of introjection, even if the authors do not follow this particular historical line. Yet, the scope of introjection in *The Shell and the Kernel* extends beyond both the purgative release of bottled-up emotions and the admittance of repressed sexual instincts or desires into consciousness. Unlike abreaction and working-through, the concept of introjection covers more than elements of therapy; it designates the driving force of psychic life in its entirety.

Abraham and Torok's concept of introjection is related as well to the Freudian processes of "psychical working out" and "binding." Both these processes are aimed at the psychical transformation of excessive quantities of excitation, tension, or instinctual energy so that they may be brought under control. Abraham and Torok were most likely impressed by Freud's use of the term "working out" in the *Studies on Hysteria* (1895), where it denotes the psychical assimilation of trauma into the network of mental associations. "Working out," in this early sense of the term, is similar to Freud's subsequently developed concept of the "work of mourning" (see "Mourning and Melancholia" [1917])—the gradual acceptance of loss and the withdrawal of the survivor's libidinal attachments from the lost object-of-love.

Viewed in the context of the Freudian theoretical legacy, Abraham and Torok's concept of introjection appears to be a synthetic enlargement of abreaction, binding, working out, working-through, and the work of mourning.[6]

But the Freudian background stops short of explaining the substance of introjection. In *The Shell and the Kernel,* introjection represents both the aim and the specific course of psychic life from birth to death. A preliminary definition might be that it is a constant process of acquisition and assimilation, the active expansion of our potential to accommodate our own emerging desires and feelings as well as the events and influences of the external world. Introjection is in fact the psychic counterpart of the child's biological development and its dependence on others as it travels through the various stages of maturation before reaching autonomy or adulthood. On one level, then, introjection is the psychic equivalent of growth, of the passage from suckling to chewing, from crawling to walking and running, from baby talk to words and full-fledged speech. Introjection accompanies the appearance of facial or pubic hair, the first erection, breasts, menstruation, and orgasm. In short, what adults define as physical growth or sexual maturation in fact requires of children a continuous process of introjection—of opening themselves to internal novelty.[7] If we follow the ramifications of this idea, we will see Abraham and Torok conceiving of life as a series of transitions that are far from automatic and

6. Freud repeatedly used or implied the term *introjection* in *Leonardo da Vinci and a Memory of his Childhood* (1910), "Group Psychology and the Analysis of the Ego" (1921), and "The Ego and the Id" (1923), among other works; however, Abraham and Torok's conception departs fundamentally from Freud's. See Torok's discussion of Freud's use of the term in "The Illness of Mourning and the Fantasy of the Exquisite Corpse"; there she traces her conception to Sandor Ferenczi's paper "On the Definition of Introjection" (1912). For an exhaustive historical overview of the widely differing early uses of the term *introjection* see S. H. Fuchs, "On Introjection," *International Journal of Psychoanalysis* 18 (1937): 269–93, as well as J. Laplanche and J.-B. Pontalis, *The Language of Psychoanalysis* (New York: Norton, 1981). No scholarly literature exists to date on Abraham and Torok's distinctive use of introjection. Most of the recent treatments of this term concern Melanie Klein's conception. For more on introjection, see the Editor's Note to part 4.

Although the authors never refer to Friedrich Nietzsche, his definition of the "will to power" as the essence of life can be likened to introjection (compare especially book II, sections 12 and 17, of *The Genealogy of Morals,* as well as book III, chapter 2, of *The Will to Power,* edited by Walter Kaufmann). The examination of introjection, as propounded by Abraham and Torok, may prove to be a valuable resource in interpreting and developing aspects of Nietzsche's conception.

7. Defined thus, the concept of introjection may be heard to resonate with Freud's suggestive maxim at the end of the thirty-first of his *New Introductory Lectures on Psychoanalysis* (1933): "Wo Es war soll Ich werden"—where id was, there ego shall be. It should be noted that in a different context Abraham and Torok reverse the Freudian maxim (stating "Where ego was, there id shall be") in chapter 8 of *The Wolf Man's Magic Word* to explain the formation of intrapsychic crypts, a pathological mechanism characterized by the breakdown of the capacity to introject.

not necessarily harmonious or pleasurable. Yet no matter how small or great, how painful or joyful, they invariably demand our more or less conscious and active participation. Transitions reach beyond childhood and puberty, of course; they continue in our lives as we leave home for the first time, take jobs, love, marry, have children, fall ill, lose our parents, let our children go their own ways, experience financial failure or success, grapple with divorce or unexpected fame, live through menopause, grow old, encounter new sources of pleasure, fulfillment, and suffering. One result of this view is that Abraham and Torok do not privilege the conflictual experiences and instinctual repressions of childhood in their assessment of the causes of psychological suffering or neurosis. Childhood undeniably presents a thicket of formative experiences and influences; still, even an ideally conflict-free childhood does not mean the adult can escape crises or catastrophes such as social humiliation, the desolation of war and bereavement, or racial persecution. All of these situations and countless others arise in adulthood without their emotional outcome having been shaped, even unbeknownst to us, by our infantile psychosexual development. Although the reader will not find explicit statements to this effect in *The Shell and the Kernel,* Abraham and Torok's view of psychic life through the lens of introjection tends to lessen the importance of childhood complexes (for example castration) and the phases (oral, anal, phallic, genital) of psychosexual development as defined by Freud and refined by some of his followers. Abraham and Torok do not appear to hold that our experiences in adulthood, our relationships to love objects, our responses to hardships and joys are necessarily determined by the degree of our fixation at (or regression to) well-defined stages and aspects of our psychosexual maturation (roughly up to age five in Freudian theory). Moreover, Abraham and Torok see no reason to separate the processes of introjection involved in assimilating the experiences of childhood from the introjections of youth and adulthood. Their emphasis shifts Freudian modes of thinking—for example, seeing early parental figures as enduring inhibitors of sexual instinct or as inevitable objects of conflictual love— toward the work of introjection or psychic opening and expansion, accomplished at any age and in the face of every sort of new experience.

The fruitfulness of the changes Abraham and Torok have introduced into Freudianism need to be argued on the basis of specific issues as well as interpretations of cases and literary texts. Freud, for example, stresses the unconscious repression of the sexual instinct and the mechanisms whereby the repressed libido makes its disguised return in symptom formation. Embracing the Freudian idea of the prominence of sexuality in psychic life, Abraham and Torok nevertheless change their emphasis to the processes of introjection, whereby the psyche gradually admits as its own the bodily manifestations of sexuality and finally makes fruitful use of the natural gift of sexual pleasure. They do not deny the significance of dynamic repression but see it as only one of several crucial factors that can inhibit the activity of introjection. Nor do they envision sexual repression as an inherent feature of either unconscious mental processes (exemplified in the Freudian concept of the superego) or social organization (as in Freud's theory of civilization and its endemic discontents). For entirely independent reasons, Abraham and Torok can be grouped with those critics who have questioned the modern-day relevance of the concept of repression when in fact society has been arguably less repressive throughout the past fifty years. While these critics of Freudianism often forget that Freud's own theories have, perhaps more than anything else, contributed to the easing of repressive social codes of behavior, Abraham and Torok continue to champion the importance of sexuality in psychic life. However, they demote the sexual instinct from its characteristic Freudian status as the principal causative agent in psychopathology. For them, psychopathology arises most often from disturbances in introjection or self-fashioning, and these may occur at any stage in life. Psychosexuality is the function of a larger whole, the continuous activity of self-creation. In sum, the authors consider the dissatisfaction or the diversion of the sexual instinct an insufficient explanation of psychic turmoil. They encourage us to ask instead what specific life-situation caused the introjection of sexuality to be suspended, diverted, or terminated. The psychological disturbances of sexuality need to be regarded in turn as symptoms of underlying individual traumas. These traumas and life-situations have the ultimate effect of stifling the free expansion of the ego or the self, limiting its field of action, by restricting or annihilating the unfettered exercise of one of its most valuable means of expression, sexuality.

PSYCHOANALYSIS WITH LITERATURE:
MAUPASSANT'S "AT SEA"

One of the central features of Abraham and Torok's work is a constant interchange between literature and psychoanalysis. This is a matter not simply of giving psychoanalytic interpretations of literature, but rather of transforming literature into a resource for clinical insight. New insights are possible because Abraham and Torok's concepts are uncommonly versatile. For example, introjection, defined broadly as the psychic process of expansion, leaves entirely open the particular subject or problem under study. Thus literature can deepen psychoanalytic understanding by giving us nuanced and artful accounts of situations that require or lead to introjection. For Abraham and Torok, the study of fictitious life-scenarios in literature parallels the psychoanalytic search for ever finer means of comprehending people and their joys or sufferings.

It is in the spirit of Abraham and Torok's recourse to literary scenarios that I now wish to illustrate the process of introjection through a short story by Maupassant. "At Sea" ("En mer," in the collection *Contes de la Bécasse*) recounts a seafaring incident involving two brothers off the coast of Normandy. Buffeted by high winds and waves, the elder Javel's small fishing boat and its crew are tossed about for several days while everyone, especially the younger of the brothers Javel, does his utmost to keep the boat afloat. The younger Javel keeps the boat from capsizing only by holding the rope around his arm like a tourniquet. A clear choice emerges in silence: the elder Javel must decide whether to save his boat or his brother's arm. Soon, when the boat has been spared, the young Javel's arm is black with gangrene. He amputates his own dead limb with a fish knife as his brother looks on disapprovingly, demanding that it be instantly thrown overboard. The amputee refuses; after all, it is his property, his own arm. So the pestilential arm is kept aboard despite everybody's protests and apprehensions of illness. Young Javel has an idea: why not salt the arm like the fish caught at sea and store it in a container? No sooner said than done. The incident seems to be over as the wound begins to heal. But the dead arm is still there, waiting to be carried home, inspected, touched, smelled by young Javel's wife and children. They marvel at "this piece of their father" while he has a small casket fitted for it. The village is summoned, the two Javels lead the procession, and the arm receives a proper burial with the blessings of the holy Church.

This tale is exemplary of the way in which we assimilate, integrate, or introject a traumatic experience. Young Javel's rescue of his dead limb from the angry dismissal of his brother (who understandably wants to discard the accusatory remains of his uncompromising choice), and all the subsequent actions culminating in the arm's burial, depict a ritual of introjection. It is as if young Javel takes leave of and buries his "old body," making his family and community acknowledge his mutilation, so that he can be reborn to a new life—with a body transformed by the loss of one arm. He keeps the vestige of his formerly complete body, awaiting the opportunity to adjust to its loss through a public display of grief. He could not continue to live harmoniously had his severed limb been discarded at sea, precisely because he would have been denied a tangible token of what he had been and what he was now becoming.

Suffering that is recognized as such by others facilitates its gradual psychic assimilation or introjection. That, distilled to the extreme, is the foundation of Abraham and Torok's theory of psychotherapy. Explicit acknowledgment of the full extent and ramifications of the patient's suffering is one of the analyst's crucial functions. Whether with our own strength, with the help of loved ones, or with an analyst if need be, we must be able to remember the past, recall what was taken from us, understand and grieve over what we have lost to trauma, and so find and renew ourselves.

The process of introjection need not be conscious to remain effective. Quite frequently, it occurs without our knowledge. We are led to introject as if by instinct. Was young Javel in Maupassant's tale fully aware that, by socializing his mutilation, he was introjecting his pain over the loss of the arm and avoiding a psychological infirmity? Surely not, nor did he have to be. With characteristic terseness, Torok states in "The Illness of Mourning" that introjection works like a genuine instinct. What this means is that the psychic work of establishing contact with oneself, the world, and others never stops. It propels itself as if it were an instinct. Indeed, much of Abraham and Torok's work suggests that the foremost psychic instinct is introjection.[8] The myriad ways of being in touch with ourselves, of enhancing our contact with ourselves, of adjusting to interior and exterior changes in the psychological, emotional, relational, political, or professional landscape, seem to derive from the inexorable force of instinct, whether or not we become aware of its workings and means of symbolization, its detours, triumphs, or failures.

Freud argued that the difference between normalcy and neurosis was a matter of degree since the disruption produced by the unconscious, the vicissitudes of infantile sexuality, and repression—the principal sources of neurosis according to his mature theory—is the inescapable lot of all humans. Supposedly, neurotics deal less well with problems that beset us all. Many agree that removing barriers between normal and abnormal behavior on the psychological plane has led to a liberation of vital energies grounded in the individual's desires as well as to a general relaxation of the moral repression of emotional and sexual conduct. A growing openness to the legitimacy of individual preferences and personal modes of expression is one of the gains we can continue to derive from Freudianism, the clinical practice of psychoanalysis, and related forms of psychotherapy. Abraham and Torok often address similarly broad issues (such as the therapeutic validity of psychoanalysis or its social precipitates) indirectly or in suggestive conclusions. A case in point is precisely the concept of introjection. As defined by the authors, introjection implies the essential

8. In shaping their own theory of introjection as a psychic instinct, Abraham and Torok implicitly took up and questioned the generality of Freud's conception of the death drive. Abraham's theory of the transgenerational phantom explains, in terms of familial trauma or secrets, psychic states similar to Freud's characterization of the death instinct.

interrelation of life and psychoanalysis. Where Freud sees degrees of neurosis, Abraham and Torok suggest levels of continuity between life and psychoanalysis, whether life is understood as the self-realization of the individual or as the activity of the social and political commonwealth. Through the idea of introjection, Abraham and Torok intertwine the therapeutic process of psychoanalysis with the very progress of life. In life, as in psychoanalysis, we continually introject; that is, we open and fashion and enrich ourselves, transcend trauma, adjust to internal or external upheaval and change, create forms of coherence in the face of emotional panic and chaos. Abraham and Torok never speak explicitly about these processes as being shared between life and psychoanalytic therapy, but we can infer their conjunction since the authors' cumulative discussion of introjection extends to both.

Introjection is the process of psychic nourishment, growth, and assimilation, encompassing our capacity to create through work, play, fantasy, thought, imagination, and language; it is the continual process of self-fashioning through the fructification of change, whether the modification is biological and internal (such as sexual maturation) or external and cultural (such as our children's gradual detachment from us). At the same time, introjection represents our ability to survive shock, trauma, or loss; it is the psychic process that allows human beings to continue to live harmoniously in spite of instability, devastation, war, and upheaval. In short, introjection coincides with life as it advances through an infinity of forms; but introjection can also rescue life when faced with the threat of destruction. If viewed as a complete process, introjection encompasses three successive stages. (1) Something new or foreign (whether good or bad) occurs in or to me. (2) I turn myself into that which this new "thing" has done to me; I familiarize myself with it through play, fantasy, projection (or any number of other activities); in sum, I appropriate it for myself. (3) I become aware of what has occurred and of my own gradual encounter with it. As a result I am now able to give the whole process a place within my emotional existence; I also understand why and how the scope of "myself" has been modified and expanded. This threefold process successively entails an occurrence, my work of appropriation, and my awareness, memorialized through naming.[9] Put succinctly, the therapeutic role of psychoanalysis is to intensify the process of introjection by making it con-

---

9. Naming—the confirmation that an introjection has taken place—may or may not occur; in addition, the naming itself may or may not be a conscious activity. When I am aware of it, naming allows me to designate what it is that occurred and what I did with "it," and ultimately what "I" became in the process of appropriation and familiarization.

When extended to the functioning of the social realm, Abraham and Torok's concept of

scious or to reestablish the possibility of introjection when the lines of communication with life have been endangered or severed.

ENEMIES OF LIFE: OBSTACLES TO INTROJECTION AND THE NEED FOR PSYCHOANALYSIS

The Shell and the Kernel may be placed in the succession of the early Hungarian school of psychoanalysis, distinguished by figures such as Sandor Ferenczi (1873–1933) and Imre Hermann (1889–1984). Ferenczi was Freud's closest friend and scientific lieutenant between 1910 and 1933; Hermann was Ferenczi's student. Abraham left Hungary in his teens and Torok in her early twenties, both with little or no knowledge of these people, and only later encountered their work as a result of well-defined interests. Abraham arranged for the publication in France of Ferenczi's *Thalassa: Origines de la vie sexuelle* and Hermann's *L'Instinct filial*, and wrote substantial theoretical introductions to both volumes (the text of these introductions from 1962 and 1972 will be included in volume 2 of the present work). It is characteristic of the authors' intellectually close connection to the Hungarian school that in 1981, upon discovering a 1929 essay by Hermann, Torok immediately arranged for its publication in French.[10] That essay, dealing with familial shame as a source of social anguish, could indeed have been written by either Abraham or Torok. Hermann suggests that the Freudian concept of superego needs to be complemented by considering some parents' dissolute way of life as a persistent source of social anguish and sexual inhibition for their children. This idea individualizes the Freudian doctrine of the internalization of universal parental prohibitions and demands such as moral yardsticks and the prohibition against incest. Attempts to particularize abstract or speculative Freudian tenets also characterize Ferenczi's work. For example, a few years after Freud introduced his second instinct theory, based on the death drive, Ferenczi virtually transformed the concept in "The Unwel-

---

introjection can be used to provide a psychoanalytic base for sociology and cultural studies. For example, the investigation of introjection and of its vicissitudes (which may include its absence) can shed light on the politics and emotional intricacies of colonization. Moreover, introjection can afford a methodological complement to comparative analysis in ethnology and cultural anthropology, since the concept is well suited to the study of social interactions in bilingual or multicultural communities and among religious or ethnic minorities.

10. Hermann's article is "La honte comme angoisse sociale" (1929), published in *Cahiers Confrontation* 8 (1982): 167–76.

come Child and His Death Instinct" (1929) by isolating a precise familial cause of destructive tendencies. Abraham, too, continually reconceives Freudian principles, often seemingly unaware of how far he has actually moved from Freud's original conception (see the discussion of the death drive in "Notes on the Phantom" in this volume). In the 1920s and 30s, the Hungarian school attached far greater importance than Freud to the field of clinical psychoanalysis and the ideal of a cure. The relative importance of clinical and theoretical psychoanalysis eventually led to disagreements between Freud and Ferenczi in the last years of Ferenczi's life.[11] The debate continues for Abraham and Torok, as they adhere more strictly than Freud to his oft-repeated ground rule that theoretical elaboration must spring from clinical discoveries. Notwithstanding major differences in execution, another point of contact between the authors and the late Ferenczi (roughly between 1925 and 1933) is their common endeavor to revitalize the spirit of Freud's early research (between 1890 and 1897) on the effects of forgotten painful memories, the nature of traumas, and their role in the development of neuroses.

The bulk of *The Shell and the Kernel* deals primarily and most explicitly with how best to understand the devastations of trauma and other enemies of life. It is Abraham and Torok's clinical experience of human suffering that forced them, as it were, to reevaluate the theoretical assumptions they had inherited and to posit hitherto unknown sources of pain. Abraham and Torok's gradual understanding of the ways in which traumas block the spontaneous work of introjection provided the linchpin for their discovery of new psychic and linguistic structures in their patients. As described in *The Shell and the Kernel*, the obstacles to introjection include the phantom, an undisclosed family secret handed down to an unwitting descendant; the illness of mourning, which the authors define as bereavement complicated by an untoward sexual outburst in the mourner at the time of loss; incorporation, or the secret and vital embrace of an alien identity; and the secret, or crypt, which "entombs" an unspeakable but consummated desire.

Although the authors do not look back at the cumulative achievement of their investigations of human suffering, readers can grasp the methodological gist of *The Shell and the Kernel* as a theory of readability (also characteristic of *The Wolf Man's Magic Word*)—a theory demonstrating the feasibility of interpretation in the face of seemingly insurmountable obstructions. While other contemporary critical approaches (for example, French structuralism, deconstruction, Heideggerian phenomenology, La-

---

11. See Torok's "Theoretra," in this volume.

canian psychoanalysis) deal with the ways in which meaning arises, functions or fails to function, the theory of readability implied in *The Shell and the Kernel* shows how signification can be reinstated after its collapse. Many essays in *The Shell and the Kernel* are concerned with converting obstructions into guides to understanding or with revealing coherence in the language of a text and in the behavior of human beings, even when the possibility of coherence is denied if not actively undermined.

This conception of psychoanalysis as the rescuer of choked or subverted signification distances the authors both from some aspects of Freudian theory and other current French trends. For example, Abraham and Torok do not admit an irreducible separation or barrier, as Jacques Lacan does, between linguistic elements and their meanings. Rather, they create avenues to study and overcome the obstructions that serve to separate linguistic entities from their potential and concealed sources of signification. Abraham and Torok view the unintelligibility they encounter in their patients as psychically motivated disturbances of meaning, as instances of psychic aphasia. Furthermore, the authors find that some patients invent particular forms of obfuscation in their speech, obscuring beyond recognition the linguistic elements that might otherwise lead the analyst to the source of their suffering. Searching for the means to retrieve signification, Abraham and Torok uncover psychic mechanisms whose aim seems to be to disarray, even to annul the expressive power of language.

One of these mechanisms, which they call cryptonymy, inhibits the emergence of meaning by concealing the significant link within a chain of words. Thus a patient's seemingly aimless speech over many sessions can hide the crucial word(s) that, once found, will provide the needed coherence. To grasp the interpretive process, let us imagine someone who continually talks about having to "keep moving," wanting to see things "function well," so that she can "perform a duty" she does not specify. Later and without any transition, she shifts her attention to wanting to find a "good job" (even though she already has one), wishing thereby to gain "upward mobility" (which, given her social standing, she does not need). Listening closely to the patient's words, the analyst realizes that the initial series of words (keep moving, function well, perform a duty) are in fact synonyms, rooted in the verb "to go," and that the other phrases used by the patient (good job, upward mobility) represent freely associated senses based on the first series (function well → good job; keep moving → upward mobility). Taking also into account the patient's persistent symptom of helpless dejection, the analyst finally hypothesizes that the apparently nonsensical geyser of words conceals the verb "to die," a secondary and excluded meaning of "to go." Abraham and Torok's interpretive method overcomes the resistance to signification by revealing the situation (for example, a shameful and traumatic death) that led to the obstructions of meaning in the first place.[12]

The concepts of secret, crypt, incorporation, and the phantom enlarge upon or redirect the Freudian definition of personal identity as beset by unconscious conflicts, desires, and fantasies. Freudian theories rely on the concept of latency: beside an emotion expressed, behind a symptom manifested, there lurks a contrary, repressed emotion. Yet this censored emotion erupts whenever repression momentarily relaxes its grip. What is forced out of consciousness can force its way back. In contrast to this Freudian structure of oppositions, Abraham and Torok explore the mental landscapes of submerged family secrets and traumatic tombs in which, for example, actual events are treated as if they had never occurred. Instead of the shifting fortunes of opponents locked in combat (repression versus repressed instinct), what matters is the preservation of a shut-up or excluded reality. This is why the authors speak of *preservative* repression, or the topography of encrypted secrets, and contrast it with Freud's concept of *dynamic* repression. Preservative repression seals off access to part of one's own life in order to shelter from view the traumatic monument of an obliterated event.[13] The discovery of obstacles to introjection— such as the disruption of signification by cryptonymy, the psychic structure of secretly perpetuated multiple identities, and the psychological implant

---

12. According to Abraham and Torok, Freud's theory of language is coextensive with his conception of the symptom as the telltale signal of the latent causes of psychological turmoil. Hence his linguistic analysis of dreams, jokes, and parapraxes stresses homophony, homonymy, pun and semantic ambiguity, malapropism, spoonerism, metaphor, metonymy, anagram, rebus, and macaronic nonsense. These techniques (widely used in poetry as well) are all characterized by a simultaneous concealment and revelation. The concepts of cryptonymy and preservative repression (the latter discussed directly below) stipulate the collapse of the revelatory properties of the symptom and language. Consequently, Abraham and Torok concentrate on the mechanisms of fractured meaning and search for new modes of comprehension. The difference between Freudian rules of interpretation and those required by cryptonymy is further explained in the final chapter of The Wolf Man's Magic Word, pp. 79–83. For a distinction between cryptonymy and Lacan's "signifying chain," see my "Translator's Introduction" to The Wolf Man's Magic Word, p. lx.

Cryptonymy can involve several languages when the patient is multilingual, as was the Wolf Man's case. For multilingual examples of cryptonymy, see The Wolf Man's Magic Word. Multilingual examples of cryptonymy can be dazzling in complexity. Yet the principle of obfuscation remains unchanged; the only difference is that several languages are constantly interchanged as if they together constituted a single phonic and semantic field.

13. Abraham and Torok's concept of preservative repression is important for understanding the mechanism of obfuscation in cryptonymy as discussed above. In this case, repression is not confined to images, thoughts, and fantasies but above all acts on words themselves. "It is not a situation *comprising* words that becomes repressed. . . . Rather, *the words themselves . . . are deemed to be generators* of a situation that must be avoided and voided retroactively." The Wolf Man's Magic Word, p. 20.

in us of our ancestors' secrets—represent the clinical fruits of Abraham and Torok's long-term inquiry into the status and essence of psychoanalysis. (Their theory of readability stands in a clear line of continuity from Abraham's early theory of the symbol in "Symbol or Beyond Phenomena.") The new mental and linguistic categories broaden the effective scope of psychoanalysis by extending its limits to what had been considered to lie beyond analysis.

PSYCHOANALYSIS WITH LITERATURE:
CAMUS'S *THE STRANGER*

The investigation of sealed-off traumas, that is, of inaccessible mental "graves," can take many forms. As we have seen, Abraham and Torok's explorations move fluidly between the clinical and the literary realms, suggesting that psychoanalysis and literary analysis are two different contexts for similar methodological insights. Torok has written that "the clinical realm works toward a better understanding of hiding in texts, while the literary analysis of the avenues of textual concealment offers allegories of reading for clinical psychoanalysis."[14] I have suggested that we read Maupassant's "At Sea" as a literary portrayal of successful introjection. In that story, a traumatic amputation is introjected through private and public mourning: we are shown how people find their own symbolic ways of transcending trauma. The story represents the type of emotional crisis in which no psychoanalytic psychotherapy is needed because life itself takes care of the gradual process of psychical readjustment or expansion. For a literary counterexample of the lack of introjection and to hint again how literature can deepen the psychoanalytic understanding of human suffering, I turn briefly to Camus's novel *The Stranger*.

Camus's story of Meursault—a Frenchman living in Algiers who attends his mother's funeral, later murders an Arab he does not know, and finally is tried and executed for his apparently motiveless crime—has been interpreted (most influentially by Jean-Paul Sartre) as dramatizing the absurdity of human existence.[15] However, Meursault's personality and actions can also be understood as the result of an unwitting, unfelt sorrow

14. Quoted from Maria Torok's Foreword to N. Rand, *Le Cryptage et la vie des oeuvres*, p. 9.

15. Essays by Sartre, Roland Barthes, Maurice Blanchot, Nathalie Sarraute, and others are collected in *Les critiques de notre temps et Camus*, edited by Jacqueline Levi-Valensi (Paris: Garnier Frères, 1970).

over a loss.[16] Meursault is chronically detached from all his actions; no events or feelings stir him except sheer physical sensation. For example, to Marie's query as to whether he loves her, he answers that this sort of question has no meaning. In response to his employer's offer of work in Paris, he says that he does not care one way or the other. Having killed a man, he is questioned by the magistrate—does he regret his action?—to which he counters that he feels weariness. Following his arrest, Meursault does nothing to extenuate his crime or save his life. "Maman died today. Or yesterday maybe, I don't know. I got a telegram from the home: 'Mother deceased. Funeral tomorrow. Faithfully yours.' That doesn't mean anything. Maybe it was yesterday."[17] Here is the picture of a man bereft of the capacity for emotion—a virtual robot.

A purely factual tone is sustained throughout the novel. "It occurred to me that I was going back to work, and that really nothing had changed" (p. 24). Meursault considers the matter of his mother's death closed, but is it? Subtle traces of his unfelt sorrow abound in the text; they emerge from circumstances apparently unrelated to his mother's death or are underscored by other characters in the book. For example, noticing Meursault's listlessness, his neighbor Raymond, rather than Meursault himself, recalls the mother's recent passing. Another neighbor, old Salamano, is desperate over the loss of a dog he acquired upon his wife's death. Meursault hears him in his room: "from the peculiar noise coming through the partition, I realized he was crying. For some reason, I thought of Maman. But I had to get up early the next morning" (p. 39). The emotions Meursault cannot feel are described or felt in his place by others. Apparently unconnected episodes and chance encounters in the novel suggest, by accumulation, the widening gulf between Meursault's grief and his ability to perceive it, to express it to himself or others: Salamano "said he supposed I must be very sad since Maman died, and I didn't say anything." Meursault is a total "stranger" to his own suffering, just as he is oblivious to the criminal nature of his murderous act and to the fatal consequences

16. The existing psychoanalytic interpretation of The Stranger differ from the one hinted at here, focusing instead on the protagonist's "oedipal struggle." Due to guilt associated with repressed incestuous love, these interpretations suggest, Meursault wishes his mother dead: the mother's death becomes a disguised murder and the killing of the Arab an extension of the son's hostility toward his mother. See Jean Gassin, L'univers symbolique d'Albert Camus (Paris: Minard, 1981); Patrick McCarthy, Albert Camus: The Stranger (Cambridge: Cambridge University Press, 1988); and, for a somewhat different perspective, Alain Costes, Albert Camus: La parole manquante (Paris: Payot, 1973).

A more detailed version of my analysis of The Stranger appears in my article "Renouveaux de la psychanalyse," Les Temps Modernes 561 (1993): 142–73.

17. Albert Camus, The Stranger, trans. Matthew Ward (New York: Random House, 1989), p. 3. Further page references will appear in the text.

of the charge brought against him. Ultimately Meursault is condemned to die because he cannot reach his own feelings of sorrow. Meursault is an "amputee" of life: he has severed all his affects and is wholly indifferent to both life and death. Prior to the murder, Meursault relives at the beach the sun-broiled scene of his mother's funeral, and by killing an anonymous man in the unbearable heat, he "kills" the intensity of his nameless sorrow. The "crime" and the ensuing "sentence" are symbolic segments in an uncontrolled but logical emotional concatenation whose (extreme) principle may be formulated as follows: an unintrojected death breeds death in life and leads to indirect suicide. The only "choice" Meursault makes in the novel is to provoke a death for the trauma of a death unmourned and thereby to relinquish his own life. The novel's air of mystery is likely due to the fact that the protagonist's unfelt sorrow is shrouded in silence and that its tragic consequences are understood by no one in the book, least of all by Meursault himself.

The Stranger helps us understand the elusive signs of thwarted introjection that Abraham and Torok discuss in *The Shell and the Kernel:* unexplained or unrecognized depression, apathy, and insensitivity or unresponsiveness to social and societal expectations. Sufferers lead apparently "normal" professional or personal lives and may even seem to enjoy themselves occasionally. Yet a sense of futility and emptiness pervades their actions; it is as if they were absent from their own lives. A dim realization of this sense of absence flickers in Meursault when he is brought to the courtroom to hear his lawyer's summation. "At one point, though, I listened because he was saying, 'It is true, I killed a man.' He went on like that, saying 'I' when he was speaking about me. I was completely taken aback. I leaned over to one of the guards [who explained] 'All lawyers do it.' I thought this was a way to exclude me even further from the case, reduce me to nothing, and, in a sense, substitute himself for me. But I think I was already far removed from that courtroom" (p. 103). Meursault could not know that the lawyer's rhetorical ploy strikes him only because the exclusion of himself, his being reduced to nothing, has been his emotional lot ever since his mother's death, if not before.

For Abraham and Torok, silence is an independent clinical and theoretical entity. Whether it characterizes individuals, families, social groups, or entire nations, silence and its varied forms—the untold or unsayable secret, the feeling unfelt, the pain denied, the unspeakable and concealed shame of families, the cover-up of political crimes, the collective disregard for painful historical realities—may disrupt our lives. Abraham and Torok's work studies the personal and interpersonal consequences of silence. According to them, silence represents that which cannot be assimilated into the continuity of psychic life, therefore works counter to and even blocks introjection, endangering or arresting the harmonious progress of our emotional development and self-expansion. Thus the concepts of crypt and incorporation denote the individual's forcible creation of a psychic tomb, arising from his or her inassimilable life experiences, while the phantom concerns the unwitting reception of a secret which was someone else's psychic burden. In these cases, psychoanalysis converts silence into speech, displaying the secret in its initial openness, conjuring up the concealed lives of the dead whose undetected machinations unhinge the mind of the living.[18]

The reader will find that the issues of introjection and the obstacles to introjection—issues this introduction has undertaken to detail—permeate Abraham's and Torok's essays. With introjection and its enemies, the authors offer a distilled theory of psychological processes: psychic life consists of the pursuit of its own harmonious progress and the afflictions or blockages caused by insurmountable trauma. This broad division has allowed the authors to widen the range of life experiences that appear clinically significant. Reading Abraham and Torok's work, we realize that it is not worthwhile or even possible to draw up an exhaustive list of traumas (let alone a list of typical traumas or universal complexes) since their number is as great and their forms as varied as human situations. Abraham and Torok also lead us to recognize that professional psychoanalysis is not needed unless the psyche's own self-propelled processes of introjection break down. The need for psychotherapy arises when the enemies of life or the obstacles to introjection overwhelm us, curtailing our ability to absorb crises and disasters. These obstacles to introjection—such as unfelt mourning, unassimilated trauma, the unwitting psychical inheritance of someone else's secrets—drive a wedge between us and our society. It is in these cases that psychoanalysis can profitably formulate and seek to answer the question, How can people be helped to initiate a process of introjection that has failed to occur spontaneously? Clinical psychoanalysis may discover the precipitating event, trauma, experience, or secret as well as the emotional context that had previously been unrecognized or had had too painful or shameful an effect to be remembered and embraced as part of life.

---

18. Although quite different from incorporation, the transgenerational phantom also shifts the balance (however unstable it may be) between consciousness and unconscious by adding the disruptions of a psychically inherited foreign presence. Psychotherapy seeks to reveal the crypt's secret content in order to effect its reintegration into consciousness, and leads, in the case of the phantom, to uncovering the shameful silence of several generations through the symptoms of a descendant.

Part I

Instruments of Therapy

Editor's Note Written in 1959, "Fantasy" has remained un-published, though it was initially circulated in a mimeographed version among the participants in a series of private seminars organized by Abraham and Torok at their residence between 1959 and 1961 under the general title "Phenomenological Psychology," later modified to "Genetic Phenomenology." These unpublished seminar papers, on topics ranging from the tempo-rality of neuroses to the role of pedagogy in the self-awareness of the child, attest to Abraham and Torok's immersion in Hus-serlian phenomenology, especially as regards the possibility of creating a bridge between the latter and Freudian psychoanaly-sis. The attempt to link the philosophical description of acts of consciousness with a clinical discipline investigating unconscious or unavailable promptings and motivations marks the distinctive methodology Torok adopted in her work on fantasy. The com-bined study of phenomenology and psychoanalysis culminated in Abraham's treatise on interpretation, "The Symbol or Beyond Phenomena" (written in 1961 and unpublished until 1978), his "Phenomenological Reflections on the Structural and Genetic Implications of Psychoanalysis" (1959), and his "Time, Rhythm, and the Unconscious: Toward a Psychoanalytic Esthetic" (1962; all three will appear in volume 2 of this Chicago edition).

"Fantasy" grows out of a dissatisfaction with the generality and pervasiveness of the concept of fantasy, especially as it came to be expanded in the writings of Melanie Klein and her followers after 1940. Pinpointing the Freudian and post-Freudian idea of *unconscious* fantasy as a source of theoretical confusion, Torok creates a new category, people's actual, *conscious experience of fantasy*. She calls this the "I am having a fantasy" experience. In her definition, fantasy is an unreal mental image or vision that is immediately recognized as such by the ego, even though the fantasy intrudes upon the chain of free-flowing associations (in therapy) or the current actions and thoughts of the self. Disruption and the awareness of unreality coincide in the experience of fantasy. Phenomenological description and psychoanalytic inquiry are combined when Torok discerns two levels in the synthesizing functions of the ego: (1) the ego is the conscious author of its own acts, assuming full responsibility for their production; (2) the ego is the site and spectator of inner events emerging from a realm not authored or controlled by the ego. The distinction has both therapeutic and theoretical consequences. The conscious experience of the discontinuous and imaginary nature of fantasy makes patients question its origin and reason for being. Torok sees in the emergence or recounting of fantasies during therapy an appeal for interpretive understanding and collaboration. The analyst functions as a mediator in the patient's as yet unformulated attempt to bring to the fore a conflict represented by the fantasy. The conflict need not be sexual or even infantile in its origin. The patient's fantasy combined with subsequent associations will reveal the problem at hand, initiating the process of its integration into the ego's active self-awareness.[1]

Torok's treatment departs significantly from Freudian and other post-Freudian conceptions of fantasy. Put succinctly, classical psychoanalytic theory equates fantasy with unfulfilled or

1. Collaboration between patients and analysts is a recurrent theme in Abraham and Torok's work, heightened at times to the idea of partnership, especially in cases where patients suffer from the disturbing effects of events or psychic matter entirely foreign to them (see Part V, "Secrets and Posterity," in particular Abraham's "Notes on the Phantom"). Torok expands on the idea of psychoanalytic partnership in "Theoretra" (see Part VII), suggesting that the revelation and gradual acceptance of past suffering is dependent on the analyst's sympathetic embrace of the traumatic emotions expressed and/or transferred by the patient.

unfulfillable desires arising chiefly along the path of instinctual development; these desires or fantasies are imperfectly repressed and therefore return in the disguised form of neurotic symptoms. Since fantasies supposedly originate and are repressed at specific moments of psychosexual or objectal (relational) development, the myriad forms of fantasy can be matched with universally uniform psychosexual or objectal stages and classified into anal, oral, phallic, depressive, schizoid, etc. Consequently, unconscious fantasy in particular is envisioned in classical psychoanalytic theory as a principle of explanation, a causative agent in symptom formation. Here is where Torok disagrees. Fantasy is not *behind* the symptom but a symptom in its own right: it is the representation of a problem seeking expression. Fantasies and dreams have the same status but not because, as Freud has said, they are both wish-fulfillments or distortions of wishes. Dreams and fantasies have similar functions because, with the patient's aid, they can become readable entities, paving the way to the free verbalization of desires, affects, or conflicts that, without the mediation of dreams and fantasies, would have remained inaccessible and unexpressed.

Abraham and Torok's work includes other treatments of fantasy, some of which enlarge upon or depart from the conception outlined here. The central idea of fantasy—according to which the boundaries of the ego may be expanded continually through the verbalization of conflicts and desires represented by fantasy—anticipates Abraham and Torok's concept of introjection, defined as the unceasing enrichment of the potentials of self-fashioning and self-awareness. (See Editor's Note to Part IV, "New Perspectives in Metapsychology.") Abraham discusses the mediating or ambassadorial function of fantasy and myth in "The Shell and the Kernel" (Part III, "Toward a Conceptual Renewal of Psychoanalysis"), placing fantasies and symptoms at the center of his conception of the psychic apparatus as a multilayered system of two-directional messages or traces. Finally, in the essays on cryptic mourning and secret love (Part IV), a crucial though largely implicit distinction emerges between as yet unexpressed and unspeakable fantasies, that is, between wordless affects and unconsciously guarded secrets. In these essays on intrapsychic secrets, fantasy loses its mediating or verbalizing function, to be understood instead as a form of desperate magic, tricking the sufferer into acting as if some actual and devastating trauma had not really occurred.

ONE

Fantasy: An Attempt to Define Its Structure and Operation

M. Torok, 1959

I. SUSAN ISAACS'S CONCEPT OF FANTASY

In an article, "The Nature and Function of Phantasy," that has already become a classic, Susan Isaacs undertook the daunting task of providing a conceptual synthesis of the various uses of the term "fantasy" in psychoanalytic literature. Her study arrives at an extremely broad definition in which fantasy is identified with nothing less than the primary content of unconscious mental processes. The present state of the problem can perhaps best be situated by quoting the conclusions Susan Isaacs draws from her definition. We will be able to see the expansionist tendencies of the concept of fantasy, which, in the end, claims the whole expanse of psychic life as its own.

(a) Phantasies are the primary content of unconscious mental processes.

(b) Unconscious phantasies are primarily about bodies, and represent instinctual aims toward objects.

(c) These phantasies are, in the first instance, the psychic representatives of libidinal and destructive instincts; early in development they also become elaborated into defences, as well as wish-fulfillments and anxiety-contents.

(d) Freud's postulated "hallucinatory wish-fulfillment" and his "primary identification," "introjection" and "projection" are the basis of the phantasy-life.

(e) Through external experience, phantasies become elaborated and capable of expression, but they do not depend upon such experiences for their existence.

(f) Phantasies are not dependent upon words, although they may under certain conditions be capable of expression in words.

Previously unpublished manuscript; translated from the French original, "Le fantasme: Essai de définition de sa structure et de son opération."

(g) The earliest phantasies are experienced in sensations; later, they take the form of plastic images and dramatic representations.

(h) Phantasies have both psychic and bodily effects, e.g., in conversion symptoms, bodily qualities, character and personality, neurotic symptoms, inhibitions, and sublimations.

(i) Unconscious phantasies form the operative link between instincts and mechanisms. When studied in detail, every variety of ego-mechanism can be seen to arise from specific sorts of phantasy, which in the last resort have their origin in instinctual impulses. "The ego is a differentiated part of the id." A mechanism is an abstract general term describing certain mental processes which are experienced by the subject as unconscious phantasies.

(j) Adaptation to reality and reality-thinking require the support of concurrent unconscious phantasies. Observation of the ways in which knowledge of the external world develops shows how the child's phantasy contributes to his learning.

(k) Unconscious phantasies exert a continuous influence throughout life, both in normal and neurotic people, the differences lying in the specific character of the dominant phantasies, the desire or anxiety associated with them and their interplay with each other and with external reality.[1]

II. CRITICAL DISCUSSION

What is striking about these conclusions is the apparently contradictory nature of the author's aims. On the one hand, she attempts to circumscribe the various aspects of fantasy: its nature, genesis, function, and topographical situation. On the other hand, she seeks to generalize the scope of fantasy, seeing it at work in modes as disparate as desire, anxiety, beliefs, pragmatic behavior, and even in defense mechanisms. Basic drives themselves, inasmuch as they must have fantasy as their psychic representative, cannot escape its control.

Gratified though we might be to see the expanding scope of such a familiar term, we should also note the disadvantages of an excessively generic definition.

Certainly, no one would disagree that the magical sentence "There is a fantasy behind that" very often does have the virtue of reconciling sets of opposing diagnoses. Yet one has to wonder whether the benefits of this purely verbal agreement do not pale before the disadvantages of

1. Joan Riviere, ed. *Developments in Psychoanalysis* (London: Hogarth Press, 1952), p. 112.

the false extension of the concept. The value of a concept is demonstrated in use, as it comes in contact with actual facts. Generic concepts do not open any doors. To be a key, a concept must fit the lock exactly, even if it opens only a single lock. For just that reason, I have placed my study on an operational plane.

The operational plane is where the effectiveness of the analyst's actions are tested. Accordingly, we need to invoke two fundamental concepts: structure and dynamism. Structure first of all, because, as Daniel Lagache has said, the analyst attempts to modify structure, and then dynamism, since this is the lever of therapy. In order to validate the concept of fantasy, we need to study it both dynamically and structurally. I will now proceed to examine this double aspect of a specific experience we may call *I am having a fantasy*. My study has three parts. First I will consider the experience "I am having a fantasy" structurally, that is, I will describe fantasy as an integral part of the general structure of the person. Second, still on the level of description, I will distinguish the concept gained in my structural investigation from a series of other, apparently related ones. Finally, I will attempt to show the operational validity of my concept, both on its own terms and in contrast to other concepts usually classified under the rubric "fantasy."

III. WHAT IS A FANTASY?

Let us start with a fictitious example, though modeled on a real-life instance: "While I was earnestly trying to fill my dinner companion's glass," says Rodolphe, "a task made more difficult by the fact that the diameter of the glass was excessively small and I wanted my gesture to be elegant, a kind of image suddenly appeared before my eyes. This was really quite surprising as the image had absolutely no connection to me or to what was around me. I had not tried to produce it and had no idea where it came from. And yet it was happening to me. My neighbor noticed nothing of course. I had the clearest vision of a knife being put through a gingerbread cookie. It was the kind of cookie I used to like in my childhood when I did tricks at Spring fairs. The whole thing only lasted for a second, accompanied by some vague emotion. A fantasy, that's all."

This is a typical "I am having a fantasy" experience. For the moment I will not try to find a precise meaning behind this unexpected representation. Initially, I think it important to describe the formal aspects of the event and situate these within the dynamic structuring of the complete person. We notice immediately the suddenness of the representation that, as is often the case, was not provoked by any intentional orientation designed either to solve a problem or to anticipate some fearsome or desired event. Now, even though the ego does participate in this representation—which is why it can say, "this is my fantasy"—it does not recognize itself directly as the active source of the fantasy. The ego has the impression rather of being the mere site of a strange and incomprehensible phenomenon. Since its reason for being as well as its aims are quite unknown, the representation gives rise to an impression of surprise, even gratuitousness. Something has happened outside the purview of the ego's concerns and suddenly *intruded* upon them in the form of a representation.

For the ego to undergo the intrusion of an inner experience invariably entails a characteristic form of passivity that is not the same as the common perceptual encounter with the outside world, or even the sudden internal realization of one's own bodily state. Fantasy stands quite apart from these two types of intrusion because what is "encountered" is immediately posited as being in the realm of the *imaginary.* Consequently, this passivity must refer to some form of activity on the part of the ego, since the intrusion of a content that signals its imaginary nature constitutes the ego's encounter with another level of itself.

This encounter is nonetheless remarkable because it catches one unawares; the ego, absorbed in its current tasks, has suffered a break in its continuity. Something was being imagined on the fringes of the ego's present preoccupations. This oncoming representation is not for the enlightenment of its inventor, leading to the solution of a problem; neither is it a retroactive type of synthesis in which hitherto disparate elements are being unified. I should like to call this untimeliness, which removes the ego from its immediate concerns, a *misfit.*

Rodolphe's fantasy can be defined as *a fleeting imaginary representation intruding upon the ego's activities and as being, in that context, a total misfit.* Structurally speaking, the sudden experience of misfitting imagination entails a momentary shift of levels within the ego's activities and is similar to the more prolonged shift that occurs in sleep. Before inquiring into the possible reasons for this shift of levels, we conclude that we are talking about a specific experience in the general structuring of the person; it will be quite easy therefore to distinguish this from other phenomena that, by misapplied generalizations, are often confused with fantasy.

IV. WHAT IS NOT FANTASY?

In differentiating fantasy from other types of inner experiences, three criteria—intrusion, imagination, and misfit—will prove useful. The presence or absence of one or more of these criteria can lead to a provisional classification of the facts at hand. I will designate these phenomena by their customary names, as I see no reason to embark on a conceptual critique, except when it comes to so-called unconscious fantasies. This concept covers too many disparate things and needs to be subdivided into (A) unconscious acts, (B) prereflexive fantasies, and (C) conversional fantasies. These events, as all human events, do have latent meaning due to the universal sedimentation of meaning, as described by Husserl. Yet their aspect of latent meaning fails to provide a distinctive characteristic to the events in question. If we claim that there is an underlying unconscious fantasy behind every human act, we strip fantasy of its specificity and operational value. The characteristic of being unconscious does not furnish a differentiating criterion: it merely states a general property that inheres in all inner experiences, a property that through its extreme generality tends to foster confusion.

Here I will list with their standard names some of the inner events that, though usually considered to be manifestations of underlying fantasies, need to be distinguished from the *experience* of fantasy: (1) unconscious acts, perverse behavior; (2) hallucinations and delusions, projection, theoretical convictions; (3) impulses, compulsions, déjà vu; (4) varieties of imaginative activity such as stories, play, drawing, inner characters, fictions, masturbatory fantasies, etc.; and finally (5) hypnoid states and dreams.

1. The first group encompasses what is usually called *unconscious fantasy*. The inner events I am classifying here (see my subdivision into A, B, and C) do not exhibit any one of the three characteristics of fantasy—intrusion, imagination, misfit—I proposed earlier.

A. *Unconscious orgasm* in hysterics is allegedly sustained by fantasy, even though the subjects involved know nothing of what is happening to them and may at best become apprised of it by the state of their underwear. *Unconscious gestures*, for example, shifting about on the analytic couch at a significant moment, as if to prepare the fulfillment of a desire, are also supposed to constitute a variety of unconscious fantasy. However, the ego is entirely uninvolved in both of these cases. That the verbalization of this type of unconscious manifestation within the therapeutic setting (a highly dubious maneuver) does not lead to any significant dynamic change lends support to my position. *To understand the meaning of an unconscious fact or gesture does not entail the discovery of an unconscious fantasy. Perverse behavior* is also understood as fulfilling an unconscious fantasy. Again, even though the ego is present when the action is performed, it would be erroneous to speak of a genuine fantasy. Of course, perverse behavior does have a latent meaning but, unlike fantasy, it does not require verbalization. The meaning of perverse behavior is interpretable in the general context of therapy, but should not be attacked frontally.

B. *Fantasies on the ego's prereflexive level.* I am particularly interested in this second variety of what is erroneously called unconscious fantasy. The recent insistence on fantasy, expecially "unconscious fantasy," marks the rapid development of child analysis to such an extent that one may wonder whether the inappropriate extension of the concept of fantasy is not somehow due to a tacit disregard for the profound differences that separate the very young child's typical modes of fashioning reality and self from the adult's established modes of thinking. The young child is constantly engaged in the construction of that which will subsequently become reality. Until the child actually arrives at that stage, it is nonsensical to speak of a clear distinction between the real and the imaginary realms, since this distinction occurs at a later point in the child's evolution. For the child, a devouring door or the wolf-obscurity equation neither constitutes reality nor derives from the realm of the imaginary. Instead these are affects in search of representatives, at a time when the representatives themselves are not yet required to take account of the intersubjective world's unity. (This theory is well known to participants in these seminars.)

The discussions focusing on the existence or nonexistence of a real mother for the child are pertinent in this context. It has been objected that Melanie Klein had no interest in the mother's reality and that she made the child's world arise from "fantasy" alone. But if we consider that the categories of the real and the imaginary prevail only in the fully constituted adult ego, the problem vanishes. The child analyst does not in fact see an endless string of fantasies, but participates in the active construction of reality and self. Moreover, it is crucial to understand that the distinct positions of the real and the imaginary do not at first form an integral part of the child's inner experience. These categories are relatively late acquisitions and many an authentic experience occurs *before* their differentiation, for example, poetry as well as other forms of artistic expression. Philippe, who is tearing me apart to eat me up, and Denis, who is killing me with an aerosol can, are actually quite worried about the consequences of their actions. At this stage of the ego's development, either everything or nothing is fantasy. Considering matters from an operational angle, we may conclude that the concept of unconscious fantasy has once again let us down.

C. *Conversional fantasy.* Rather than being transferred onto a representation, it happens at times that affects appear in the form of bodily states: yawning, the urge to urinate, headaches, a form of coenesthesia. These conversional phenomena are usually classified as manifestations of unconscious fantasy. In therapy, they stand apart because the real issue is not whether one should supply an unconscious fantasy in their place but rather how to understand why these bodily states could not find imaginary or verbal representatives.

2. What of *hallucinations* and *delusions?* To equate them with conscious or unconscious fantasies (which ones?) would really make no sense. Neither hallucinations nor delusions entail any kind of reference to the ego as supposed by my guiding categories of fantasy. Considered operationally, a hallucination or delusion functions in much the same way as a prereflexive fantasy might: it can at times serve to initiate a process of therapeutic working-through. Pathological projection is quite different in that, though also sustained by concealed aims, it remains resistant to interpretation. More work needs to be done here, but it is clear at any rate that the fantasy which is supposedly submerged behind the projection has no operational value.

Certain types of *theoretical conviction* need to be placed under the same rubric; their manifest content is often a rather thin disguise for their hidden meaning. To remain within our specialty, we may consider the conviction held by many a psychoanalyst that, fated to be incomplete, women are both castrated and essentially masochistic, whereas men are intrinsically autonomous, active, endowed, and masters of the sex act. Were such a conviction not motivated by some unconscious fear of castration, its proponents would not be prevented from taking up a position somewhat closer to the obvious, arguing, for example, that sexual intercourse accomplishes the union of two narcissistically complete and genitally complementary beings. No doubt this conviction, which happens to be my own, has a number of latent meanings as well. I am quite prepared to admit this, with the stipulation that these meanings will not be branded unconscious fantasies.

3. There is a third group of experiences that satisfy two of my criteria, the intrusion into and misfit with the ego's ongoing concerns. *Impulsive actions* fall into this category. However, they are not to be equated with fantasies because they are never posited as being imaginary and the realization of their being misfits does not coincide with the actions themselves but generally occurs after the fact. *Compulsive acts* also possess latent meaning yet they too, just like impulsive acts, are devoid of any reference to the ego. In addition, compulsive acts cannot be classified in either the real or the imaginary realm.

The illusion of déjà vu is also understood as harboring a repressed fantasy. Though this illusion appears suddenly and stands in contrast to the subject's immediate concerns, it does nevertheless refer to reality; no imaginary representation accompanies it. Déjà vu is the return of an affect attaching itself unexpectedly to the spectacle of reality. The illusion is due to a momentary confusion between the recognition of a previously experienced affect and a new reality that is being currently unveiled. Here, as in many other cases, it is more correct to say that, rather than a fantasy, there is an affect behind the experience.

4. A fourth group of experiences is palpably closer to fantasy. These are inner experiences that are definitely posited as being imaginary. This is precisely why these experiences are perpetually being confused with fantasies. I mean here *imaginations,* grouping under this generic name a number of disparate experiences that possess an undeniable structural affinity with each other: imaginary tales, play, drawing, the creation of internal characters, the contents of a fiction as well as another form of imagination, improperly called masturbatory fantasies. All of these experiences are quite distinct from fantasy because the ego is knowingly responsible for producing them, and this full assumption of responsibility by the ego voids two of the criteria of fantasy: being an intrusion and a misfit. In fact, whatever their form, imaginations never entail an actual shift of level within the ego. On the contrary, imaginations are the ego's genuine products, designed to anticipate a satisfaction. Understanding the latent meaning of imaginations need not lead the analyst to interpret them. Whether they are expressive of the narcissistic freedom authorized by therapy or alternatively a form of resistance to the reliving of objectal conflicts, imaginations do represent a relatively high level of working-through inasmuch as they are the ego's active products. Consequently, to interpret an imagination does nothing but degrade it; the interpretation will at any rate have no dynamic effect.

5. There is a fifth and final group of experiences that, though in some respects similar, are ultimately distinct from fantasies because they do not exhibit any intrusiveness: *dreams and hypnagogic representations.* With these phenomena we stand at the threshold of fantasy proper since we can speak of fantasy as a waking dream. We can conjecture that the interpretation of dreams in therapy is at its most effective when the memory of the dream appears as unexpectedly as a fantasy.

V. FANTASY IN THE ANALYTIC SITUATION

If, with good reason, the dream is called the "royal road" to the structural understanding of the patient, fantasy can lay claim to just as much, if not more, since it moves the analyst beyond partial understanding, offering truly propitious occasions to effect dynamic change in therapy.

Let us examine a fantasy in the psychotherapeutic situation. Germaine suffers from near total blindness due to affective causes; she wears "protective" sunglasses. During her sessions she is negative for a long time, anxious, even feeling persecuted. "What's the point of this moral exposure?" she asks. She is talking about her confessor whom she sees once a week to be absolved of her sins of gluttony. A long silence follows, interrupted by some insignificant comments about the furniture and the threads of my sweater. That is when she suddenly has a fantasy. She has an abrupt vision of something like a "plant" ("Where is that coming from?"), a plant with thorns, she says. Her associations lead her to a date palm that she "raised" while she worked in a children's home. She had to, in her own words, "punish" [*mettre en pénitence:* make it stand in the corner—*Trans.*] the date palm by surrounding it with thread, because one of its prickles nearly poked out its mother's eye (i.e., Germaine's). The accident resulted in nothing more than slight injury, making it necessary for Germaine to wear sunglasses.

This is the fantasy and the immediate memories associated with it. Note the fantasy's characteristically abrupt shift of level in the ego. What is the significance of this shift in the analytical situation? In everyday life, the ego is generally concerned with pragmatic reality. A fantasmic shift calls attention to itself because of its incongruous relation to one's immediate concerns. Now, in the therapeutic setting the pragmatic concerns of everyday life are bracketed in order to preserve the spontaneity of associations. Under these circumstances, is it correct to speak of shifting levels? Yes, because even during the spontaneous flow of associations, the ego continues to see itself as the seat and author of its own psychoanalytic discourse, so that here too the intrusion of fantasy causes the ego to give up its own self-government for a moment and to be content with observing its own vision like a spectator. While remaining the seat of its actions, the ego momentarily refuses to be its author. There is no need to belabor the difference between an ego that is simply a spectator and one that is the author of its own acts. In therapy this kind of shift in levels constitutes a privileged moment: an anonymous affect has just found a representative, but the ego is as yet incapable of assuming responsibility for either the affect or the representation. The fact that an affect is on the verge of abandoning its anonymity, conferring a representative on itself, should be interpreted as an appeal for help from the analyst. The moment the fantasy is *communicated* seems especially favorable to the integration of an affect by the ego.

To return to Germaine, the affect seeking a reference point in the ego is of an aggressive nature and has to do with her masochistic dialectic. The first interpretation notes the masochistic aspect of the patient's personality. Like the plant, she too is being punished: she goes to confession every week. Her laughter indicates her realization of this as she continues the interpretation on her own by comparing her glasses to a thread surrounding her head. Yes, she is punishing herself, but it is because she has been wanting to do harm to somebody. Her "protective" glasses are supposed to protect her aggressive tendencies like the threads tied around the date palm. At the following session she is relaxed, takes off her glasses, tells of a game of "patience" [*réussite:* game of success—*Trans.*] she won, and for the first time she envisions her future with less resignation.

Why was the interpretation of the fantasy effective? No doubt the immediacy of a conflict drove the ego to abandon its usual level and to transpose the solution to a lower level of its activity. But the effect is also due to the call for help that is implicit in fantasies patients choose to communicate without delay. As opposed to other instances of momentary shifts in level—like slips of the tongue and the use of equivocation, whose interpretation is often a matter of indiscretion rather than psychoanalysis—fantasy constitutes a positive attempt to transcend the pure affect and arrive at a representation of it, an attempt in which the analyst is invited to participate. Need I insist that in the case before us the affect found its way to actuality *in the transference* and had no objectal pole other than the analyst herself? In this sense, fantasy is to be considered as the expression in *statu nascendi* of a relational moment, the expression itself being a part of the relation. It is as if my patient had told me: I know that I can communicate my fantasy to you—a fantasy I actually produced for you—because I know you are not going to push me over the cliff of my conflicts. On the contrary, you will help me resolve them.

Fantasy is expressive of an attempt at working through a problem and is combined with a desire for collaboration; without exception it constitutes the privileged moment when the therapeutic transcendence of problems is operative.

VI. CONCLUSION

Structurally, fantasy appears to be the product of an abruptly actualized affect. The affect's corresponding representation intrudes, is a misfit in the current context of the ego, and is immediately posited as being imaginary. These characteristics of fantasy derive from a temporary shift of levels in the ego; the transformation of affect into a representation indicates that a lower level of the ego seeks to make contact with a higher level of its conscious activity. Viewed operationally, only the representations that emerge under the conditions enumerated above possess the requisite dynamism to become a lever of therapy. To interpret such a fantasy at the time of its emergence is to respond to the patient's call for help. That is the operational value of fantasies.

Part II

Femininity
in Psychoanalysis

Editor's Note   Maria Torok's article "The Meaning of 'Penis Envy' in Women," written in 1963 and first published in 1964, predates contemporary feminist discussions of female childhood development as well as feminist critiques of the Freudian conception of femininity. The essay invites us to reconsider the Freudian concept of penis envy. Understood by Freud as the inevitable psychosexual result of a biological lack and as such virtually insurmountable, penis envy leaves only one therapeutic avenue open: encouraging the patient to renounce her desire or to replace it with the birth of a male child. Torok argues that if anything like a penis envy exists at all, it is not based on the biological fact of sexual difference. The alleged incompleteness of women is a misconception flowing from Freud's assumption that a common phallic phase characterizes the infantile development of both sexes. Freud offers penis envy as a universal principle of explanation; Torok treats it as a symptom. Penis envy is not an anatomically determined and therefore inalterable cause of women's behavior, but rather the effect of a suffering that requires psychoanalytic elucidation. Torok asserts that in a woman's desire to be (like) a man "nothing matters less than the penis itself." Penis envy, in Torok's view, is a mere fantasy, a belief or myth, invented by the little girl to mask an inhibited and therefore inexpressible desire for her own orgasm. It is the prohibition against approaching her sexuality that constrains the little girl to imagine the plenitude of the other sex, to fantasize the boy's penis as an idealized object. Ultimately, penis envy is the symptom of a fixation on the mother who prohibits auto-erotic libidinal contact. As long as girls fantasize about privileges enjoyed by boys, they do not recognize their repressive environments. By the same token, the fantasy or myth of penis envy allays the fear of losing the mother, should the child/woman's underlying wish to free her sexuality be fulfilled. Understanding the meaning of penis envy through psychoanalysis as a symptom of the little girl's inhibitions results in the sexual liberation of the adult woman she has since become.

This argument's larger implications become manifest only when set in the context of Abraham and Torok's later writings. Torok studies the pathology of dissatisfaction with being a woman and traces it to repressive mother-daughter relationships. It seems reasonable to expand this thought and to suppose that the mother in turn suffered in childhood from a similarly inhibitive relation. The mother's aggression and jealousy toward the daughter are born of the frustrations and repressions to which she was subjected by her own mother. There is then a generational legacy, a transmission of sexual inhibitions along genealogical lines. The ultimate aim of analyzing women who suffer from penis envy would be to understand the specific source and configuration of their mothers' thwarted sexual fulfillment. This type of transgenerational therapy was subsequently developed by Abraham and Torok in the mid-1970s and served, in conjunction with Abraham's theory of the phantom, to treat certain forms of obsessive behavior and phobia. (See Part 5, "Secrets and Posterity.") In the psychotherapeutic context envisioned by Abraham and Torok in the mid-1970s, liberating the daughter would imply liberating the mother, even in her absence. Enlarging the transgenerational perspective, we can throw psychoanalytic light on the social and historical aspects of the subjection of women. The succession of inhibitive mother-daughter relationships enacts the perpetuation of dependency over the ages; mothers effectively function as the frustrated and impotent instruments of the subordination of women. Men may thus have reaped the benefits of a mechanism whereby women contributed to their own subjugation. The question why women should have been subjected to male rule may be raised in light of the evidence offered by Torok that girls can achieve full-fledged orgasm at a substantially earlier age than boys. The liberation of women's sexual development presumes a liberated social fabric in which the orgasmic self-sufficiency of the very young female child is recognized and allowed to develop and reach maturity in the desire for union with a partner seeking complementary fulfillment. Torok's ideas can be brought to bear on the political sentiments first formulated by John Stuart Mill in the opening paragraph of his pamphlet *The Subjection of Women* (1861): "The principle which regulates the existing social relations between the sexes—the . . . subordination of one sex to another—is wrong in itself, and now one of the chief hindrances to human improvement; . . . it ought to be replaced by a principle of perfect equality, admitting no power or privilege on the one side, nor disability on the other." Reflecting on Torok's essay, we realize how essential it is to understand the relationship between the systematic rejection of the little girl's pleasurable inner feelings and the history of women's social subjugation. The sexual liberation of women and their unhindered entry into society are inextricably linked.

TWO

The Meaning of "Penis Envy" in Women

M. Torok, 1964

I

In the psychoanalysis of women there comes a period in which an envious desire for the male member and its symbolic equivalents appears. Episodic for some women, for others "penis envy" constitutes the very center of the therapeutic process. The exacerbated wish to possess that which women believe they are deprived of by fate—or by the mother—expresses a basic dissatisfaction some people have ascribed to the fact of being a woman. Surely, the conviction that their own privation is balanced by the enjoyment of others is common to patients of both sexes and is found in all analyses. Jealousy and demands, spite and despair, inhibition and anxiety, admiration and idealization, inner emptiness and depression: such are the diverse symptoms of this state of lack. Yet it is remarkable that, of men and women, only women should trace this state of lack to their very sex: "It's because I'm a woman." By which we should understand: I do not have a penis; hence my weakness, my inertia, my lack of intelligence, my dependency, and my ills.

> Ultimately, all women are like me and I cannot help feeling contempt for them, as I do for myself. It's they, the men, who possess all the qualities, all the attributes that make them worthy of admiration.

How is so radical a depreciation of one's own sex conceivable? Is it perhaps rooted in real biological inferiority? This idea came to seem inevi-

Previously published as "La signification de l'envie du pénis' chez la femme," in Janine Chasseguet Smirgel et al., *La sexualité féminine: Nouvelles perspectives psychanalytiques* (Paris: Payot, 1964), pp. 181–219; and in *L'Écorce et le noyau* (Paris: Flammarion, 1987), pp. 132–71; as "The Significance of Penis Envy in Women," in Janine Chasseguet Smirgel et al., *Female Sexuality: New Psychoanalytic Views* (Ann Arbor: University of Michigan Press, 1970), pp. 135–70; and as "The Meaning of 'Penis Envy' in Women," trans. N. Rand, *Differences* 4, no. 1 (1992): 1–39. Editor's brackets are marked *Trans*.

table to Freud following his unsuccessful attempts to cure the problem of desire for an inherently inaccessible object. We might as well "preach to the fish"—so Freud's colorful phrase would put it—as overexert ourselves in the hopeless endeavor to make patients give up once and for all their childhood wish to acquire a penis. Given the failure of so many attempts, was it not inevitable for Freud to yield in the end, conceding some legitimacy to "penis envy" and ascribing it to the nature of things: "the biological inferiority of the female sex"? From another point of view, that of the child's affective development, Freud drew the same conclusion. So when he saw fit to insert an intermediary phallic phase between the anal and genital phases, he conceived the phallic phase as similar in both sexes, as wholly given to the male member. If it is true that the child at this stage knows one sex only, the male sex, then we should understand the little girl's frustration at being deprived of it. All her conjectures concerning her state of castration and the value of the opposite sex would spring from her frustration and from the phallic phase's inherent psychobiological phallocentrism. That is why both "penis envy" and the attempts to make women relinquish it are doomed to come to an impasse in Freud's psychoanalytic perspective. Yet, even if fantasies relating to the phallic stage may confirm Freud's thesis of its universality, it would seem that this state of affairs might still allow a genuinely psychoanalytic explanation without our having to admit defeat by resorting to biology.

I understand Freud's exasperation on hearing: "What's the use of continuing the analysis when you can't give me *that*." But I also understand his patient's despair at being asked to *relinquish* a wish she holds so dear. And Freud would have been the first to agree that it is not the analyst's function to promote the surrender of a desire, whatever it may be.

Now, precisely because it is envious, the woman's desire to have a "penis"—to be a "man"—can be exposed as a subterfuge through analysis. A desire can be satisfied, envy never. Envy can only breed more envy and destruction. It happens occasionally that envy disguised as desire achieves a semblance of satisfaction. Such is the so-called "phallic" attitude of some women who are completely estranged through their imitation of the other sex or, at least, through their imitation of the image they have of it. The fragile structure thus constructed merely houses emptiness, anguish, and frustration. The task of analysis is to bring to light a genuine but forbidden desire lying buried beneath the guise of envy. Here as elsewhere, taking literally the analysand's protestations closes the door to analysis. One sure way to achieve this result would consist in legitimizing women's "penis envy" by declaring that the supposed state of castration is a phylogenetically determined destiny. Another guaranteed means of falling short of analysis would be to posit extra-analytical motives—for instance the real inferiority of today's women as regards their social and cultural fulfillment—behind the demand to have a penis.

Analysts who do not recoil from "penis envy," this "stumbling block" of therapy, will want first of all to clarify the nature of the conflict giving rise to such a desperate compromise. They will also need to evaluate fairly the benefits this compromise solution of "penis envy" nonetheless does provide the patient, to take advantage ultimately, for the purposes of treatment, of the painful contradictions into which "penis envy" locks her.

Among post-Freudian authors, Ernest Jones and Melanie Klein have the signal distinction of no longer placing "penis envy" beyond the scope of explanation. Both consider the quality of the initial relationship to the maternal breast as decisive. As soon as analysis improves the initial maternal relation (by deconflictualizing the introjection of the Breast), envy in general and "penis envy" in particular lose their reason for being.[1]

It is perhaps useful to add and underscore the following: for the purposes of analysis object-things are mere *signs* of conscious or unconscious desires or fears, that is, they are reminders of the subjective moments that caused the subject to create them. In the libidinal economy love objects (and even the internal object) are considered by Freud as simple *mediators* toward attaining the aim of instinct: satisfaction. Admittedly, *object-things* have names and spatial dimensions and therefore are indeed *objective:* their being the same for everyone makes them apt for exchange, but also for disguising desires. Is it not the task of analysis to recover from behind the *thing* the desire it at once negates and fulfills? Analyzing via the *things* an envious patient might covet, such as the "penis" or the "breast" (even if they are the analyst's), thus amounts to exacerbating the contradictions that relate to love objects (and internal objects). Transcending these contradictions would involve, instead, the revelation (and hence dissolution) of the internal conflicts implied by the *satisfaction* of a vital desire. The fulfillment of desires is not a matter of objective realities; it is dependent on our capacity to satisfy ourselves and on our right to satisfaction, that is, on our freedom to accomplish the relational acts of our bodies. The objective realities, invoked as so many— usually inaccessible—objects of lack or of envy, are traps in therapy; they are meant to mask (and therefore sustain) the inhibitions linked to relational acts. These traps—all too often—imprison desire for life.

---

1. [The term "introjection" (as well as "incorporation" further on) is used here in Melanie Klein's sense; Torok's definition is to be found in "The Illness of Mourning and the Fantasy of the Exquisite Corpse" in this volume.—Ed.].

For this reason I must exclude from this study on "penis envy" the penis itself insofar as it is considered a thing, an objective, biological or social and cultural reality. Though a seeming paradox at first, the fact is that in "penis envy" nothing matters less than the penis itself. This "partial object" appears to me as a stopgap invented to camouflage a desire, as an artificially constructed obstacle thrown in the way of our becoming one with ourselves in the course of being liberated from inhibited acts. What is the purpose of this artifice? What does it protect against? This needs to be *understood* before it can be exposed.

However deformed or estranged from itself it may have become, the desire underlying "penis envy" cannot fail to show through. As all others, this symptom deserves therefore our respect and attention. If through luck my analytic endeavor manages to reach the source of "penis envy," rendering it superfluous, I will not substitute acquisition for renunciation. "Penis envy" will disappear by itself the moment the painful state of lack responsible for it has ceased to exist.

II

The way is opened for a genuinely psychoanalytic approach, provided that we abandon objectivistic views about the coveted "penis" and suspend all questions about the social and cultural legitimacy of the envy. For the psychoanalyst, "penis envy" is not the symptom of an illness, but the symptom of a certain state of desire—the state of unfulfilled desire—no doubt due to contradictory demands. When the symptom is examined in this light, we will be surprised to find that such an examination, provided it does not stray from the analytic stance, is itself enough to reveal the general meaning of this phenomenon, the nature of the conflict it tends to resolve, and the manner in which it attempts to do so.

Freud's idea comes to mind: the little girl's discovery of the boy's genitals was sufficient reason to provoke envy and, concomitantly, hatred toward the mother, the person responsible, according to the girl's hypothesis, for her state of "castration." And of course, "penis envy" could not derive its *content*, that is, its pretext, from anything but experience. A problem still remains: under what conditions must this experience take place for it to result in an insurmountable and lifelong envy? After all we meet only what we are ready to meet. "The polar bear and the whale . . . , each confined to his element . . . , cannot come together," as Freud himself says. If indeed a decisive meeting occurs between the little girl and the boy, they meet not as different from each other but precisely as similar, namely as marked by sex. We may legitimately surmise that the girl's discovery of the boy's genitals occurs within the framework of the exploration of her own. The discovery of the penis must have come at a fitting moment for it to escape being reduced to a mere childhood incident. When the girl tells herself: "My mother didn't give me *that;* that's why I hate her," she takes advantage of a convenient pretext. Yet she merely gives voice to her hatred without in the least explaining it.

The association of "penis envy" with conscious or unconcious hatred for the mother is a matter of common observation. But there is another no less remarkable clinical fact whose study allows us to understand the deep-seated motivation of this hatred. This clinically constant and highly significant fact is what I might call the *idealization* of the "penis." Many a woman has fantastic ideas about the male organ's extraordinary qualities: infinite power, good or bad, that guarantees for its owner absolute security and freedom as well as immunity to any form of anxiety or guilt; a power that brings him pleasure, love, and the fulfillment of all his wishes. *"Penis envy" is always envy of an idealized penis.*

> "When you've got *that* ['the penis']," says Ida, "you've got everything, you feel protected, nothing can harm you. . . . You are what you are and others have no choice but to follow you and admire you . . . it represents absolute power; they (the men) can never sink into a state of need, of lack of love. Women? Incompleteness, perpetual dependency; they have the role of Vestal Virgins guarding the flame. It's no use speaking to me about the Virgin Mary. . . . God the Father is a man! The word pure reminds me of purée. . . . I've always held women in contempt."

> "I don't know why I have this feeling," says Agnes, "when it has nothing to do with reality, but it's always been like that for me. It's as if men were the only ones made to be fulfilled, to have opinions, to develop themselves, to advance. And everything seems so easy to them . . . , they're a force nothing at all opposes . . . , they can do anything they want. And I simply stagnate, hesitate; I feel there's a wall in front of me . . . I've always had the feeling that I was not quite completed. Something like a statue waiting for its sculptor to make up his mind finally to shape its *arms.*"

> When she was little, Yvonne always believed that boys "succeed in everything . . . , they are instantly fluent in several languages. . . . They could take all the candles in a church and no one would stop them. If ever they encounter an obstacle, they just naturally jump over it."

These are eloquent descriptions of an *idealized* penis. It is clear that we are dealing with created meaning: "the *thing,* whatever it may be, *that one does not have.*" Now, so vital a lack cannot be natural; it must be the effect of deprivation or renunciation. And so the question arises: how does it happen that one deprives oneself of so precious a part of oneself in exchange for an external "object" that is inaccessible and, going by the patients' own words, even nonexistent? For the time being let me limit myself to registering the fact. Its name is *repression*. Every idealization has a repression as its counterpart. But who benefits from this repression? The mother, of course, since the hatred is directed at her. In fact, though the idealized penis has no real existence at all, its counterpart for the subject—depression, self-depreciation, rage—does, and how! I will not believe for a second that affective states of such intensity could spring from an *idea* one fabricates about an object one has encountered. When the girl says to the mother living within her: "I hate you because of that thing you never gave me," she also says: "My hatred is as legitimate as the absence of that thing in me is obvious. But rest assured, I do not consider legitimate the real hatred I feel because of the repression you force on my desire."

What is this repression? It is surely no accident that precisely the penis—absent from the girl's anatomy—should have been invested with values from which the subject has had to divest herself. The genitals one does not have lend themselves famously to representing inaccessibility, especially since they are by nature alien to the experiences of one's own body. Here is then a marvelous way of symbolizing the prohibition affecting those very experiences of the body that relate to one's own genitals. In sum, the naming of an inaccessible thing as the coveted object masks the existence within the subject of a desire that has been refracted by an impassable barrier. The overinvestment of the coveted thing merely demonstrates the primary value attached to the desire renounced. Women tend to overlook the agency responsible for repression, the faceless prosecutor dwelling within them. To unmask it would imply coming face to face with shadowy areas where hate and aggression smolder against the Mother they cannot help but love.

A complex unconscious speech, directed at the maternal imago, condenses in "penis envy." It can be made explicit in the following statements:

1. "You see, it is in a *thing* and *not in myself* that I look for what I am deprived of."
2. "My attempts are *useless* since the thing cannot be acquired. The obvious futility of my efforts should guarantee my final renunciation of the desires you disapprove."
3. "I want to insist on the value of this inaccessible thing so that you may see the extent of my sacrifice in allowing myself to be stripped of what I desire."
4. "I should accuse you and strip you in turn, but that is exactly what I want to avoid, deny, overlook, since I need your love."

5. "In short, idealizing the penis so as to covet it all the more is a way of reassuring you by showing you that I will never be at one with myself, that I will never attain such a thing in myself. It is, I tell you, as impossible as changing into another body."

This is the pledge of allegiance on which "penis envy" affixes its seal.

The forbidden part of herself—which corresponds to "penis" in the little girl's imagoic speech—is in fact her own sex, struck by repression.

An astonishing statement. It seems to mean that the girl's actual lived sex can be symbolized through the boy's penis *thing* or, put another way, through an anal understanding of the penis. In point of fact, a link is missing in the genesis of this symbolization: the anal relation to the mother. The idea of an accessible or inaccessible, condoned or forbidden "thing" clearly alludes to this. The girl speaks to the Mother through her appeal: "I want that *thing*." Yet the demand's futility, as regards both its form and substance, implies reassurance toward the Mother. Her prerogatives will remain intact. It is quite remarkable that the Mother's authority or superiority in fact concerns less the "things" that "belong" to her than the acts of sphincter control, acts she claims to command at will. Hence the difficulty of the child, and later of the adult, in accepting these acts without first passing through the agency of the imago. "Penis envy" needs to be situated in this context. It can be understood then that what is coveted is not the "thing" but the acts allowing for mastery of "things" in general. Coveting a *thing* amounts to displaying for the imago the renunciation of *acts*. In the anal relation the child will have transferred its acts of sphincter control to the Mother. The result is incredible aggression toward her. Let us consider the following process. The child cannot interpret the mother's exercise of control otherwise than as a show of her interest in possessing the child's feces, even while they are still inside the body. The result: *the body's interior falls under the sway of maternal control.* The child can free herself from this domination only by a reversal of the relation: hence the birth of killer fantasies such as evisceration, evacuation of the maternal body's insides, as well as destruction of the place and function of the mother's control.

This is why the mother has to be reassured. That the show of desire for the penis-thing—inaccessible anyhow—can perform this role of reassurance marvelously is now abundantly clear.

Let us return to the final question: What motivates this specific choice? Why precisely the "penis"?

I shall use another, complementary way of examining symptoms in order to define the problem more precisely. In addition to my previous attempt to reconstruct the symptom's *retrospective* genesis, I now want to consider another equally crucial aspect, the symptom's *prospective* dimension. This examination will perhaps reward us along the way with some insight into the question of genesis itself.

I understand by the prospective dimension of a symptom (as well as of its underlying conflict) its genuinely negative aspect, one that provides no solution to any problem whatever and is solely defined by something not yet realized, not yet existent. The prospective dimension is the step ahead that was thwarted. At the same time, the prospective moment gives repression all of its dynamic features. The obstructed stages of affective maturation demand their realization. Even though a hint of these stages does shine through the repression blocking them, the symptom's prospective aspect is not articulated in the imagoic speech. The little girl could not, even unconsciously, state the following to her imago: "Though I can tell you that I covet the penis-thing for my possession so that I can become a boy, what I cannot even feel is my aborted desire *to experience pleasure with* the penis as women do and as it is *preordained* in the destiny of my own sex." This very fact of genital nonattainment should put us on the road to identifying the repressive prohibitions. At stake is the experience that should have *prepared and set forth the girl's genital project and identification,* an experience obviously related to the "precious part" of herself that underwent repression.

We have seen that this "precious part" is a *set of acts* transferred to the anal Mother as her prerogative. The little girl had at her disposal, nonetheless, an indirect means of reclaiming what was taken from her: *identification* with the Mother, sovereign in her powers. And yet what we observe is a lack of identification, a lack "penis envy" richly bespeaks. Thus I am led to incriminate not only the repression of pregenital anal conflicts but also a specific inhibition: the total or partial inhibition to masturbate, to have orgasm, and to engage in attendant phantasmic activities. "Penis envy" emerges then as a disguised demand not for the genitals and attributes of the opposite sex, but for *one's own masturbatory and self-developmental desires realized through encounters with oneself in a combination of orgasmic and identificatory experiences.* This is the first conclusion we may draw regarding the general significance of "penis envy" considered as a symptom in the Freudian sense of the term.

III

M. Klein, E. Jones, K. Horney, and J. Müller have already indicated the early discovery and repression of vaginal sensations. As for me, I have observed that encounters with the other sex always entail a reminder or occasion for becoming aware of one's own. Clinically speaking, "penis envy," i.e., the discovery of the boy's genitals, is often associated with the repressed memory of an orgasmic experience.

> For a few sessions Martha had wild fits of laughter and crying. Her emotions gradually found their content: when she was a little girl, she met some boys in a swimming pool. Since then she had often repeated the sentence: "I can't live *like that.*" In the course of her analysis this sentence would reappear when she was deeply depressed. "Like that" means consciously: "deprived of the penis." But I came to understand with her that at the same time she "pressed her thighs together," "pushed part of her swimming suit inside," and felt something like a "palpable wave." The combination of laughter and tears [joy combined with guilt] refers to the idea: if I am "like that" [feeling "this wave"], "will they still have me at home?" At puberty the same patient felt such intense guilt toward her mother that she kept her ignorant of the onset of her periods—the mark of her genital attainment—for an entire year.

Far from being neglected, her own genitals were a constant source of latent preoccupation, since the need to please the mother triumphed at that time over the pleasure of orgasm. During the session, however, the desire for orgasm came to the fore through fits of laughter; previously it had had to stay repressed, precisely by means of "penis envy." At first there had been an "inexpressible joy," "tremendous hope." But then, she does not know how, she came to be convinced: There is, not in me, but out there, not in my body, but in an *object,* something infinitely desirable, though entirely inaccessible. Note the contradiction: "the palpable and infinitely good wave" makes the little girl lose her sense of *being good* for her environment. The "penis" is perceived in this case as the "good" sex organ, the one providing pleasure to its owner without any guilt. This sex organ is not linked to guilty acts of masturbation and incorporation; it combines pleasure for oneself and harmony with one's environment, resulting in conditions of truly perfect harmony. To feel "this wave" must appear arrogant and evil to others. So this "good" is relinquished in exchange for an external object, the idealized penis. The emptiness thus created within the subject fills with sadness, bitterness, and jealousy. Yet smoldering aggression cannot replace what has been missed: the progressive and sensuous awakening to maturity. Only analytic therapy can perform the reawakening by freeing the instruments needed to accomplish it.

The joy of maturational awakenings reaches beyond instant gratification. It signifies for the subject a sudden opening toward the future. It is the joy of great discoveries, of "Yes! I understand." "So, that's how I can become *myself,* an adult. I acquire my value through the joy that turns me into myself." (J. Müller notes aptly that the free play of infantile sexuality guarantees self-esteem.) True enough, the orgasmic joys of early childhood constitute the means whereby genital sex, and therefore the budding personality itself, are foreshadowed and developed. What do we discover on the way to orgasm? The power to fantasize our identity with our parents and the power to picture ourselves in all the positions of the primal Scene, in accordance with the various levels at which it is apprehended. *The completed orgasm actually functions as verification: the fantasy is valid since it "provoked" the climax.* Clearly, every inhibition of such a self-to-self encounter leaves a gap within the subject in place of a vital identification. The result is an incomplete "body of one's own" (some might say Body Image) that has as its corollary a world peopled with fragmentary realities.[2]

There are dreams which aptly call to mind the meaning of orgasmic experience, its joyous sense of opening toward the future.

> This is how Agnes recalls the memory and excitement of her early orgasmic experiences. She first dreamed of an "incredible joy" turning into despair. At the seashore, she was waiting. An excited crowd thronged about her [= she awaits an orgasm]. Behind her there were restrooms [= memory of a place where she masturbated]. She was seated: all of a sudden, a wonderful animal, soft and silky to the touch, landed on her taut skirt. She is breathing heavily, extending her arms, caressing the animal. The admiring crowd vibrates with her. Everything was "so full," so "wonderful." That moment, she says, *gathered together everything, all that I've been, all that I will be.* As when you say to yourself: I want to be in a beautiful place, I want it badly, and you've hardly thought it when you find you're already there.

As the dream also shows us, the repressed fantasy of orgasm concerns the incorporation of the penis in its instinctual function as the *generator of orgasm.* This same patient felt that her body was incomplete, and wished that a "sculptor" would "make her *arms.*" Barred from masturbatory activity, she was limited in the use of her hands, whose fundamental fantasmic function is that of being the *penis for the vagina.*

Ferenczi taught us that masturbation brings with it a doubling of the subject; s/he identifies at once with both parties in the couple, performing intercourse self-sufficiently. Let me add that this doubling—touching oneself, the "I-me" experience authenticated by orgasm—also means: "Since

---

2. Masturbation might, of course, reappear later with a fantasy content corresponding to a different level, but the previous repression will have imprinted its negative mark on the personality as it develops subsequently.

I can do it to myself all alone, I am liberated from those who, up to now, have provided or forbidden pleasure at will." From a maternal relationship of dependence the child moves to autonomy through masturbation, through self-touching in both the literal and specifically reflexive sense of fantasy. In the process, the child sets up an independent maternal imago, which is seen as capable of having pleasure otherwise than with it. This possibility is clearly lacking when the maternal imago prohibits masturbation. The imago develops in this case during excessive or premature anal training and carries over its despotism to all other analogical realms. An excessively demanding mother will produce a jealous, empty, and unsatisfied maternal imago. How could she be self-sufficient when her control over the child is her only satisfaction? Of course, she is jealous and irritable when she sees the child escape her grip during its maturation. The effect of forbidding the child to masturbate is precisely to chain the child to the mother's body, hindering the child's own life project. Patients often express this situation by saying: "A part of my body stayed in my mother [hand, penis, feces, etc.]. How can I take it back? She needs it so very much. This is her only pleasure."

The hand that "belongs to Mother" cannot symbolize for the patient what the Mother forbids to herself; the hand will resist penile representation.[3] The road toward the Father is thereby blocked, and the relation of dependency on the Mother becomes permanent. The little girl experiences an insoluble dilemma: her only choices are either to identify with a mother deprived of value and dangerously aggressive, who needs to supplement herself by means of possession, or else to remain the futile appendage of an incomplete body. Women are likely to repeat these two positions in their relationship to their spouses. In analysis the aim is thus precisely to open the spellbinding circle of being and possessing. No, surely it is not a penis-appendage that is to be conferred; the "arms" Agnes recovers correspond to the penis as complement, which represents, beyond being or possessing, *the right to act and to become.* When the "penis-appendage envy" no longer masks the wish for a penis-complement, closeness to the Father need not falter on a sense of having too dangerous a body for the penis. This means at the same time that masturbation, as well as the [maturational—*Trans.*] identifications, are no longer perceived as destructive of the Mother.

During analysis a sense of power always accompanies the removal of orgasmic inhibition. Analysis could not lead a woman toward genital maturity without first resolving the "penis envy" that disguises the underlying

3. It is surprising to note that, as an instrument for introjecting the primal scene, the hand always represents the genitals of the opposite sex.

anal conflict. It is especially inconceivable that "penis envy" could be turned directly into a "wish to have a child from the Father." In fact, if the child is considered as playing the part of a coveted penis-object that fills a prior lack, the Mother—who without the child would lapse once again into bitterness and envy—will never be able to accept, desire, or encourage the evolution and fulfillment of the child's life project. Such a Mother has only one wish: to keep the child-penis in a state of perpetual appendage, as the illusory guarantee of her own plenitude.

To the extent that "penis envy" is based on repression and shields the child from the return of *pregenital* anxieties, it is an obstacle to genitality and in no way can lead to it. The road going from "penis envy" to genitality must go through an intermediary stage, the stage of tolerated fantasy. The child that is desired will no longer carry the meaning of what one *has,* but will represent something that is integrated into life's very becoming.

IV

Arrested in her genital attainment, the woman who suffers from "penis envy" lives with a feeling of frustration whose core she barely suspects. She has only an external idea of what orgasmic genital fullness might be. In any case, she cannot achieve it as long as the repression remains.

As we have seen, the symptom consists in idealizing the penis, in investing it with all that one has lost hope of for oneself: one's own life project, that is, genital maturity. This is what fulfillment means for the child, since she does not yet have it. Surely, desire springs eternal, it never relents, yet it is forced to "run on empty" or to fix itself to conventional images. Meeting a man in full orgasmic fusion is both the deepest wish of a woman suffering from "penis envy" and the thing she most avoids. Daily clinical observation shows us women yearning for the penis-complement—for the means of feminine fulfillment—only to see them grappling with a threatening and jealous imago. This is how envy emerges, envy of the idealized penis along with hatred for its supposed owner. Thus disappointment triumphs over love and frustration over fullness.

The passage to the so-called genital phase goes hand in hand with the feeling: I am no longer "castrated" since "I can." This means first and foremost the removal of inhibition from masturbatory acts and fantasies, which otherwise would block the analytic process itself. Repression being equivalent to a gap in the ego, to a restriction of one's power and worth, the removal of repression brings with it strength, self-esteem, and especially *confidence* in one's power and becoming.

"I don't know how to put it," says Olga, "the feeling your words left me with. I can't get over it. It's as if you had *transferred power* to me. Even so, I was very depressed the other day. But after leaving here, I repeated what you told me. All my anxiety melted away. I have rarely cried as I did this week. . . . It's like a sudden source of light. . . . And last night, I . . . no, I've never talked to anyone about those things. Anyway, it was like an *awakening*. I felt pleasure. Now I feel like trying things out and I've been flashing smiles at men and, you know, they respond nicely. I just can't get over it, people pay me compliments!"

During the previous session the two of us had understood how, by means of idealization, she forbade herself access to a reality within her reach and also to what extent this refusal was in full agreement with her mother's prohibition against approaching her father's virility. The rejection of the imago opened the road to the heart of the problem, masturbation. Olga came back a few sessions later with "*one* utterly cold hand," so cold that it seemed not to be hers. We talked about this in connection with all the objects her mother would not let her touch, including her own genitals. The "utterly cold" hand was simply a show of compliance with the forbidding maternal imago.

Tracing the idealization of the "penis" to the repression of masturbation frees up energy and clearly empowers one with one's own sex. This power, once taken from the child and now reclaimed, is the capacity to identify with the characters in the primal Scene of each successive stage of development and the capacity to verify the transient accuracy of these identifications through the orgasmic pleasure produced by them.[4]

To give the reader a more concrete grasp of these ideas it may be useful to provide a short sequence of analytic therapy (about 20 sessions). Ida, a young woman of Hungarian extraction, resorted to psychoanalysis

---

4. This is so true that even the identification with the castrating prohibitor of "autoeroticism" entails masturbatory fantasies. In the absence of such an identification—paradoxical and distressing though it may be—the prohibition acts as an effectual castration and manifests itself through a state of shock and great tension. Psychotic self-castration has this meaning of attempting to effect a lethal identification in despair so as to remove a no less lethal inhibition.

There are two ways of endangering the child's maturational identifications, either by forbidding the orgasm that would confirm the validity of the child's attempts at self-elaboration, or by annihilating fantasy life through the substitution of objectal reality in the form of seduction. In the latter case, the process of identification through fantasy is short-circuited by an effective but premature realization. The crippling effects of the inhibition resulting from this traumatism are in all respects comparable to those that derive from the other extreme. This is why women suffering from masturbatory inhibition can at times reach for mythomaniac fantasies of rape, whereas those who suffered rape early behave as if they were inhibited orgasmically.

in order to free herself from numerous emotional and professional difficulties.

> It really startled me to see Jacques do the dishes. I felt ashamed, as if
> something had been exposed to me. I can't do any needlework, mending
> or sewing . . . I'm ashamed of having a female body. I was ashamed of
> seeing Jacques become . . . how can I put it? a woman. Of course, that's
> not why he's . . . but why did it upset me so much? *Perhaps because for*
> *you "woman" does not have the usual sense. Being a "woman" for you is*
> *to be "sexless." What might have been upsetting to you is the idea that*
> *Jacques would become "sexless."* I don't know. I'm really confused. Why
> did I think that when you had a torch [the name given to the penis] you
> had everything, that it was great. Why did I think men had so much
> strength? Are they really like that? No, they aren't really. *In any case, if*
> *they are as you describe them, I understand your desire for the torch.*
> Jacques isn't like that, neither is my father or my grandfather, nobody is.
> It was my own idea. For my mother, women were enemies. But not Oliver.
> Oliver, my brother, he could be a friend. He could say to men: this is my
> mother and she's great. She was abandoned by her own mother. She thought
> babies were born through the navel. It's really like what we said last year:
> the baby didn't give her a "lower body." For me babies represent the life
> "down there," they're all you have down there, they're all that can grow
> from below. And my mother had had jaundice. Really, I should be like her.
> [She remembers a dream in which she gives birth to a yellow-orange child.]
> In fact, I must have been kind of an enemy for her. But I was also a friend.
> Why did she say to me: you'll never be pretty, never as clever, as sensitive
> as Susan? She never protected me, she's never been a real support for me.
> I've never had anything for myself. I've never kept anything, I always gave
> away my things.

It is clear that for Ida "woman" means "castrated." Trying to castrate
men is justified by the desire to possess the only sex, the male sex with
all its "advantages." The interpretation attempts to raise awareness concerning the idealized characteristics of the coveted penis as well as the
subjective nature of this idealization.

Having recognized in herself the source of the meaning that "woman"
and "penis" have for her—having by the same token understood that it
is not a matter of external, absolute, and unquestionable facts—Ida can
now go beyond meanings to their genesis: "my mother." It is because my
mother lives in me thus that for me "woman" must mean "castrated,
without a lower body, monstrous" and that I have to envy and idealize
the penis. Incomplete, empty, and frustrated, the Mother devalues and
castrates her in her very becoming. That is the reason why, as she now
understands, she can never keep anything for herself.

Poor mom, she feels left alone. She thinks from now on I'll only care for my baby. I dreamed about a snake. It came out of my breasts and was going to sting people. The midwife told me the baby was almost ready to come out. Poor mom. She called today, but she wanted to talk to Jacques. She must be very lonely. In the day care center there were only girls. And the doctor, this nice old man, I really liked him. He gave me shots. At school there were boys, too. My mother never sent me to school on time. I always had to start out late to stay some more with her. She always wanted to extend my vacations too. She didn't like school. But school represents strength, authority, regularity, and security. I like school. [Ida has strong inhibitions about going on with her college education.]

Ida continues to deepen the meaning of her relationship to her mother. She now grasps that: if she has a baby, mom will become "poor." Daughter and mother are inseparably linked; the one completes the other's emptiness.

The serpent-baby that *stings* [*pique*] and the good old doctor *giving shots* [*pique*] are equivalent: they are pleasure-objects for Ida, but dangerous for the mother. She definitely senses that by means of these pleasure-objects she could free herself. This clarifies for her why her Mother keeps her from coming in contact with the "strength and authority" that school means to her. Ida comes late to her sessions for the same reason. The "empty" Mother "with no lower body" needs to keep her close as *her own* pleasure-object in order to fill her own lack. In short: her choice is either to be autonomous and have pleasure *with* the penis or to be the Mother's annexed appendage. If I have my own pleasure, Mother will be destitute and empty; I cannot bear this idea.

I dreamed that we begged my mother for a little dog. Not me, my husband. When I was little, I liked to hold back my pee. The old cleaning woman would tell me to go to the bathroom when she'd see me shifting from one foot to the other. It's funny. I go after making love, too. . . . I was always told that girls didn't have anything, only a hole things come out of. They have nothing to hold back. This little bear makes me laugh. I bought it for the baby, but I keep it for myself for now. I'm tight like a virgin. I can't put in a diaphragm. It bleeds and falls into the toilet. I'm going to pay you today.

Something is to be claimed from the Mother: the freedom to hold back her "pee" in her body in order to play and have pleasure with it. Speaking of it starts to dissipate the depressing link to the Mother. Ida needs to reassure her Mother: she does not mean to make her destitute, on the contrary, she is paying her; in any case, it is so tight inside that she could hardly hold back anything. "No chance of making myself happy by myself; no danger for you, you can keep me as your appendage." Here, being able to hold back amounts to saying that one can have pleasure by oneself and therefore become independent. We also see that Ida's own "lower body" enters speech.

> When I was giving birth, I had a lot of trouble pushing out the baby. Then, suddenly I thought of everything we've said here, I called you very loud, really loud and that did it. It calmed me down. I was late today because of my kitchen. By the way, I quit my job, you know. I just said to myself: I'm a real woman. *A real woman: What's that for you?* Oh, dresses, a hairdo, a few minutes rest from time to time, a well-prepared *boeuf bourguignon* [beef stew—*Trans.*]. But you're right, there is something strange. I saw Jacques at his desk, he was writing. I wanted to write, too. I was . . . well, jealous. My studies, that's still what makes me anxious. I still have mountains to climb. [This recalls a dream in which she hiked in the mountains with her mother. There was an abyss below; "it was terrible," a crab crate, a big red crab.] My mother in that kitchen . . . awful. That day I had the feeling I had two mothers. An everyday one, who smiles nicely, talks, and does all kinds of things. The other is an unknown, unreachable, absurd woman [reference to a scene in the kitchen: her mother hurt her father during a violent discussion]. I dreamed that there was a fabric store, they sold buttons. I wanted to buy a sewing box.

Ida reassures me: I am good for her; thanks to me she was able to push out the baby. There is no danger that she will assert her independence. But would I allow her another pleasure, the real one, precisely the one forbidden by the Mother: her studies? It is impossible, she says. Now she feels like a "real woman," that is, like a castrato. But this is better than breaking loose from the relationship of belonging. If wounded and deprived, Mother would become dangerous as in the kitchen scene. At the same time, renouncing her own completeness, as when Ida pretends she is a "real woman," implies the same threat, namely the aggression born of dissatisfaction. No escape except total inhibition. To study, to hold back, as in "holding back her pee," or to have pleasure in intercourse— these are forbidden realms. The empty Mother clings to Ida; she prevents her from moving away toward that "strength."

> I just can't get here on time. I'm always late. *Like at school.* I felt that you were unhappy the other day. Now I'm handling the baby well. When my mother wouldn't send me to school, I was unhappy, I wanted to throw a tantrum, but finally I always gave in. The idea of continuing my studies makes me anxious. You talked about my mountain dream. I was with my mother, behind her. I was really scared. Down below, it was awful. *Like*

the life "down below." And I was also really scared of falling. I had a dream last night. I'm in the sand or something like clay. It gives way and I sink in deeper and deeper. I have the feeling that to save myself I would have to make some gesture, some movement. I had to let go without resisting. . . . I had to, I don't know, make some specific gestures. At the edge of the hold: an unknown man, I couldn't see his face, I didn't know who he was. A neutral, undefined character [the analyst]. I had the feeling he could save me, but also that he was powerless and couldn't be of help to me. And I was sinking in deeper and deeper, looking for the gestures. I had to find them. But then, it wasn't so bad, I thought. I could be saved anyway. I don't know anymore. I don't know. It was also like when I was giving birth.

The memory of the "mountain dream" (she is at the top with her mother, down below: an abyss and a crab) reminds her of a more recent dream. This time she is herself "down below" with a man in the very abyss: she now dares explore it. She goes inside it (like a baby inside her body). She now conceives of identifying with the penis penetrating her. She felt reassured: the penis was not at risk and would even climax. To penetrate herself, allowing herself to be lured "inside," as in a masturbatory splitting of herself in two, means being capable of picturing a relationship with a man, thereby freeing herself from "the mountaintop," namely the maternal relation that renders "down below" an "abyss of crabs." The dream's orgasmic aspect became more explicit a few sessions later. "It was also like when I was giving birth" as the child separated from the mother. The separation occurred by means of orgasm through penetration. As a result Ida is now in control of the doll she had been for the Mother; she now knows how to handle it and can broach another problem, the genital relation.

I panic when Jacques holds me. I thought of your inner hallway. I went to my gynecologist. This time I wasn't afraid at all, I was very relaxed. When Jacques holds me and I can't get free, I stomp my feet. I hate it when someone wants to hold me down. When he caresses me, though, it feels good, but I still feel panic. Then I think of something else [of his hometown where his mother still lives]. I was ugly as a child. It was because I wanted it that way. I said to myself: I'll make up for it with willpower and hard work. I was fat because I ate bread all the time. That was one pleasure they allowed me. *Instead of another one that was forbidden?* [Ida laughs.] I get it. You mean that I'm just as afraid of you as of Jacques. Maybe that's why I always come late?

The Mother is now endowed with an "inner hallway": her body is no longer empty. Ida can now speak of her own inside. The woman with "no lower body" no longer threatens to chain her to herself. She will now envision working through (in transference) the panic she feels when faced with sexual intercourse.

To my mother I was always a doll to be dressed. I'm ashamed to think that I walked naked in the woods, in the country [where her father is from]. Jacques says that I avoid him, too, just like you. He's nice anyway, even if I do make scenes. . . . I left him and went to sleep on the carpet. He came after me and we both ended up sleeping there. I'm looking at the things here. When I was little, I couldn't stand being in bed. I thought it was boring. I used to look at the things in the room for a long time. For my mother, it's really strange. . . . I was her little doll. Sometimes she wants me to be her mother. When I'm with her, I disappear, I have no right to exist as myself. She wants me to pay attention only to her. She called me up and I told her I was tired and sick, that I had metritus. Actually, it's funny with the baby. He almost fits in a basket. Babies are strange. Now I handle the diaphragm well, but I'm a little scared. I told Jacques I was bleeding . . . *and that it wasn't good inside.* I dreamed last night. But I'm not going to tell you about it. I'll keep you in suspense, I'll keep you waiting for nothing. It was at the Galeries Lafayette. Jacques and I were there to buy curtains. We were on the fifth floor. Then suddenly a fire broke out, there was smoke. Jacques went up to the sixth floor. It was better to go up than down. Once he really was a fireman in a burning house. I have a girlfriend who says: I'm on fire when I make love. I tried to figure out why he went up, but I stayed behind on the floor below. I fainted. It left me with the same feeling as the dream in which I was sinking into the sand. Why did I dream this? Sometimes Jacques sticks his tongue out at me and it's just awful. [We are analyzing a problem related to fellatio.] It's good to be able to talk about all this. You're not afraid of fire.

"It left me with the same feeling," but did not create the same symbol. Whereas in the dream of the "abyss" Ida entered her own inside, in the "fire" dream she imagined putting a man's tongue inside her (penile function). She is not afraid of "fire" (torch was the name she gave the penis in her childhood) just as the analyst, representing the paternal imago, is not frightened by Ida's own "internal fire."

I'm not staying with you, I'm going to quit. By the way, I got a price reduction on the train. *You reduce me, so that nothing from me should pass into you. You were always told not to take anything from daddy.* I had a dream. There was Brigitte Bardot and me; I threw a temper tantrum like a kid, I stomped my feet: I want it, I want it! It was a dress. I think of my father at the beach. He had something in his shorts and because of that I wasn't supposed to play with him. *There isn't supposed to be any BB* [short

for *Brigitte Bardot* in France; pronounced *bébé*—baby = penis—*Trans.*]
in the trunks either, right? Something happened to me. I bought a little
bird and took it home. A little later it was dead and I felt terrible. Yes, at
the beach I thought: if I'm going to play with him, he shouldn't have that
in his shorts. When they talked about the divorce, I was told he might
kidnap me and that I had to hide at my grandparents' house; they would
protect me. That bird, that poor little bird, I wanted so much to give it a
warm nest. *You really wish you could nest the "bird"* [weenie] *warmly
inside you. But it seems to you that it will not be comfortable inside. So,
it's better to leave than come near it. You were told, weren't you, to keep
away from daddy. Would the encounter have been dangerous for both of
you maybe?*

The Mother's prohibition surfaces precisely at the moment desire is
defined: "You're not supposed to have a BB." Thus Ida "reduces" the
Father's penis so as to make it ineffectual. She shields herself from the
desire to take hold of it and to put it inside her. The ideas of danger and
of the forbidding Mother surface simultaneously. The interpretation bears
on this movement.

I went back to my mother's house. I felt sick, I vomited. My mother never
wanted to let me in on the secrets of the kitchen. She would only let me
chop onions and parsley. Chopping and cutting, nothing else. Nothing about
the art of cooking. *Just as she never taught you anything about the art of
having access to your father.* I dreamed last night. It was bizarre. Just like
going to the office; boring and pleasant at the same time. There was an
arena. The lion should have been inside, but instead he was outside. He
would run, run around the arena. I was with a friend and I asked him to
protect me. I was next to him and we were also running. The lion ran in
the same direction as the two of us. He looked like a man. Strange. I turned
around and I saw that he was leaping like a dancer, he did the splits in the
air. I introduced myself when I went for my job. It's nerve-racking to have
to talk in front of 50 people. I did it. How much do I owe you this month?
I had stage fright, I didn't dare speak. I'd like to tell you something. You
know, I always thought that it was all dead inside me, completely dead.
And now I've felt something . . . , that my vagina responded. It's amazing.
I've felt that I could have pleasure. I used to be very scared. Now "it" is
coming. I can't be scared. Yes, I do feel that it's going to happen, that it's
already happening. I don't know. Jacques and I never talk about it; I have
a feeling he's scared. If it doesn't work out, he'll have to go see an analyst.
Funny, I talk as if you weren't there. It's almost as if I had nothing to say.
Do you think perhaps that your pleasure frightens me? I don't understand
why I suddenly thought of dad and mom as well as the Germans. Mom
didn't like it when he came to see me. She was jealous. And then it was as

if things could happen while dad was holding my hand. People were hostile. He was handsome, though. But then everyone knew they would be divorced. I also thought that I could have been born to a mother and father who were not together. I was also afraid something would happen to mom. That she would be unhappy. I feel happy. . . . I was really scared she might act in a certain way toward me. I picture her angry, shouting, saying unbearable things to me as she did to dad. I would have done anything to avoid that. She was never happier than when I was away at boarding school. But nowadays I don't know. I don't hold it against her. Sometimes, not too long ago, I used to be full of hatred. It's fading. I think I'm not responsible for them. I'm thinking something stupid: I have a baby and you don't. Maybe it's not even true, I don't know. But this is how I see it and . . . I'm a bit sorry. It's stupid. I'd like to know how much I owe you? *For the baby?* (Ida laughs.) No, that's not what I meant. It's strange, I feel as if now I get pleasure out of depriving you. These things are stupid.

Now that the obstacle has been named, the desire of admission into the body can be formulated. The complex "lion" symbol (a man-eating man) condenses the image of the penis (pleasure-object) and the movements of love-making between man and woman (the "leaps"; the "split"). The desire to have orgasm through insertion of the penis aims at being integrated (the lion "runs after her"), but Ida cannot as yet fully accept it: the lion remains "outside." Desire (to climax with the penis) is ever more precise, but Ida is frightened by the very fact that she begins to feel the orgasmic sensations discussed during the previous session. These sensations would signal the breakup of the maternal relation. If frustrated and hurt, would the Mother hurt her daughter as she had hurt the Father? Nevertheless, the mere fact of catching a glimpse of the outcome leading to orgasmic pleasure allows Ida to envision taking up her previously inhibited professional pursuits.

I'm having insomnia. I didn't sleep at all last night. As if I had other things to do besides sleep. I did dream, though. Next to a pool there was a sort of brothel. There was a woman, a prostitute, pretty nice, not nasty at all. It was warm. I really wanted to take a dip in the pool. She didn't at first, but finally gave in. Then four men appeared; it was terrible. They wanted me to make . . . to act as though I were on call. I was horrified and we left. Then I was in a train. I said: I need help, people want to do terrible things to me. In this case I was effective. I spoke to a soldier and told him that it was his civic duty to help me out. He gave me a phone number. I think I remember that in the end I failed. I'm awfully sleepy, so sleepy that I can't make things out around me. How much do I owe you? My husband told me that I was intelligent. It felt good, as if I was being reassured from the outside. I don't know why I think women are worthless. It's always the men who are in control, who do things. Oh, I cut my finger. It bled all day yesterday. I don't even know how I cut myself. With a knife? It bled a lot. Why? How could I do that to myself? Oh, I'm sleepy. I didn't want to fix myself up or get dressed. I never know how much I owe you for the month, it's annoying. *For the moment, you think that you owe me a finger for the pleasure you had in your inside.* On the beach at home, I was always by myself. The other kids were always with their parents, but I was alone, always. *Are you quite sure?* Oh, not quite, I think you're right this time. In the dream it was the same beach where I saw dad.

Ida has a tendency to nullify the previous movement because of her feelings of guilt. "You see," she tells me, "I didn't put anything inside. I did nothing; anyway, women have nothing, they have no "lower body," so you have nothing to fear—I will go on being your doll." The correlation between penis and finger comes to the fore. How did she cut her finger? She is convinced that the Mother is responsible for this wound. After all, it is she who prevents Ida from putting her finger-penis inside and keeps her from becoming freed. But considering that this "finger" (her pleasure-object) is withheld by the Mother, Ida, in cutting it, manages to represent—even if by an aggressive act directed at herself—the desire to break loose from the relationship of belonging to her mother.

I dreamed last night that dad had died. We were in C. . . . In real life I haven't received any letters from my parents for a while. Dad's death could explain their silence. He was in a car. Mom was with him. He hadn't yet reached the monument to the dead when he started to feel sick. He had trouble driving. Mom asked another man for a light. That was a sign that he wasn't well. I said to myself, he should take care. And then he died. It was his heart. But there was nothing sad about it. A feeling just like the one I had when my grandmother died. A strong emotion, yet somehow foreign. In any case, it had nothing to do with anything I could understand. It was more like a feeling of shame. In the dream I had to leave town. I was with my mother. I wanted to leave but she was against it. Always the same blackmail: she had a fit. . . . I said to myself, I'd rather give in; I was never sure what might happen. When I learned that dad had died, there was no more doubt. I thought of mom and said to myself: he must have suffered a lot, but now no more problems. No need to worry anymore about the dead. I'm less and less afraid of death. I've started doing some work again, reading, thinking. It's important. I went to a meeting later. I felt like saying something but I didn't. I'm still waiting to get the job. That would give me time for my studies. My poor father was always threatened by my mother, he was always in danger of being abandoned. I also dreamed that fires broke out everywhere, to the left, to the right, below, above, in front, and behind. Very odd.

She makes her "mother's fire," the "father die"; she detaches him from the Mother. This Father, of course, is also Ida herself, since she too has suffered from constraints and threats of abandonment. Ida's desire becomes ever more precise: to come loose from the Mother's grip, but this time through the autonomy acquired in the context of oedipal erotic pleasure. Guilt feelings reappear, however, and the second half of the dream shows Ida becoming once again the Mother's complement. Still, her fear of breaking up diminishes. She looks forward to regaining her professional status and invests everything, that is her body, with "fire" ("fire is life").

> I'm late again. Yesterday was our wedding anniversary. I gave him a pipe. Last year I hardly talked to you about my marriage. I had to keep it from you, I had to steal it, in a way. I'm very happy. It's not the same as before, but there's more to do. I always expected you to make decisions. Now I decide on my own. I had a very strange dream last night. There was a kind of semipolitical meeting at my house. Something suspicious. My husband was in the house across the street. I wanted to brush my hair and I was looking for a mirror. I went to the bathroom and, it was awful, I realized . . . I saw my skull. On top there were some tufts of hair left . . . like a brush, a few hairs. The hair on the back of my head was left, it was falling off as if it had been burned. It was awful, ugly. . . . I called out for help. Come quick! "Yes," I was told, "it's a serious disease, it needs attention right away." Then I went back to my husband. I said to him: it's very dangerous, a disaster, but he didn't want to understand. When I was ten I wondered what would happen to me if they died and I became an orphan? I still care about having parents. I met an old girlfriend of mine in the dream and I hugged her warmly. There are lots of things hidden in my relationship with women. It makes me happy to think that fire doesn't scare you. It means I'm going to be able to live. I've discovered that people don't really live. Their fire is out. My husband is a smoldering fire. He trusts me a lot. I want to say: I'm happy, but then right away I think of some disaster.

"To brush her hair, to touch herself," that is, to masturbate amounts to being in danger, to being a threat. The dream's intent will become clearer subsequently. Ida tries to recapture the memory of a scene. The idea of masturbation implies for her the desire to be liberated by means of her parents' death. The "meeting" means that in touching oneself, one accomplishes a self-to-self meeting similar to the one the parents accomplish when uniting in the sexual act.

> A friend once told me: You're a slow starter, but once you start, you go all out. I dreamed of an engine and of a child threatened by kidnappers. The train passed between the beach and the bathers. I had to cross the tracks.

I'm thinking of a lion who bit the arm of someone who petted him. I'm afraid of Jacques. I've always been very clumsy with my hands. When I sew, I always prick myself or cut my finger. Come to think of it, how much do I owe you? *Come to think of what?* I don't know, I can never figure out what I owe. I wish you'd tell me. I don't like to handle money. It's my mother's job. She's the one who held the purse strings. Money, opening the drawer, touching it . . . for me that's like touching fire! *Like touching the torch?* (Ida laughs.) Strange. I'm pleased by the idea that last time, when I didn't show up, you were waiting for me. Maybe you waited for me minute by minute since this hour is mine, it's my session, no one else can come in my place. And I'm pleased that you . . . you were thinking of me. But when I'm well, I mean, when everything is all right, when I have a job again and can study, what will happen to you? *Will my purse be empty? Will my room be empty?* In fact, my husband gave your address to some-body. Because he thinks you're good and that's rare. I don't know what I think of it all. *That it might fill me? That it might console me?* I don't know. For the first time in my life I really have something for myself.

While autonomy, the development of the self, and identifications en-sue as a result of masturbatory contact with the genitals, this very contact falls under the sway of an intense form of anal guilt. The Mother has the right to manipulate the "purse" [*caisse:* stomach], filling and emptying it. Ida forces herself to restore to her Mother the power of the fingers she usurped for a moment. She thereby also reinstates herself as the manipu-lated object.

Shocking. What do you think of someone who kisses her baby on the lips? I thought I had to tell you right away. It felt like when you're convicted, I mean, in my dream. There was a stagnant river with big worms in it. You had to eat them or was it that if you ate them, you died? It happened at my grandparents' house. It left me with a feeling of horror. Great big worms. It makes me think of this lump of ground meat I left in a plastic container and it rotted and there were worms crawling inside. I was in the typical situation of a woman not wanting to show her fear. My husband, who was just as disgusted, acted brave. Finally I pulled myself together. I put the small container in a larger one and put it all outside in the garbage can. I almost passed out. I really wanted to show that I was brave. And then, it's stupid, but can you imagine I interpreted this dream. I don't know anything about psychoanalysis and I didn't even give it any thought, it just came to me. I just did an interpretation. I said to myself that I must be afraid that people might die during sex. It does happen, you know, newspaper stories . . . , well, I don't know who, a president or somebody died that way. It's stupid to want to interpret your own dreams. *Why is it stupid?* Because I don't know anything about psychoanalysis; it's your job. It's exactly the same thing as with my mom. She always tells me: you're stupid, there's a cross bar stuck in your head. She always wanted me to depend on her, she wanted me to need her completely. This dream at my grandparents' house is strange. I feel that the kitchen is very important. I think of my grandfather in the kitchen when I lived with them. I was just as tall as his . . . so that my face . . . , these things are terrible. *The fact that you might have done the same thing with his penis as with your baby?* That reminds me, I also dreamed about a tiny, tiny baby, hardly bigger than my pen. He was in a transparent case and I put him inside everything I had, in my pocket, in the drawer, on top, below, in front, and in back. It was very funny.

Ida's guilt is no longer expressed in unmitigated inhibition. She limits herself to paying lip service to the Imago. Despite the seemingly depressing dream, she does not shrink from handling herself and from stating it: "to brush herself, to do interpretations, to put the baby inside, to eat somebody's worm." This brings with it at the same time an introjection of the analyst's function. A crucial modification of the maternal imago is taking place.

[We are talking about a girl being "kidnapped" in the street.] It gives me a weird feeling. It reminds me of something in the kitchen. I can't get this kitchen off my mind. I dreamed: there was dancing, I accepted an invitation to dance, then the room became a lecture hall, I was seated. Then the lecture hall turned into a kitchen. A woman held out a crab to me, something gelatinous, just about disgusting, for me to eat. I hesitated. Then I took it. I cut off a little piece and gave back the rest. At the convent school I prostituted myself. Last night I made a scene. I said you had to let people be stupid, after all, if that's what they wanted. Why did I say that? Everyone looked down on my father. I was the only person who loved him. My mother must have been influenced by her parents. That woman, all the things she used to say about my husband. I dreamed that I had binoculars and that my baby had a small detachable penis; it could be taken off, put back on, manipulated. I've never had it so good with my husband and even so I'm jealous. I'm afraid another woman might take him away from me. *Perhaps precisely because the two of you are doing well together?* I'm also scared of having a fire in the house. I'm afraid of hurting my husband. Yes, I'm afraid of hurting him. *Doing the same thing as your mom when she hurt your dad in the kitchen.* You should analyze my husband.

A new difficulty arises. Even though Ida can now, in fantasy, achieve liberation from her Mother—by introjecting through her acts of masturbation the Mother's anal power—she has difficulty assuming this power because she views it as dangerous for her partner. There is something of a contradiction in the imago. This is why she can assume only a partial introjection by accepting a piece of the crab. Yet, only the complete introjection of the "crab" would remove the inhibitions concerning "dance" and "studies" (objectal orgasm and intellectual activity). The contradiction consists precisely in the fact that, to achieve this, she would at the same time have to be the violent and frustrated Mother who "cuts" but "does not eat" (who cannot procure pleasure for herself). Violence toward the Mother also implies the castration of her own genital object of love.

> I have the feeling there are some kind of hidden vibrations among people. I look for other people's secrets. What are they like? What do they do? They'll see that my shoes are badly polished, that my skirt is rumpled. When I was a teenager, I wanted everyone to look at me, to fall in love with me. To be seen and looked at. That's how you become an actress. I read about the Russian Revolution on the bus coming over here. Yesterday Jacques left on a trip and I cut my finger with the scissors. My mom didn't like to take care of me: You shouldn't be sick, she would say. I think I'd like some herbal tea. When mom and dad went to bed at night, I often had a stomachache. I was happy with dad on Sundays. Jacques' mother is sick. She might have a really serious problem with her uterus.

Jacques' leaving on a trip is compared to the scene in the kitchen. This time Ida used the scissors herself to "cut away" Jacques from her mother. This gives rise to guilt, self-mutilation, and the fear of illness. Nonetheless, the oedipal movement is gradually defined.

> I can't swallow anything. I'm on a diet. I might have an ulcer or something in my stomach. I need to be x-rayed. I never used to complain when I was little. Never! *Even when you were in your little bed?* Well, yes, actually, I cried a lot. I dreamed last night. A mountain: on the inside there were some things of great value, old gems. It was a very, very hard mountain. Jacques went inside it.

Ida cannot "swallow" her parents' intimacy at night. The dream mountain (the Mother) hides great values inside. Ida does not mean to enter it—she implies—to take possession of the valuables. On the contrary, she seems to restore Jacques to the "mountain." Yet, this may also be understood to mean that she secretly turns her husband into an ally; he will be capable of fetching what is "valuable" and give it to her.

> I went to a doctor about my stomach. That's why I didn't come here. And I don't have much money this month. Analysis irritates me. *You're irritated to acknowledge that you have to take some "valuables" away from here for yourself. That's why you think you have to be sick, weakened, and impoverished. But, in the end, if you're poor, I'm impoverished, since I'm the one*

who is not being paid. That's true. By the way, I don't know what's happening to me. I'm overexcited, aggressive, and I don't know why. I love my husband, you know that, and still I'm so angry with him. I don't know what I might do to him. *When you're mad at yourself, this is what you do: you prick yourself, cut or hurt yourself, you deprive yourself of intellectual nourishment and of love. You would perhaps like to do this to someone else when you're angry.* There were no mirrors at the convent school. I could never look at myself in a mirror. *You did so in a dream.* Oh, yes, when I had my hair all burned? *Yes, and you had the feeling there was something "suspicious" about it.* I remember that. I couldn't wash my whole body in the convent school. I mean, we had to do it bit by bit. It was ridiculous. I never looked at myself down there. Strange. When my arm falls off the bed between the mattress and the wall, and I touch the carpeting, it feels silky and soft down there, but I have the feeling someone might cut off or bite my arm. Often it makes me so uncomfortable that I pull back my arm suddenly. *What's down there is dangerous.* I think, at the convent school, this soldier, he came in one day . . . , I can see him clearly, he was German. I was . . . , anyway, I was asleep . . . I think I was in the midst of . . . and he said to me: if you don't behave, baby . . . *and you put your hand down there. . . .* No, just, if you don't behave, I'll cut your arm off. Then it was Christmas and I could ask for a present. I asked for a little brother. I was three years old. I was sure it was all right to ask for that. Actually, I did have a teddy bear, but it wasn't the same. It was no fun at all. A little brother is alive, you can play with him. And besides, a little brother could be proof! *Proof of what?* That . . . my parents were somehow alive; they made a baby, so they must exist. *If it had proved simply that, a little sister would have been just as good, but you specifically wanted a little brother.* A little brother is like an extension. Yes, he does have a penis, and really I hardly knew my father. There were no men in the convent except for the priest and the old doctor . . . , really that teddy bear. A little brother would have been like an extension in my father's direction. It's funny that I should think this way, I'm embarrassed not to know this. Where is the hymen? It can't be right at the opening, it must be a little higher. A little girl can put her finger on it. I always used to sweep the stairs from bottom to top. At first I didn't want to sweep, just hold the broomstick in my hand. You could manipulate it. I'm thinking of the way children climb stairs: first they put one leg on the step, then the other one right next to it. I liked to handle the broom going up, you could put it between your legs. . . . *It extended the finger, the arm, and it would lead toward your father.* You see, I could have played with a little brother; a little baby is nice, well behaved, it's good. *He's not an enemy for your mom, that's what you explained to me one day.*

Ida draws back from the aggressivity of her desire to "empty" her Mother of her "value." She flees me in order to protect me. She refuses to face in herself that which drives her to "deprive" me, to "cut" me, to "prick" me, namely the desire to reclaim her autonomy which I "withheld." This session shows *in statu nascendi* the movement leading to "penis envy." We see here the exacerbated conflict with the anal Mother. This kind of conflict is usually resolved by means of masturbatory acts and fantasies. In point of fact, Ida finally recalls memories having to do with masturbation and she is also led to remember the traumatic moment that made her relinquish this solution. It is precisely at that moment, in desperation, that she invented "penis envy" in the context of a "little brother" utopia. Having a penis like the boy would, in the girl's mind, represent many advantages, all of which boil down to this one: the ability to maintain a harmonious relationship with the Mother. What is the magic power of the "penis"? The answer needs to be sought on three different levels, not always easy to distinguish. On the literal anal level, it would seem that the penis—construed as the undetached fecal column—might signal that its bearer has not been dispossessed of his sphincter control. He has therefore no reason to show aggression toward the Mother ("a boy is well-behaved, nice, and good"); he is also free of guilt. On the level of the development of the self, the penis, placed where the [girl's— *Trans.*] genitals are, serves the same end; it eliminates masturbatory conflict (no need to put your finger there since a "finger" is there permanently). As a result there is no conflict with one's surroundings; the boy can have pleasure without becoming "evil." The road to the future is open to him. Finally, on the level of prospective genital anticipation, the penis is an extension in the father's direction, as Ida noted, and it allows the little girl to approach her genital object. This then is the collection of childhood meanings that underlie Ida's "penis envy," an envy which, as we have seen, has very little to do with the male organ of procreation. The envy expresses the repression of autoerotic fantasies of identification with the anal Mother.

I had a strange dream last night. I forgot it, but then I did remember a little bit, anyway. . . . I wouldn't mind this job. It would be good for me, I would have to make myself presentable, do my hair, make myself attractive. I don't know. I sing, then I want to complain, like dad. I do contradictory things. I'm going to start work. I think that Jacques' mother is doing fine. Everything is all right there. Strangely enough, I think I'm ashamed of working and studying. It's as though I didn't have the right to. When I was little I couldn't do my work in peace and quiet. It was like an outrageous privilege. I wasn't supposed to do work for the fun of it. My mother would often say: stop, you can think of yourself later. And then the more I studied the more fun it was, but mom would become sadder and sadder. It feels like a thorn that's stuck in me. She needed me so much, then one fine day, she could be happy all by herself! She didn't need me any more . . . ! Before, I was totally enslaved, she had an absolute need for me and I thought to myself: this way you won't be alone. When I was little, she left. . . . This dependency also had a positive aspect to it. It was like being dependent on God. It allowed me not to exist alone. At times we were buddies like two high school kids. But that was just on the surface. And poor dad, he was totally excluded from this strange paradise. It was a kind of hell. And even so he was scared of us: two women joining forces, that's nasty. She wanted to turn me into an ally. Sometimes he felt affection for us; it hurts so much. Actually I'm ashamed of him, ashamed of my dad. *Ashamed of your dad, ashamed of your studies. . . .* Dad thinks that from now on I'll write to him and not to mom. That really upsets me. I wonder why?

Recalling the scene with the soldier leads Ida to envision the possibility of identifying with her father. But here a new difficulty arises. The solution provided by the identification is condemned to fail on account of the Father's weakness; he is subject, like the daughter, to the Mother's ascendancy.

I'm tired. I went to see about the job yesterday. I'm delighted. I went and got myself some curlers, lipstick, etc. I'm having a good time. I'll be paying you late. At first, when I couldn't pay you, it was awful. Now I think, after all, you can wait a while. And besides, you didn't have to choose this profession. You make money off other people. It's an outrage to earn a living that way. *The other day you told me that working and studying were a privilege for you, an "outrageous" pleasure. It seems that today you act with me the way your mother did with you. You reproach me for my pleasures, my work, my career, the fact that I make money. . . .* [Ida laughs.] Yes, you'd think that I was angry with you just as with. . . . But let me talk about the dream, the nightmare. I was at home with Jacques. This had to be kept secret. There was something illegal. Some authorities were on our trail; it was a frightening thing. Soldiers were supposed to be looking for him. He explained to me that I had to hide him under the covers in the bed so they wouldn't find him. It's funny. The higher authority of these same soldiers showed me how to escape its own power. But Jacques took it all too lightly. He was moving around, he came out. I thought to myself: they're going to knock, they'll come in, but he didn't want to keep still; he was moving around the whole time. As though there had been a baby in there. I was on the lookout. They could be coming back. Someone knocked on the door. I told Jacques to keep quiet, but there was no way. He got up and opened the door. An old woman came in. You're here, she said, hello! Then she left and I saw her talking to the soldiers. I thought we had been betrayed. I was afraid they might take him away from me and kill him. Last night . . . we made love, usually I'm . . . , but this time I felt like going on. I was very sensitized. [However, an external event intruded and interrupted the act.] I felt amputated. It's strange; there seemed to be mysterious, bizarre things attached to dad. I wasn't supposed to be with him. Everyday life was actually full of mysterious things. The German soldier . . . loaded with handguns and machine guns. He said to me, Hello baby! and I answered saying, Hello André. *Hello. Just like the old woman in the dream, the one with the soldiers?* Yes, exactly. And then I thought in the dream, my God, she saw what she shouldn't have seen. The situation was treacherous. Maybe these Germans were looking for members of the FFI [Independent French Forces—*Trans.*] or something else that might have been hidden away in me. I mean, in the bed. There were my arms and maybe, at the ends of them, my hands. [Ida laughs.] It's funny to say it that way. Actually hands are always at the ends. *Perhaps when they're threatened, it feels like they're detached from the ends.* You know, in boarding schools that's exactly how the sisters do things. We never slept with our hands under the covers. It's strange but sometimes I don't dare look at people in the street, I don't dare watch them, see what they're really like. Before, even when I was talking to them, I wouldn't dare look at them. . . . I'm reminded of the Mother Superior. She was a witch. Everybody knew she was stealing fruit. And I wondered why she slept in a big bed. We only had our little beds, our little blankets.

Ida continues to nullify her projects and achievements with her mother's very words. Yet the dream shows a significant shift as regards the imago's expectations: this time the supreme authority itself shows how to escape its ascendancy. Ida can thus relive the "scene of the soldier" while keeping her pleasure-object (hand, penis, husband) under the covers. The external event unexpectedly interrupting the coitus is interpreted by Ida in terms of her guilt: I felt "amputated," she says. Let me note though that this "castration" does not concern the male member but the acts and enjoyments attached to it. In her dream the pleasure-object she keeps under the covers still appears "stolen" and, in any case, linked to an act of aggression (she is being persecuted). As the persecution lessens ("hands are always at the ends"), Ida acquires the right to make use of the pleasure-object, and "penis envy," losing its reason for being, will dissipate.

Ida's analysis goes on, but we can already see a movement toward liberation in various realms. Ida has an increasing sense of self-confidence; she is starting to show her qualities in professional pursuits.

V

At the close of my study the time has come to formulate a question avoided so far in this paper: Why do the sense of castration and its corollary, "penis envy," constitute the almost universal lot of women? Why do women so frequently give up activity, creativity, and their own means of "making the world"; why do they accept being locked up in the gyneaceum, "keeping still in church"? In short, why do they prefer to accept a dependent position? The question is far from simple and would require research in a variety of fields as well as information to which I have no access. I may be allowed, however, to consider the problem from the psychoanalytic angle and to formulate no more than a hypothesis, based on elements within my reach.

From the psychoanalytic point of view an institution does not emerge, nor does it stay alive, unless it resolves a problem among individuals. In principle the institutional solution brings advantages for the parties involved in relation to their prior situation. Our task is to display the advantages resulting, for both men and women, from the institutional inequality of the sexes, at least as far as this obtains in the area available to psychoanalytic study, that is, within the affective realm.

It is reasonable to suppose that this state of affairs, prevalent for several millennia, requires the woman's complicity despite the apparent protestations she registers through "penis envy." Men and women must be in the throes of specific and complementary affective conflicts for them to have instituted a *modus vivendi* that has stayed so tenaciously alive through diverse civilizations.

As far as the woman is concerned, let me start with the following consideration. Emerging from the anal stage the little girl should be able to accomplish a simultaneous identification with both sexed parents through her masturbatory fantasies. Yet this movement encounters a twofold difficulty. The first is anal, since the little girl's autonomy in masturbatory satisfaction inevitably implies that the Mother is sadistically divested of her prerogatives. The second difficulty is oedipal to the extent that the phantasmic realization of the primal scene, through identification with both parents, implies the Mother's eviction. As long as this twofold difficulty is not surmounted—and this occurs only in a few exceptional cases—a gap will remain (1) in the identification with the Father as regards the specificity of his sex and (2) in the identification with the Mother, considered as his genital partner. This fundamental gap goes hand in hand with a special imagoic configuration: a demanding, castrated, and jealous Mother; a Father who is envied, depreciated, and magnified at the same time. The only escape from this impasse is through the construction of an inaccessible phallic ideal (the mythical image of an idealized Father) which entails both the Mother's being reassured that she can hold on to her prerogatives and the little girl's wish to see the fatal gap in her genital destiny filled through her identification with the Father. When a woman laden with these imagos approaches married life, she is abruptly confronted with her own latent genital desires. At the same time, her affective life remains immature since—by dint of a lack of heterosexual identification—it is dominated by problems descended from the anal phase. Short-lived oedipal hopes often give way to a replay of the anal relationship to the Mother, this time, however, with the spouse, in a relationship marked by "penis envy." The benefit derived from this position is not having to come face to face with the maternal imago and thus being able to avoid the deep-seated anguish at tearing oneself free from her dominion.

The drama of the girl's particular maternal relation becomes concretized through the following fact: in trying to free herself from the anal Mother she leans on the Father, only to find herself with the Mother's heterosexual object, that is, once again in a conflict of interest with her. Attacked *on two fronts simultaneously,* the Mother does not cease appearing highly dangerous: about to be destroyed completely, she threatens complete destruction. The superimposition of both mastery and rivalry *in the same object* blocks the emergence from the anal stage and forces the girl to renounce her desires. She will turn herself into the Mother's anal appendage ("the baby of the family" [*le bouchon:* also feces, as in *pousser le bouchon:* to take a crap—*Trans.*], "the doll") and later into her spouse's phallus [hanging on him in a relation of dependency—*Trans.*] It would seem that we see here a universal difficulty in women's development, a difficulty which explains roughly why they accept a relationship of dependency on men, that is, on the imagoic heirs of the anal Mother. This is the price to be paid for a few disguised genital fulfillments that, in some fortunate cases, women allow themselves.

At first sight the advantage men gain from this propensity for dependence, due to the guilt feelings of women, seems easy to grasp. But on closer examination it is not a priori obvious why men should naturally desire such a relationship of mastery. The insincerity, ambivalence, and the refusal to identify with the other that this type of relationship entails should appear to men as so many obstacles thrown in the way of their own complete and authentic fulfillment. And yet. . . . Who can doubt that, going against the grain of their own higher interests, males are almost universally party to the woman's state of dependency and that they find it agreeable to raise this state of dependency to the level of religious, metaphysical, or anthropological principles. What benefit does the male derive from subjecting to his mastery the very being through whom he could both understand and be understood himself? Self-to-self revelation through the opposite sex would be the realization of our humanity, and this is what eludes nearly all of us.

After considering the specific problems of women, let me examine the ones that impede men's fulfillment. Moving away from the anal Mother, the little boy can lean on his identification with the Father who possesses the "phallus." He thereby escapes maternal control: the phallic Father is his ally and the Mother is not yet his genital object. He will thus have avoided two anxiety-producing moments in his development: (1) winding down his relationship with the anal Mother through a particularly dangerous identificatory incorporation of her—doubly dangerous because of the dismantling of her mastery and because of a reverse oedipal eviction of the Mother; (2) the oedipal movement strictly speaking, which implies identification with the genital rival as well as his being eliminated. This twofold gap in the boy's identifications is clearly symmetrical with the one we noted in the girl. In both cases the unrealizable desire of [genital—Trans.] attainment condenses in the parallel envies of the same illusory object: the "penis." Clearly, these envies are not dependent on genital differentiation in the strict sense but bespeak rather an unassimilated anal relationship to the Mother. If a difference between the two sexes does appear at this stage, it concerns the equally illusory possession or lack of possession of the penis-thing and its symbolic derivatives. The phallic trap thus sets the stage for the institutional relationship of the sexes. Active and passive fascination disguises, by means of the fetish, the problem of missed identifications. The possession of the fetish is so contrived as to elicit envy, and envy itself confirms its value. This then is the deep-seated reason why men foster "penis envy" in the opposite sex and why they extend it to institutions. If it is understood that the exclusive owners of the fetish are men, then this supposed privilege—created and sustained solely by covetousness—is itself nothing more than a variation on envy, a reverse envy projected onto woman. The penis-emblem is thus revealed to be a means of setting oneself up as enviable in order that, logically speaking, one does not have to be envious oneself. Men cannot help but be envious as long as they are in need of objectifying and masking at the same time, through a fetish, the gaps in their own attainment. By means of this ploy men continue to disregard their formidable desire to take the Mother's place in the anal primal scene. The guilty and envious woman serves as the unacknowledged "feminine part" men need to master and keep under control at all costs. That is why men prefer a mutilated, dependent, and envious woman to a partner who blossoms in the plentitude of her creativity.

The biblical myth of the first couple provides a telling illustration of this problem. Eve is a detached part of Adam, representing that which he rejects in himself. She is accused of the original sin so that he will not be made fully responsible for it. Eve is supposed to have disobeyed the divine prohibition; she is supposed to have castrated the celestial Father. That is why she has to bend under a double guilt, her own and man's which is projected onto her. She is constrained to double slavery, in relation to God (the castrated Father), and in relation to her husband (the Mother who must not be castrated). She will live henceforth on terms of intimacy with the Serpent; that is the divine decree ushering in "penis envy." A part of Adam's body, Eve is at once his thing (his servant) and his attribute. A base for projections, enslaved and kept under control, she is constrained to live in submission not with a partner of the opposite sex, but with a tyrannical representative of the anal maternal imago.

This is, briefly, my psychoanalytic hypothesis as to the affective aspects of the institution which posits a "female" dependency and passivity at the same time that it forces onto the woman the envy of an emblem leading to her becoming estranged from the desire of her own sexuality. As opposed to various cultural and philosophical conceptions, this hypothesis has at least the advantage of being derived from clinical experience and, as such, is destined to facilitate therapy. I do think in fact that the resolution of "penis envy" on an individual basis is a matter for analysis, provided of course that analysts themselves are freed from phallocentric prejudice, as old as humankind.

Part III

Toward a Conceptual Renewal of Psychoanalysis

Editor's Note Written in 1967 as an extended review of Jean Laplanche and J. B. Pontalis's encyclopedic manual, *The Vocabulary of Psychoanalysis,* "The Shell and the Kernel" outlines Abraham's approach to the conceptual organization of psychoanalysis. Abraham's concepts of anasemia, symbol, messenger, trace, introjection, antisemantics, nucleoperipheral conflict, metapsychology of myth, etc., are either developed here for the first time or are given more systematic treatment than elsewhere. "The Shell and the Kernel" builds directly on two of Abraham's previous essays, "The Symbol or Beyond Phenomena" (1961, published 1978) and "Time, Rhythm, and the Unconscious: Toward a Psychoanalytic Esthetic" (1962, expanded version 1972), which combine psychoanalysis with philosophical inquiry. "The Symbol . . ." presents the ontological implications of the psychoanalytic concept of the symptom, while "Time . . ." concerns itself with the genesis of time as a mental category and its relationship to the unconscious dimensions of literature. (Both essays will appear in volume 2 of this edition.)

"The Shell and the Kernel" treats Freudian psychoanalysis from the philosopher's point of view, presenting psychoanalysis as a coherent system of thought even when disassociated from clinical practice. Abraham also suggests that Freudian psychoanalysis is capable of giving entirely new answers to problems traditionally raised by philosophers, such as: what is the nature of the self, object, subject, intersubjectivity, consciousness, experience, feeling, pleasure, unpleasure, etc. At the same time, Abraham provides both explicit and implicit definitions of psychoanalytic concepts (for example, fantasy, sex, symbol, unconscious, affect, symptom, the Oedipus complex, mental topography) that are often quite different from Freud's own. In fact, Abraham aims at giving a unified view of Freud's theories, being aware nonetheless that such a unity may represent only the spirit and not the letter of Freudian thought. The result is a highly original account of psychoanalysis, startling both in its loyalty to and its distance from Freud's tenets as originally expounded.[1]

Abraham sees the power of psychoanalysis in its combination of two basic ideas in the history of Western thought, the unconscious and the symptom. The import of these concepts far exceeds their initial domain, the treatment and psychological theory of neurosis. With the unconscious, psychoanalysis has introduced a principle of noncoherence at the root of identity. Definitions of personal identity based on the possession of self-awareness linking the present to the past as well as to the future fall short because the unconscious has the ability to overwhelm conscious awareness at any time. Yet in psychoanalytic thought, the unconscious, this principle of incoherence, is also regarded as the very foundation of any form of identity. At this juncture the idea of symptom complements that of the unconscious. The symptom links the disruptions of identity to the possibility of tracking down their unconscious reasons for being. Psychoanalysis may be defined then, according to Abraham, as an apparently paradoxical discipline pinpointing areas of incoherence, discontinuity, disruption, or disturbance in self, reality, object, experience, meaning, present, past, other, etc., even as it postulates

1. Attempts are made at times to smooth over aspects of Freud's theories (for example, the phallic phase of genital development) that either Abraham or Torok or both criticize in other contexts. Concerning the phallic phase in particular, see Torok's "The Meaning of 'Penis Envy' in Women" in this volume.

the need for finding a level of coherence which can absorb the noncoherence.

Abraham introduces the concept of anasemia to define the paradoxical status of psychoanalytic thinking and interpretation. In its descriptive sense, anasemia designates the status of concepts which, though deliberately disruptive of a unifying, conscious self, outline the ultimate unconscious sense or source of the disruption. At the same time, the concept of anasemia is central to Abraham's view of the specificity of psychoanalysis as an interpretive discipline. In this context, anasemia serves as an active analytic tool, enabling us to search for the meaning of phenomena in something that is by nature inaccessible to direct apprehension. Thus, anasemia explains the apparent with the nonapparent, observation with nonobservation, speech with silence, presence with absence, inclusion with exclusion. Abraham calls this sort of interpretation an inquiry into the sources of signification (*les sources de la signifiance*). The methodological originality of psychoanalysis lies in its capacity to transcend phenomena or rather to attach them to a realm that justifies or motivates their existence. This is the realm of "transphenomena" or "symbols" in Abraham's terminology. Going beyond the domain of psychopathology and the description of unconscious mental processes, Abraham makes the methodology of psychoanalysis into a general theory of the genesis of phenomena, or "transphenomenology."[2]

Abraham's depiction of psychoanalysis—as both the theory of the sources of phenomena and the methodological instrument capable of uncovering the hidden underside of phenomena—differs in its emphasis from Freud's many attempts at definition and stock-taking. "Recognition of the simultaneous presence of the three factors of 'infantilism,' 'sexuality,' 'repression,' constitutes the main characteristic of the psychoanalytic theory" (Freud, "On Psycho-Analysis," *S.E.* 12:210). For Freud the most enduring discoveries of psychoanalysis include (1) the theory of the dynamic nature of unconscious mental processes, consisting of an interplay of forces that inhibit each other or enter into compromises with one another; (2) the theory of the

2. The elaboration of transphenomenology as a methodological discipline encompassing fundamental research in diverse fields, such as the biological sciences and the humanities, is the subject of Abraham's essay "The Symbol or Beyond Phenomena."

instincts, according to which the inhibitions of instinct are the characteristic lot of humans, whether considered singly, in the family, socially, or through the mirror of civilization; and (3) the theory of the infantile determinants of mental life, that is, the theory of general mental development. Freud's emphasis falls more often than not on the elucidation of the vicissitudes of psychic energy (whether in the form of excitation, appeasement, substitution, transfer, cathexis, displacement, or repression) as rooted ultimately in the instinctual or sexual life of children. In Abraham's view the most distinctive feature of psychonalysis resides in the idea of symptom as a fragmented yet telling compromise formation. Hence his characterization of psychoanalysis as anasemia, a general method of investigation, inquiring into the substratum, the justification, motivation, and efficiency of compromise formations, whether they derive from instinctual sources or not. It is this shift of emphasis from the theory of mental energetics (as championed by Freud) to the theory of symptomatic memory traces (also outlined but not privileged by Freud) that leads to Abraham's critique of the Oedipus complex. By defining incestuous desires and frustrations in the instinctual development of the boy as the model formation in his theory of mental energetics, Freud seems to have put aside his methodological discoveries on the nature and functioning of symptoms, discoveries that can be (and perhaps should be) distinguished from his characterization of the universal content of infantile mental processes.

THREE

The Shell and the Kernel: The Scope and Originality of Freudian Psychoanalysis

N. Abraham, 1968

THE SHELL OF WORDS

A t last psychoanalysis possesses its Lalande.[1] Technical, critical, and even historical, the first dictionary of this science, now well over seventy years old, undertakes to define, tabulate, prescribe, and proscribe the meanings, the uses, the misuses, and abuses of a language which, despite its growing dissemination, has remained esoteric and arcane. This mighty effort of clarification, to which the authors devoted eight years of research and reflection, aims, over and above lexicographical questions, at "the conceptual organization," in the words of Lagache,[2] and at "the conceptual apparatus," according to Laplanche and Pontalis, of a body of knowledge and practices whose originality has challenged those who have sought to codify it. To establish the inter- and intradisciplinary status of each psychoanalytic concept, tracing their vicissitudes and transformations in Freud's works and beyond, while exercising critical watchfulness as to their extensions, connotations, implications, and overlaps— such was the undertaking, such the challenge.

Previously published as "L'Écorce et le noyau," *Critique* 249 (1968): 162–81; and in *L'Écorce et le noyau* (Paris: Flammarion, 1987), pp. 203–26; and as "The Shell and the Kernel," trans. N. Rand, *Diacritics* 9, no. 1 (1979): 16–31. (The subtitle of this chapter is provided by Nicholas Rand for the purposes of this translation.)

1. [This essay was written as a critique of the *Vocabulaire de la psychanalyse* (Paris: Presses Universitaires, 1967) by Jean Laplanche and J. B. Pontalis, which is now available in English as *The Language of Psychoanalysis* (New York: Norton, 1973). All quotations in the text refer to the French edition; page references will be followed by the numbers of the corresponding pages in the English edition. André Lalande is the author of a widely used reference work, the *Vocabulaire technique et critique de la philosophie*, whose reputation is such as to allow Abraham to designate it simply by the author's name.—Ed.]

2. [Daniel Lagache, editorial overseer of the project carried out by Laplanche and Pontalis.—Ed.]

The importance of the task determined the project's scope and conduct: rereading (in three languages) and abstracting some five thousand pages of the complete works of Freud, not to mention the far from simple works of Sandor Ferenczi, Karl Abraham, Melanie Klein, and others; setting up an enormous file with at least four hundred entries and innumerable cross-references; using the file by means of subtle and detailed comparative studies; ruthlessly detecting all metasemias, contradictions, aporias, and open questions; in addition, recording the results of the scrutiny in condensed and substantive notes; and finally, crowning this long preparation by establishing definitions for the over three hundred concepts, to be set in boldface type, providing an authoritative answer to the legitimate questions of all, scientists, philosophers, jurists or even psychoanalysts: what on earth are "transference," "hallucinatory fulfillment of a wish," "libido," "instinct," "ego," and so forth?

The execution measures up to the aim. With its five hundred fifteen pages tightly bound in royal octavo, the book—showing terms in five languages, and complementing definitions with historical and critical discussions, which are supported in turn by direct quotations from and references to the primary texts—appears to be at first glance the analytical repository of the instruments of thought authorized by psychoanalysis. And even if, having long perused *The Language of Psychoanalysis*, we are led to reconsider this first impression, it does nonetheless reflect the function assigned to the book: to constitute a *corpus juris* having the force of the law henceforth no one can ignore. It is not for us here to scrutinize the foundations, whatever they may be, of such a jurisdiction. They may lie in a commentary on Freud's works, the effectiveness of clinical practice, or epistemological considerations. (In fact all three are invoked.) The result demonstrates a vast effort to define the status of the psychoanalytic "thing" in its relationship to the external world as well as in its relation to itself.

Here then is an accomplishment called upon to fulfill, for all of psychoanalysis, the functions of that psychic agency on which Freud conferred the prestigious term "ego." Now, in making this comparison to Freudian theory itself, I want to evoke the image of the ego struggling on two fronts. Turned toward the outside, it moderates appeals and assaults; turned toward the inside, it channels excessive and incongruous impulses. Freud conceived of this agency as a protective layer, an ectoderm, a cerebral cortex, a shell. This cortical role of twofold protection, directed inward and outward, can be readily recognized in *The Language of Psychoanalysis*; it is a role that understandably is not unattended by some concealment of the very thing to be secured. Yet the shell itself is marked by what it shelters; what it encloses is disclosed within it. And even if the kernel of psychoanalysis need not come to light in the pages of *The Language of Psychoanalysis*, its secret and elusive action is attested all the same at every step by its unbending resistance to encyclopedic systematization. The remarkable merit of the authors is that they never disguise the difficulties inherent in their task, thereby making us understand the following: if a conceptual organization of psychoanalysis is to exist, it cannot yield its unity within the bounds of traditional thinking, and its apprehension requires a new dimension yet to be found.

THE FIRST STAGE OF THE EXEGESIS

Whatever the banal objections to which the theoretical developments of psychoanalysis lay themselves open may be, nobody any longer thinks of contesting its real clinical import. Nowadays it is generally agreed that the choice between rejecting the theory for lack of cohesion or adopting it as a last resort should be transcended. Some would be tempted to object: granted, but then we would need a theory better adapted to *facts*. The difficulty with such scientific liberalism applied to psychoanalysis is that the "facts" themselves would be denatured if we were to change the discourse defining them. This became apparent each time attempts were made to absorb psychoanalysis into systems of different prompting (behaviorism, existentialism, phenomenology). It is so because psychoanalytic concepts, however awkward or incoherent or even scandalous they may appear, possess a sort of power, and they cannot be included in alien systems of reference without deadening their nerves. Psychoanalytic theory energetically refuses to submit to any kind of recasting or readjustment. Given this observation, only one road remains open for us: to search out what the theory manages to communicate from behind its contradictions and lacunae.[3] Freud's texts invite us to engage in an enterprise of exegesis, provided that this enterprise supports and sustains the originality of the texts it purports to illuminate. Such an exegesis must proceed by steps and requires at least two stages. During the first stage, it will be indispensable to collect everything that furnishes material for commentary. In other words, it will be necessary to make up a list of everything that, for various reasons, is problematic in Freud's body of ideas. Such a directory of problem clusters, set up by means of traditional instruments (conceptual specification, comparison of the various stages of thought, semantic concordance and discordance, viewed both synchronically and diachronically, filiation of ideas, constants, thematic variation, etc.), is precisely the aim of the historico-critical part of *The Language of Psychoanalysis*.

3. Cf. Pontalis, *Après Freud* (Paris: Juilliard, 1965), pp. 113–54.

The authors are to be highly commended for having prepared, by their patient and careful labor, the second stage of the exegesis. Given the inventory of the paradoxical and irregular aspects of psychoanalytic theory, this is a decisive stage, since we can no longer evade the true question, which is as follows: if Freud's theories form the protective shell around his intuition, simultaneously concealing and revealing it, what of the actual kernel? For it is the kernel which, invisible but active, confers its meaning upon the whole construction. This kernel, the active principle of psychoanalytic theory, will not show through unless all the apparent contradictions have found their explanation in the unity I ascribe hypothetically to Freud's intuition. To say that the second stage of the exegesis lies outside the intended realm of *The Language of Psychoanalysis* is to appreciate the moderation and prudence that have presided over its writing, especially since the authors are engaged in more personal works of exegesis.

THE PLOY OF CAPITALIZATION

Meanwhile, we would look in vain under the entry "Psychoanalysis" for a definition that might bring to light the originality of its discourse or the paradoxical character of its status. To catch a glimpse of these, however, it will suffice to refer to the innumerable discussions which, usually without offering a solution, are content to point out conceptual difficulties. Let us choose for our purposes the terminological problem, noted on p. 334 [p. 324], concerning the "pleasure principle": "to speak, for example, of unconscious pleasure which would be attached to an obviously painful symptom could raise objections from the point of view of psychological description." I might add that pleasure, as an affect, does not have its origin (according to *metapsychology*) in the Unconscious, in the strict sense of the term, but in the conscious ego. After all, what is a pleasure that cannot be felt, that might even be perceived as suffering? One could reply: it matters precious little whether or not pleasure is experienced, provided that theoretically the underlying process is bound to produce it, and that, of course, this can be observed objectively. Pleasure would no longer be an affect then, but, by metonymy, that which might be its cause, the discharge of tension. Such a shift from the introspective to the psycho-physical realm would require at the very least that pleasure and discharge consistently overlap on the various levels. But this is not at all the case. Following a similar train of thought, let me also cite the challenge to conditioned-reflex behaviorism constituted by the concept of the ineducable wish (p. 120 [481]). Such concepts are not reducible to any known system of reference, and we would do well to resign ourselves to that fact from the start. If we want our work of exegesis to move ahead, we will have to recognize that psychoanalytic theory demands a genuine mental conversion of us.

As a token of such a conversion, we might decide to write the metapsychological concepts of Pleasure and Discharge with capital letters. It will appear then that this ploy acts as revelation showing unequivocally the radical semantic change psychoanalysis has brought to language. To be sure, the nature of this change is not clearly or directly accessible, hence the innumerable misconceptions on which psychoanalytic literature feeds. But the first French translators of Freud, having perceived this change, reinforced its imprint by generously bestowing capitals on most metapsychological concepts. Lacking such distinctive spelling in German, Freud advocated the use of special abbreviations to designate the unconcious (UBw), the perception-consciousness system (WBw), the system ψ, etc. These designations, esoteric in appearance, reveal—but do not yet define—the semantic originality of the plane on which, from the very start, psychoanalytic discourse unfolds.

BETWEEN THE "I" AND THE "ME"

What then is the principle of coherence of a discourse in which Pleasure no longer means what one feels, in which Discharge refers to something other than what one sees? In this confusion some would be tempted to resort to a phenomenological description of the meanings at issue. To do this, one would bracket the term Pleasure with reductive quotation marks whereupon it would be ready to undergo—according to the Husserlian method—the examination of its noetic-noematic structure. Yet, strangely enough, metapsychological capitals incontrovertibly reject the quotation marks of the phenomenologist. The concept of Pleasure cannot be bracketed. The same is true of the terms Conscious and Unconscious[4] and— upon closer examination—of all other metapsychological concepts. This one incompatibility is sufficiently characteristic of a domain, proper to psychoanalysis, to locate it instantly outside the field of phenomenology, reserved for the so-called objects and experiences of intentionality. The graphic ploy is suggestive enough to attract attention to the following: the effect of capitalization invokes a mystery, the very mystery of the un-

---

4. Unless one were to misconstrue the Unconscious, as Husserl did in *Ideen* II, by tracing it to the forgetting of the once-conscious experiences that the associative method could recover. *Husserliana* IV, pp. 222–24.

thought that burdens reflexive philosophy with a congenital naivete. The ploy reveals the opaque indeterminacy of the *distance* that separates the reflecting subjects from themselves, a distance endangering even patent notions founded on an illusory proximity to self. The condition sine qua non of the relation to self, the space that separates the "I" from the "me," necessarily escapes reflexive thematization. It is in this space, in this nonpresence of the self to itself—the very condition of reflexivity—that phenomenologists unwittingly place their foothold in order to scrutinize, from this terra incognita, the sole horizon visible to them, the inhabited continents. But psychoanalysis stakes out its domain precisely on this *un-thought* ground of phenomenology. To say this is already to designate, if not to resolve, the problem facing us: how to include in a discourse—in any one whatever—the very thing which, being the precondition of discourse, fundamentally escapes it? If nonpresence, the kernel and ultimate ground of all discourse, is made to speak, can it—must it—make itself heard in and through presence to self? Such is the form in which the paradoxical situation inherent to the psychoanalytic problematic appears.

PSYCHOANALYSIS AS ANTISEMANTICS

Hence a double conclusion: first, psychoanalysis cannot be allotted a determined place in the order of the sciences; and second, although psychoanalysis is "located" outside of any place, the psychoanalytic domain is nonetheless contained in a well-defined interval, the interval which extends between "I" and "Me," between subject and object of reflexivity. And it is of course understandable that the two frontiers of this domain should be the only places from which it is possible to set out to explore the space they enclose and which has erected them. Moreover, this is why psychoanalysis uses forms of speech in the therapeutic situation to achieve ever more self-awareness and self-affect, proving to the listener that the frontiers are dependent on a beyond that Freud named the *Kernel of Being:* the Unconscious. Yet, emerging as they do in the interplay of toucher-touched—as images alluding to the untouched nucleus of nonpresence—Pleasure, Discharge, the Unconscious (as well as Consciousness and Ego, in their relation to them), do not strictly speaking signify anything, except the founding silence of *any act of signification.* This, then, is the role of the capitals: instead of resignifying them, they strip words of their signification, they *designify* them, so to speak. This does not occur by some contingent telescoping of meanings, as in the "exquisite corpse" of automatic writing. Psychoanalytic designification *precedes* the very possibility of the collision of meanings. The capitals carry out designification in a particular and precise mode, capable of defeating signification and of laying bare, at the same time, the very foundation of the signifying process [*signifiance*]. Their rigor resides in the always singular way in which they oppose semantic actualization—that *Pleasure* should mean *pleasure*—all the while referring precisely to the nonpresence from which "pleasure" emerges and which at the same time manages to be represented in "pleasure." To make such a capitalized discourse into something other than mystical or religious illusion, the second stage of the exegesis should take it upon itself to define the requirements, constraints, and the universe proper to this scandalous antisemantics of concepts designified by the action of the psychoanalytic context and revealed to be such through the ploy of capitalization.

Let us take any term introduced by Freud, whether he coined it or simply borrowed it from scientific or colloquial language. Unless one is deaf to their meaning, one is struck, as soon as Freudian terms are related to the unconscious Kernel, by the vigor with which they literally rip themselves away from the dictionary and ordinary language. The allusion to the nonreflexive and the unnamed in fact induces this unprecedented and strange semantic phenomenon. The language of psychoanalysis no longer follows the twists and turns (*tropoi*) of customary speech and writing. Pleasure, Id, Ego, Economic, Dynamic, are not metaphors, metonymies, synecdoches, catachreses; they are, by dint of discourse, products of designification and constitute new figures, absent from rhetorical treatises. These figures of antisemantics, inasmuch as they signify no more than the action of moving up toward the source of their customary meaning, require a denomination properly indicative of their status and which—for want of something better—I shall propose to designate by the neologism *anasemia*.

Thus, psychoanalytic theory speaks in an anasemic discourse. What justifies such a discourse? At first nothing except its sheer existence. But that suffices. The very fact that, running counter to the known laws of discursive ratiocination, such a discourse actually occurs—that it evidences genuine impact and fruitfulness—amply confirms that its allusion meets a resonance in us capable of founding the discourse and allowing it to reveal, by its advance toward this nonpresence in us, the place from which all meaning ultimately springs.

In his preface to *The Language of Psychoanalysis*, Lagache is right in saying: "Ordinary language has no words for the structures and psychic movements which, in the eyes of common sense, do not exist." In fact, the anasemic structure, proper to psychoanalytic theorizing, does not exist in any known mode of language. It proceeds entirely from Freud's discovery. Before it, one could not say Pleasure or Anxiety without designating the experience which founded its meaning. Symmetrically, with Freud we can speak of a pleasure experienced as such that would nevertheless not be designated as Pleasure with a capital, of a pain that would be Pleasure, and even of a Pleasure that would be suffering. Most of the misconceptions about psychoanalytic concepts come from the constantly tempting confusion between the subjective (introspective) or objective (for example, neurological) plane, on the one hand, and the anasemic plane, on the other.

THE SOMATO-PSYCHIC AS ANASEMIA AND THE SYMBOL OF THE MESSENGER

I shall choose one example in order to illustrate what is baffling and original in the universe of anasemic discourse, and also what is rigorous and fruitful. The following fundamental statement by the authors of *The Language of Psychoanalysis* provides the example: "The relation between the somatic and the psychic is conceived of neither as a parallelism nor as a relation of causality. . . . It must be understood by a comparison with the relation existing between a delegate and a sender" (p. 412 [364]). Anasemia, here, is found in the term *somatic*. Clearly, we are not dealing here with the biological sense of the word and the same can be said for *organic* in similar contexts. To speak of a relation of mission, it would be necessary to attribute to the emissary traits in common with the sender, on the one hand, and with the accrediting agency, on the other. The emissary's mediating function should be that of communication through interpreters and would imply merely difference of language, not of nature, between the two poles of the relation. It is understood that, under these conditions, *somatic* can no longer mean "somatic" but something else, and that, similarly, *psychic* finds itself designified as well; only the *representative*, the mediator between the two poles x, seems to have preserved its meaning, inasmuch as it is a term known by comparison with a known relation of mediation. From a purely semantic point of view, psychic representatives, like the symbols of poetry, are mysterious messages from one knows not what to one knows not whom; they reveal their allusiveness only in context, although the "to what" of the allusion must necessarily stop short of articulation. The philistine claims to translate and paraphrase the literary symbol and thereby abolishes it irretrievably. We have seen, on the contrary, how Freud's anasemic procedure *creates*, by virtue of the Somato-Psychic, the symbol of the messenger. Later on we shall understand how it serves to reveal the symbolic character of the message itself. By way of its semantic structure, the concept of the messenger is a symbol insofar as it alludes to the unknowable by means of an unknown, while only the relation of the terms is given. In the last analysis, all authentic psychoanalytic concepts may be reduced to these two structures (which happen to be complementary): symbol and anasemia. What is the precise content of this symbol of the messenger, of the representative we have just been considering? It is called either Instinct or Drive, complete with its accompanying affects, representations, or even fantasies. If we examined this somato-psychic liaison agent more closely as a symbol, we could throw new light on its two anasemic poles. Let us begin with this enigma, as old as it is unresolved: how does it happen that fantasy has the power to move our bodies, be it sexually or by creating real diseases? This enigma could be reduced to another: what is the sense of the nonsensical "organic sources of Instinct or Drive," or of the deployment of either one "on the limits of the somatic and the psychic"? This is nonsense, obviously, if we give to *somatic* and *psychic* the meanings of naive empiricism. Nonsense again if we constitute them phenomenologically as the body proper and the habitudes of the Ego, respectively. Both of these alternatives—the body with its anatomical and physiological objectivations and the phenomenological Ego's habitudes, with its repeatable acquisitions—belong to the same set of representations which, according to Freud, defines merely a part of the whole: the Ego. The *somatic* must be something quite different from the body proper, which derives from the psychic as one of its functions, the psychic having been described by Freud as an exterior layer, an envelope. The *somatic* is what I cannot touch directly, either as my integument and its internal prolongations or as my psyche, the latter given to the consciousness of self; the somatic is that of which I would know nothing if its representative, my fantasy, were not there to send me back to it, its source as it were and ultimate justification. The *Somatic* must therefore reign in a radical nonpresence *behind* the Envelope where all phenomena accessible to us unfold. It is the Somatic which dispatches its messengers to the Envelope, exciting it from the very place the latter conceals. Under the influence of its solicitations, the whole of the Psychic is moved, the body proper included. Its emotions as well as its fantasies are nothing but modalities of the reception given by the Envelope to these delegates of the one and the same Kernel. Thus the relay between fantasy and affect passes through the Organic from which they both emanate.

HYSTERICAL DESIGNIFICATION AND EROGENOUS ZONES

The false enigma of the effectiveness of fantasy dissipates by itself. There remains the mystery, impenetrable in quite another way, of this so-called organic Kernel. At the moment, we have—for clarity's sake—merely converted the Somato-Psychic into another anasemic couple, the Nucleo-Peripheral, thereby ridding ourselves of the ever-present threat of confusion between the everyday use of terms and their derivatives of designification. Yet this substitution, however essential it may seem to us, does not release us—quite the opposite—from a need to discover why Freud chose precisely these two terms, "somatic" and "psychic," to be designified and, concurrently, to what extent their initial content survives in this designification, so as to justify its basis. The starting point of his choice was undoubtedly the "mysterious jump of the psychic into the somatic" whose detection in conversion hysteria begat psychoanalysis as a theory. Now, in order to arrive at the designification of the *somatic,* it was necessary to pass through the *sexual* and to designate the "stigmatic" loci as erogenous zones. Since in hysteria any area of the body can become an erogenous zone, depending on the fantasy which confers this quality, it became obvious that the erotogenicity of the body proper could not be primary. Erotogenicity arose, passing through diverse mediations, from a so-called organic source. But between the zones and the sources there had to be a relation of homology, as though there were a particular function in the Kernel corresponding to each bodily organ. Thus, mutilation of the sexual organs does not entail the elimination of the homologous nucleic function and, vice versa, anasemic Castration does not imply the excision of the genitals. It is by virtue of this correspondence between the Envelope and the Kernel that Freud localized the source of sexual drives in the somatic zones, meaning thereby the Erogenous Zones, with capitals, that is, the ones originating in the Kernel. Without this implicit but effective distinction, it would be hard to understand, for example, how the source of the drive could be a representation and, as such, be its own emissary (see pp. 449–59 [424–35]). The motive for designating the Kernel as organic lies in this: the phenomena belonging to the Envelope, such as conversion hysteria, would not make any sense if they were not rooted in the transphenomenal nonsense of nucleic Organicity.

THE SEX OF SEX AND THE ORIGIN OF FANTASY

We shall acquire a still better sense about the nature of the Kernel if we examine the aspect of it revealed by the anasemia of Sex. The authors of *The Language of Psychoanalysis* are right to ask: "What authorizes the psychoanalyst to attribute a sexual character to processes from which the genital is absent?" (p. 144 [419]). Nothing, of course, except designification. Surely, in the Envelope, sex occupies a circumscribed place, both as localized genital organ of the body proper and as affective and fantasmic function with an overtly sexual content. The extension of sex is in fact minimal with respect to the vast domain it seems to exclude. Yet, as an anasemic figure, the Sexual does not have this partial character at all: it concerns the totality of the Kernel. Here is something that, if we return to the level of fantasmic delegates, acquires far-reaching effects. This new anasemia implies, in fact, that the Kernel's message, transmitted to the Envelope through the channel of the Drive and received in the form of fantasy—whatever its modes and disguises—is always, and necessarily, connected with Sex inasmuch as the latter governs the interiority of nucleic life. The pansexualism of Freud is the anasemic pansexualism of the Kernel. This means simply that in the Envelope, in the "I" and the "me" of reflexivity, in the body proper, including the genitals, in what is experienced and in fantasy, extending even to what is called the external world or others, there is nothing that would not have a constitutive relation to Sex as the universal requirement and origin of all phenomena. Of course, nucleic Sex has nothing to do with the difference between the sexes. Freud said, again by anasemia, that Sex is in essence masculine. Indeed it is, in the sense that it is the active instigator of everything and displays itself in the Envelope as a phallus penetrating it from the inside. It is not surprising that fantasies of "passivity" should be the ones which, in the course of treatment, prefigure the outcome of the analytic process as the Ego takes charge of the solicitations of the Unconscious. We can also understand the many theoretical and practical misconceptions arising from the failure to recognize and appreciate the phallic nature of the Kernel in its relation to the Envelope. I will merely cite the very common misconception which consists in confusing an objectified phallic image (to be the phallus or to have it) with its nucleic source or in rejecting penis-envy in the woman as unfounded instead of recognizing it as an instrument of repression, a means of warding off contact with the Phallus of one's own Unconscious. Let me also mention various other psychoanalytic conceptions of femininity that lend credence to the fantasy that "the woman is castrated of the phallus," the better to misconstrue psychoanalytic reality: men and women are endowed with an Unconscious whose phallic representation simply objectifies repressed demands.

The origin of fantasy—whose substance Laplanche and Pontalis have so remarkably elucidated[5]—overlaps with the problem of the metapsycho-

5. In "Fantasme originaire, fantasmes des origines, origine du fantasme," *Les Temps modernes* 19, no. 215 (April 1964): 1833–68.

logical relation between the Kernel and the Envelope. Fantasies of the so-called Primal and Primordial Scene, in the different modes of seduction and rape, are prototypes for staging various dynamic moments of that relation. . . . No need to enlarge upon the Freudian theory of fantasy here for us to perceive an essential point: far from being gratuitous or arbitrary, the attribution—by anasemia—of the male Sex to the Kernel provides a real key to understanding fantasy life. To fantasize is to translate into an imaginary objectivation—conscious or not—the Kernel's concrete momentary relation to the Envelope. We shall say, again by anasemia, that this relation is *sexual* to the extent that every fantasy aspires to have contact with the Unconscious and thereby concerns the phallus. Along the same lines, the pregenital mother, as the pole of oral and anal relations, is said to be phallic, i.e., the giver of the phallus in these archaic modes. Thus, even though there are psychic processes that seem to exclude "genitality," all of them, whatever they may be, nonetheless have as a condition of possibility the nucleic Masculinity of Sex.

THE HIERARCHICAL EMBEDDING OF KERNELS

With the second stage of the exegesis thus sketched out, we are sufficiently prepared to examine one of the most profound passages of *The Language of Psychoanalysis*. Commenting on certain aspects of the Ego, the authors cast new light on the whole of metapsychology. Their remarks will acquire greater unity if I am allowed some synonymic substitutions: "Endogenous excitation is successively described as coming from inside of the body [= *from the Kernel, from the Organism*], from inside the psychical apparatus [= *the Unconscious = secondary Kernel*], and finally as stored in the Ego [= *the Envelope of the Unconscious*]: this presents a series of successive embeddings which . . . gives rise to the idea of the ego as a kind of actualized metaphor for the organism [= *of the so-called organic Kernel*]" (p. 446 [135], my parentheses).

To elaborate on this perceptive commentary, we shall have to examine the Kernel's anasemic complement, the so-called psychic Envelope. Here the essential point seems to be that, in Freud's intuition, the Periphery itself includes a Kernel with its own Periphery, which in turn includes a Kernel, and so forth. The secondary, tertiary, etc., Kernels, along with those that precede them in rank, are related by analogy. Thus the primary Kernel, termed organic, has on its periphery a so-called psychic counterpart or secondary Kernel, which is the Unconscious properly speaking. This, in turn, has in its own Envelope its exterior nucleic counterpart, Consciousness. In summary, the set of Unconscious-Preconscious-

Conscious constitutes the doubly nucleic Periphery of the primary Kernel: the Organic.

THE MEMORY TRACE AS MESSENGER OF THE ENVELOPE

If we follow Freud in his scheme of analogical embeddings, the relation of the Unconscious to the Conscious should be of the same type as that, on a deeper level, of the organic Kernel to the psychic Envelope. Just as drives translate organic demands into the language of the Unconscious, so it utilizes the vehicle of affect or fantasy in order to move into the realm of the Conscious. Thus the appropriate emissaries enact a passage each time from a Kernel to its Periphery. Are there messages moving in the opposite direction, from the Envelope to the Kernel? This might be the case of memory traces in particular, the "vestiges of perception." At first sight, Freud's response seems to be negative as the problem of the so-called dual inscription would attest. Given that the trace of the same past receives different functions in the various psychic systems, one would be inclined to conclude that it is inscribed simultaneously and separately in each one of the systems. Hence the recollection of a repressed memory in the course of therapy would not modify its localization in the Unconscious, but would only liberate—not without dynamic effect, moreover—its *twin* inscribed in the Preconscious. This would explain how, even after being brought to consciousness, dream representations retain their value of sexual symbolism. Obviously, if the inscription is double, the duplicated trace cannot serve as a nucleo-peripheral relay. However, there is another well-known Freudian model of mnemic functioning, the "mystic writing pad," suggesting that the inscription must occur once and for all, provided that this happens neither in the Unconscious nor in the Preconscious, but in a typically intermediary region: in the region of contact, so to speak, between the Kernel and the Periphery. Without itself being double, the trace of the inscription could lend itself to a twofold use: nucleic, through its side turned toward the Unconscious, and peripheral, through its view toward the Conscious; the former obeying the laws of the Primary Process (in feeding hallucinatory realizations with representations), the latter adapting and bending the trace to the demands of the Secondary Process (discursiveness, temporality, objectality). From this point on, we could proceed to radicalize the concept of the trace and offer the following idea for consideration: the inscription is made possible precisely as a result of different uses to which the trace is put on the two sides, and this doubleness is constitutive of both the Envelope and the Kernel; these would then be simply the poles on the *near* and *far side* of the dividing line where the perpetual nucleo-peripheral differral [*différencement*] pulsates. Envelope and Kernel would have this frontier as substance, instrument, object, and subject simultaneously. Conceived in this manner, the trace would no longer be a static vestige, a Janus figure or two-sided medallion. On the contrary, it would be constant activity, repeating endlessly the alternation of its duplex discourse.

Returning to the restricted psychoanalytic sense of such a universal operation, we would learn that, forming the surface of communication between the two systems, memory traces could have the same mediating mission as representations, affects, and fantasies. Memory traces are to be distinguished from the latter only by their orientation: their mission is centripetal while the others' is centrifugal.

This interpretation at any rate allows us to overcome many of the difficulties indicated on numerous occasions by the authors (for example, p. 199 [248]). To mention only the difficulties entailed by the theory of repression, we could ask: how can repression be both the product of censorship and of the attraction of the Unconscious? How can repression respond to the demands of the Secondary Process when it is supposed to follow the laws of the Primary Process? Such questions cease to arise as soon as memory traces are situated on the nucleoperipheral boundary. Doing so, we define the trace as the reception given by the unconscious Kernel to the emissaries of the Preconscious-Conscious system. Received on the surface of the Kernel, the trace can then be sent back to the Envelope in the form of representations or affects, or else be excluded from it by Censorship. Repressed, the trace continues nonetheless to act in relation to the unconscious Kernel, but henceforth obeys its laws exclusively—both to attract into its orbit the other traces that concern it and to erupt into Consciousness as the return of the repressed.

It is important for our purposes to note the dual quality of the trace as it acts upon the two systems simultaneously. Considered in this way, memory traces would be literally identical with the Freudian description of symbol and symptom. "Freud compares the hysterical symptom to a monument erected in commemoration of an event: thus the symptoms of Anna O. are 'mnemic symbols' of the illness and death of her father" (p. 474 [253]). A monument, by all means, and a monument which lives on and does not cease being active. The symptom is a memorial that bespeaks a willfully disregarded event: identifying perception with fantasy, identifying the centripetal emissary with the centrifugal one. The "mnemic trace" is a monument as well, raised on the occasion of such an establishment of identity. Fantasy and perception, insofar as they are memory traces, form an indissoluble unit. It is in this that their structure resembles both symptoms and symbols: they derive their being from the unity they effect between two opposing demands: the Envelope and the Kernel.

THE NUCLEIC ROOTS OF CONSCIOUSNESS

We have come a long way both from the naturalist point of view and the reflexive approach. In this present view, which requires the name "transphenomenal," what is the place of Consciousness? In Consciousness, says Freud, the "perceptions of the self and the other" become actualized "in difference" (*Gesammelte Werke* XVII, p. 79).[6] "The psychical apparatus"—Freud notes as early as *The Interpretation of Dreams*— "turned toward the outside world through the sensory organs of the Perception-Consciousness system, constitutes the external world for that sensory organ which is Consciousness" (*GW* II-III, p. 620). This appears to be a barely disguised paraphrase of Brentano's doctrine concerning "secondary consciousness," "lateral consciousness," or "perception of self," postulated as part of any external perception. Freud's originality in relation to his teacher of philosophy consisted in rooting this intentional consciousness in a nucleoperipheral system and endowing it with a fathomable depth; the same is true of the Object, the symmetrical outside of the system. Freud was not content with maintaining that Consciousness makes the external world emerge in its relation to itself. He went further, declaring that self-perception passes at any rate through an "internal foreign territory," the Unconscious, and entails a form of exchange with it (Ferenczi's term is Introjection); by this means the internal foreigner will establish the external one, the Object. Using the Object-Unconscious play of symmetry, we are able to recognize ourselves as the Object of the Object, the prerogatives of each being reciprocal. In other words, Consciousness is only possible by virtue of the Unconscious whose image comes back to it by way of the Object. Such an understanding of Consciousness as doubly and reciprocally auto-objectal greatly deepens the somewhat mathematical rationalism of the toucher-touched of intentionality. Consciousness is not limited to acknowledging the coincidence of diversity in a unifying Ego and a unified object, but brings nucleoperipheral dramas onto the internal stage in the innumerable figures of objectal reciprocity.

Consciousness, resistant to any definition by reflexive philosophies, is conceived of psychoanalytically as an organ of the Envelope, capable of objectifying the various modes of the nucleoperipheral relationship in the Ego's diversified relations to external Objects. All psychoanalysis, clinical and theoretical, rests upon this cardinal tenet.

But what exactly is the vocation of metapsychology? It has to translate the phenomena of Consciousness—auto- or hetero-perceptions, represen-

6. [London: Imago, 1940–48.]

tations or affects, acts, reasoning, or value judgments—into the rigorous symbolic language which reveals the concrete underlying relations that, in each particular case, join the two anasemic poles: the Kernel and the Envelope. Some of these relations are typical or universal formations. We shall pause to consider one of them, the Oedipus complex, as it constitutes the axis of both psychoanalytic therapy and of the theoretical and technical elaborations which derive from it.

THE METAPSYCHOLOGY OF MYTH

It is no accident that this formation took its name from a myth. A myth is in fact no more, at least in my view, than a collective imaginary objectivation of the varying nucleo-peripheral relations, inasmuch as these ultimately ground the concrete organization of specific social groups. Allusive of the anasemic domain, and at the same time communicable, myths lend themselves particularly well to the representation of various metapsychological positions. However, one should not see in myths what many theoreticians seem to allow—a simply reflection of the relationship between the Kernel and the Envelope. On the contrary, myths are efficient ways of speaking by means of which some situation or other comes about and is maintained. We know how: by carrying out, with the help of their manifest content, the repression of their latent content. Myths, therefore, indicate a gap in introjection, in the communication with the Unconscious. If they provide food for understanding, they do so much less by what they say than by what they do not say, by their blanks, their intonations, their disguises. Instruments of repression, myths also serve as a vehicle for the symbolic return of the repressed. Any study of myths, whether ethnological or psychoanalytical, should take this aspect into account.

This position is the more strongly warranted when a myth is taken to be exemplary of a metapsychological situation. It would be naive to take myths literally and transpose them purely and simply into the domain of the Unconscious. No doubt, myths do correspond to the numerous and varied "stories" that are "recounted" at the confines of the Kernel. Yet, the fact that it is possible to carry out treatment innocently, so to speak—simply by allowing unformulated, disguised, or implicit fantasies to become explicit in the order of their emergence—shows only this: the rationalization of fantasy, that is, its transformation into a provisional myth, gives rise to dynamic changes between the unconscious Kernel and the Ego. Melanie Klein followed this procedure with extreme rigor, as is well known. This level of elaboration leads nonetheless to both theoretical and practical impasses which occur especially when the infantile system of fantasies, raised to the rank of mythology, comes to be substituted for theory: castration, primal scene, Oedipus complex. To take myths and fantasies literally is to grant them excessive dignity at the expense of metapsychology. To turn a blind eye to the contingency of fantasies or, worse, to claim to formalize them in the mode of descriptive structuralism, is to fail to recognize their true mainspring: the specific tension that arises between the Envelope and the Kernel.

THE OEDIPUS COMPLEX TRACED BACK TO NUCLEOPERIPHERAL CONFLICT

It is important to know that in general a Complex is a "group of representations and memories of great affective force, partially or totally unconscious" (p. 72 [72]), and that, in particular, the Oedipus complex is a "body of loving and hostile wishes which the child experiences toward its parents" (p. 79 [282]), and that it "plays a fundamental part in structuring personality and in the orientation of human desire" (p. 80 [283]). But it is also important to emphasize that if the oedipal formation is a "story" the child "tells" itself, it does so in accordance with the contingencies of the cultural codes already in force. Do we find a constant in the oedipal mythologies of the child? If we do—according to the authors, it is the reference to a "prohibitive agency"—there still remains the question of its ultimate metapsychological meaning, that is, its symbolic value in relation to the two anasemic poles. For we can wonder whether the fact that the child interposes this "prohibitive agency (prohibition against incest) which bars access to a naturally sought satisfaction and ties the wish inseparably to the law" does not derive from the manifest content of the child's discourse and whether, in stopping at this level of interpretation, we do not still remain accountable for unearthing the latent content, the key component of the symbol functioning between the Envelope and the Kernel. Surely, the play of contrasts, which in this case opposes desire and prohibition, derives from the requirements of the discourse through which the child makes itself heard. But to take the child's discourse literally, would that not amount to ratifying the social and moral order in which the expression of its misleading wish is embedded, and to condemning the child to suffer the inexorable sanctions of its own verdict? In that case, psychoanalysis would be more bigoted than the most narrow-minded of religions and more conservative than the most reactionary parties. Lest the child be trapped as an adult in its own game of make-believe—lest it and the society it constitutes congeal in a relational structure the child both presupposes and tends to perpetuate—it is crucial for the child to be able to relive the inaugural moment in which its pseudology is rooted. To whom is the discourse of the boy or girl addressed? Is it not to the mother in both cases, and is not the intention always to speak to her of an object other than herself—in this instance the father—in order to let her know, in accord with the contingency of the operative code, that she will not be abandoned in favor of this third party? Does this not, by the same token, already introduce a third party into the maternal relation, in the form of denial, to be sure, but all the same foreshadowing an imminent detachment from the mother? Until then the mother had the functions of the Envelope; she was everything: amnion, warmth, nourishment, mainstay, body, cry, desire, rage, joy, fear, yes, no, you, me, object, and project. However, the child has been progressively able to appropriate this exterior maternal Envelope. As a result, the child has nothing more to expect from the mother. Once accomplished, maternal introjections must yield to other introjections, the introjection of the vast domain encompassing all that is not part of the motherhood of the mother, the whole of social life, as represented by the non-mother, whatever form the non-mother may take, that is to say, in our civilization, the "father." It is to reassure the mother of their faithfulness that children of both sexes invent, each in its own way, the fantasy of the Oedipus complex, the idea of incest and its prohibition, the fear of the phallus and of castration, the wish to kill the father. All these are conventional means, implicitly offered by the whole cultural fabric, which allow children—unless there is a fixation—to bring about a smooth detachment from the mothering mother, even as they indicate a dilatory attachment to her. The metapsychological moment of the Oedipus complex, in the sense Freud gives it, coincides with the introjective exhaustion of the maternal Envelope. Henceforth, the introjection of the Kernel's libidinal Masculinity will be accomplished through social life wherein the Phallus of the Kernel is objectified in a thousand and one ways. Hence the reverse of oedipal fantasizing, the secret representation of coitus with the father, suggesting the necessity of constituting the Envelope by introducing the nucleic libido into it. Freud emphasized many times that during the phallic stage, when the oedipal conflict is born, the child knows only the male sex, either through its presence or its objectified absence. Torn between the Phallus and the mother, Oedipus does not yet know the differentiation of the sexes. His incest is pestiferous, not because it strikes a blow at social order, but because it stifles his own desire to introject his sex in favor of a mother who had not found hers. I do not think that incest would provide a "naturally sought satisfaction." Such a statement derives precisely from the pseudology of the child, paying a last tribute to the mother before leaving her. We can see clearly the hypocrisy of thus pitting the order of nature against the order of culture. In reality, the oedipal conflict does not weigh the pros and cons between nature and culture, but rather between the maternal relation and sexual attainment in the social order. For this reason, I am equally disinclined to think that the "prohibition of incest ties the wish inseparably to the law." Everything seems to indicate that once again we allow ourselves to be duped by a child theory. In a society where some form of incest prohibition reigns, the child will not fail to utilize it as a mode of expression and to make use of it as an alibi. If there is a prohibition, it does not, in the last analysis, concern "incest," which in any case is impracticable before puberty, but rather the excessive prolongation of mothering, the continuance beyond what is necessary of the mother-child circuit of the conservation instinct (= instinct of the Ego, of the Envelope). The universality of the Oedipus complex finds its explanation in the equally universal fact that human beings come from a maternal Envelope and, by the introjection of the social order, constitute their own sexualized Envelope. Moreover, the prohibition does not strike the child, but the mother; and the "rift" or "castration," which some take pleasure in elevating to an anthropological principle, affects essentially the maternal propensity to derive satisfaction from mothering. Jumping to the statement that an agency of the law is capable of revealing desire— in the final analysis, the desire of returning to the breast—derives from a particular attitude toward the mother. With this precautionary note in mind, we will all most likely come out ahead by opting for the true desire: the introjection of the unconscious Kernel through social channels. This theoretical solution would offer no obstacles to psychic equanimity, were it not for the opposition to progress, the moralism and insincerity implied by society. I, for my part, prefer to see in Freud's discovery the beginnings of a radical renewal of culture, laying bare the myths of the Oedipus complex, castration, and the law—a renewal to be wrought at the point of origin of all these objectivations, at the meeting place between the Envelope and the Kernel, the place where, between two poles of non-meaning, the superior rationality of the symbol is born, where the innumerable forms of civilization disintegrate, originate, and bloom.

Here then are a few, all too rhapsodic remarks concerning the structure and functioning of some of the key concepts of psychoanalysis. We can observe in retrospect that they do not yield to the norms of formal logic: they relate to no object or collection of objects, nor in any strict sense do they have either extension or comprehension. They are "ways of speaking," means of disclosing the unspeakable in nonsense and contradiction.

However, this language does respect rigor and rationality to the highest degree. Having its starting point in clinical facts, constantly returning to them for verification, it reveals with implacable logic the taint of constitutive contradiction in the "facts" themselves. Under the cover of seemingly traditional definitions, and pretending, in its discussions, to follow the rules of naive rationality, *The Language of Psychoanalysis* reveals, inside the shell of words, the existence of discontinuities and entanglements. In so doing, it allows us to glimpse what words cannot name, the transphenomenal Kernel of this nonscience, which, for more than a few, is already the science of sciences.

Part IV

New Perspectives in
Metapsychology:
Cryptic Mourning and
Secret Love

Editor's Note   Abraham and Torok wrote the essays on cryptic mourning and secret love in a steady succession between
1967 and 1973; with one exception, they were published by
1975. This section should be viewed as a whole since each article
expands on the others: elaborations, connections, or interactions
become increasingly apparent. The explicit focus is on secrets
formed in connection with the trauma of loss and on love situations that become both traumatic and secret through the violent
loss of a partner.

   Abraham and Torok's conception of a secret does not coincide with the customary definitions of this term. For the authors,
a secret is not primarily a hushed-up fact, a covert plot, a private
feeling, or confidential knowledge kept from others. "Secret" is
not synonymous with "hidden," "unknown," or "latent," even
in the Freudian sense of a person's unconscious or repressed
desires, apt to reappear only in opaque, symptomatic compro-
mise-formations. In Abraham and Torok's sense, the secret is a
trauma whose very occurrence and devastating emotional consequences are entombed and thereby consigned to internal si-

lence, albeit unwittingly, by the sufferers themselves. The secret
here is intrapsychic. It designates an internal psychic splitting;
as a result two distinct "people" live side by side, one behaving
as if s/he were part of the world and the other as if s/he had
no contact with it whatsoever. The "two people" know nothing
of each other and their fundamental disparity appears only to
the trained observer. Abraham and Torok deal with the causes
and possible cure of these secret psychic formations, aptly rendered by the popular terms "split" or "multiple personality"
but called by the authors the illness of mourning, melancholia,
incorporation, preservative repression (distinct from the Freudian dynamic repression), and more generally, the topography of
denied or excluded reality, and the metapsychology of secrets.
The idea of the secret, in Abraham and Torok's sense, casts new
light on the process of mourning as well as a great number of
other psychological and bodily afflictions, habits, preferences,
or states: manic-depressive psychosis, fetishism, anorexia, pedo-
philia, neurosis of failure, sexual apathy, impulsive behavior,
kleptomania, juvenile delinquency, in addition to the so-called
psychosomatic diseases, for instance, colitis and asthma.

The essays on mourning and secrets indicate yet another,
less explicit strain of thought, which serves to connect these
writings to Abraham and Torok's previous or concurrent work
on topics ranging from the acquisition of emotional and sexual
autonomy, the construction of self and reality, the union of
mother and child, and the metapsychology of myths to femininity and fantasy. The guiding principle here is introjection, the
idea that the psyche is in a constant process of acquisition,
involving the active expansion of our potential to open onto our
own emerging desires and feelings as well as the external world.
Though featured only once as the main subject of an informal
lecture ("The Crime of Introjection," 1963, to be printed in
volume 2 of this work), "introjection" lies at the root of Abraham
and Torok's conception of psychoanalysis. Yet Abraham and
Torok give no systematic account of their distinctive view of
psychoanalysis as based on the vicissitudes of introjection: en-
richments and disturbances in the process of self-fashioning.
The synthesis of this overarching theoretical common denomi-
nator, the definition of introjection as the constantly renewed
process of self-creating-self, is left to the readers. In a very
broad sense, the idea of introjection is implicitly operative in
Torok's earliest essays on "Fantasy" (1959) and "The Meaning
of 'Penis Envy' in Women" (1964), both of which deal with

the reception and the rejection of inmost affective and sexual promptings, the reception being mediated in this case by the analyst and the rejection performed by someone (for example the mother) who has been in her turn an unwitting victim of the disturbances of self-fashioning. Acquiring ever more complex facets when set in the context of Abraham and Torok's evolving theories of psychopathology and psychoanalytic interpretation, the concept of introjection is useful in understanding Abraham's idea of the psychoanalytic symbol: a twofold memory trace that encompasses death-dealing traumatic occurrences and the infinitely varied mechanisms of successful survival. (See "The Symbol or Beyond Phenomena," 1961, to be printed in volume 2 of this work.) Introjection is also the cornerstone of Abraham's reworking of Imre Hermann's concept of dual unity between mother and child, expressed by Abraham in "Introducing the 'Filial Instinct'" (1972) and *The Case of Jonah*, written in 1972, published in 1981 (both will appear in volume 2).

For Abraham and Torok, introjection represents both the very substance of psychic life—the unhindered activity of perpetual self-creation—and the ultimate result of psychotherapy. Hence the sharp distinction, indeed the mutually exclusive opposition, that first Torok, then Abraham and Torok together established between introjection and incorporation, two mechanisms that in the authors' view embody, on the one hand, an ideally harmonious progress of life and, on the other, its traumas, obstacles, or near deaths. Thus, from the opposition between introjection and incorporation emerges Abraham and Torok's understanding of the two basic principles of psychic functioning. Though the authors never formulate their ideas in the following terms, readers may see in the introjection-incorporation pair an avenue for recasting some of Freud's major theories, for example his identification of the pleasure and reality principles as the opposing forces of psychic life. The idea of introjection—the principle of gradual self-transformation in the face of interior and exterior changes in the psychological, emotional, relational, political, professional landscape—has the capacity to embrace the Freudian pleasure and reality principles as well as Freud's precept of the psychological prominence of infantile sexual development. Likewise, the afflictions of introjection—the traumatic impossibility of self-fashioning and readjustment, of which incorporation is the primary though by no means the only mechanism—encompass the psychic processes of conflict, censorship, and repression as outlined by Freud, whether these processes constitute responses to endogenic or external factors. Abraham and Torok's theory of introjection and incorporation synthesizes in one sweep the mechanisms and the aims or results of psychic processes. Viewing psychic life in terms of the vicissitudes of introjection, self-making versus the obstacles to self-making, has the compelling virtue of simplicity even as this conception potentially broadens the field of vision beyond the scope of Freud's theory of the instincts and their vicissitudes.

Both introjection and incorporation are terms inherited from the early theoreticians of psychoanalysis, such as Sandor Ferenczi, Freud, Karl Abraham, and Melanie Klein. Any attempt to summarize here the complex history of these two concepts would result in hair-splitting and fruitless terminological controversy. It may be helpful, however, to note several points. Ironically, the more familiar readers are with the widely varying uses of the terms "introjection" and "incorporation" in the psychoanalytic literature of the past seventy-five years, the more baffled they will be, unless they move beyond the terms to the substance of Abraham and Torok's arguments for creating a dichotomy in the principles of psychic functioning. Although the authors derive their concept of introjection from Ferenczi's 1912 definition, Ferenczi himself repeatedly uses this term to designate psychic mechanisms other than the one he initially described. Despite their attribution of the concept's paternity to Ferenczi, Abraham and Torok are the genuine creators of the concept of introjection in the very broad sense they intend. The distinction drawn by Abraham and Torok between introjection and incorporation has no precedent within psychoanalytic thought, either in the depth and scope of the distinction or in its theoretical consequences and clinical effectiveness.

"The Illness of Mourning or the Fantasy of the Exquisite Corpse" (1968) is the first in a series of articles focusing on the psychological weight of unwanted, shameful, or untoward reality and on our tendency to isolate painful realities, thereby removing them from the free circulation of our ideas, emotions, imaginations, creations, responses, initiatives, and contact with other people. This removal of an unbearable reality and its confinement to an inaccessible region of the psyche is what Torok calls "incorporation" or "preservative repression." Deriving her ideas from clinical experience, Torok finds support in a suggestion Karl Abraham made to Freud in 1922 concerning an increase in the sexual activity of people following a death in the family.[1] Combining K. Abraham's observations with her own (or rather seeking whatever precedents there might be for her startling discoveries), Torok proposes a new category of psychopathology, the illness of mourning. The crux of this illness is not the loss of the love-object but the secret the loss occasions, which Torok calls the "psychic tomb." The secret is formed because an unwelcome intrusion of sexual desire (at times erupting in involuntary orgasm) accompanies or closely follows upon the love-object's death. If we rid ourselves of prejudice, we, the readers of Torok's essay, may view this intensification of desire as the final, climactic outpouring of love for the departed. Complications may ensue, however, when the departed is a parent, grandparent, sibling, or other nonsexual associate. In these cases, the sexual outburst appears personally and socially unacceptable to the mourner; the involuntary effusion constitutes an occurrence the mourner cannot combine with his or her somber feelings of bereavement. The erotic effusion is transformed into an intrapsychic secret.

Beyond the mechanism and consequences of libidinal invasions or irruptions, Torok is interested in their causes. No such intrusion or untoward explosion of sexual feelings occurs unless the mourner has a past of unsettled desires as connected with the deceased. The distinction is worth stressing. It is not a matter of children's unfulfilled desire for their mother or father, as in the Freudian Oedipus complex. Rather, in these cases a situation existed in which the child's and adolescent's inchoate passions, provisionally directed at family members, encountered a parent's own conflictual or paralyzed history of desire. We can infer from Torok's essay that the mother or the father is an object of erotic love for the child not for the purposes of sexual possession but as a kind of training ground for the child's discovery and autonomous exercise of its budding desires. Though not overtly expressed, according to Torok, parents are not desired primarily after an oedipal fashion; they are the mediators of their children's process of self-creating, or introjection, a process of discovery and acquisition that includes the encounter with one's own desires as they spontaneously emerge and gradually grow to maturity, trying their wings on any and every cir-

---

1. Karl Abraham (1877–1925) was no relation to Nicolas Abraham. The former's full name or first initial is used throughout to avoid confusion.

cumstance of love, including parental affections. When complemented by Abraham's explicit critique of the Oedipus complex in his contemporaneous article "The Shell and the Kernel," Torok's argument can be extended: it is not the children's failure to accept the adult's rejection or prohibition of incest wishes that is most likely to lead to neurosis, but the degree of disarray in the parents' own state of desire.

The far-reaching implications of this view come into focus if considered in the context of Abraham's subsequent work on the mother-child union (dual unity) that gives rise to the gradual and potentially problematic detachment of children from their parents in the process of self-creation or introjection. The scope widens once again when the influence of the parents' emotional situation on their offsprings' psychic progress is viewed through the lens of Abraham's theory of the phantom, dealing with the unwitting transmission of family secrets, and through Torok's extension of this concept in the "Story of Fear" (1975) to the unexpected legacy of our unconscious fears, or conflicts in the lives of our descendants. The whole issue of the interrelationship between the parents' own history of hindered self-fashioning or failed introjections, as a factor in children's emotional and sexual unfolding, is an implicit sequel to Torok's early essay on "The Meaning of 'Penis Envy' in Women" (1964).

"Mourning *or* Melancholia: Introjection *versus* Incorporation" (1972) extends the idea of the illness of mourning to the unconscious refusal to mourn although in reality the person involved is overwhelmed by his or her grief. The essay deals primarily with the mechanism of setting up a psychic enclave—the crypt—"housing" the departed love-object in secret because the survivor is being deluded into behaving as if no trauma or loss had occurred. The full import of this essay emerges in the next one, entitled " 'The Lost Object—Me': Notes on Endocryptic Identification," a genuine sequel in the sense that it includes several detailed case studies illustrating the mechanisms described somewhat more abstractly in "Mourning *or* Melancholia."

The idea of inexpressible or cryptic mourning, the foundation of Abraham and Torok's theory of secrets, leads to a highly characteristic view of language, culminating in the concept of cryptonymy or concealment in language. Abraham and Torok follow Freud in viewing language as a product of psychic processes. Consequently, the authors expect little from the discoveries of modern linguistics in the way of illuminating unconscious mechanisms. On the contrary, their contention would appear to be that linguistics and in particular semiotics or the theory of signs (and by implication rhetoric and literary criticism) will find new avenues of methodological inspiration if they integrate the contributions of psychoanalysis into their conceptual stock, particularly the study of the disturbances of the expressive functions of language. Abraham and Torok found that patients suffering from a secret identification with a departed love-object invented particular forms of obfuscation in their speech. The patients obscured beyond recognition the linguistic elements that might reveal their secret's existence and contents to themselves and to the world. The authors' fundamental query in analyzing these patients can be formulated as follows: what leads people to make themselves unintelligible? Abraham and Torok's answer entailed the discovery of new linguistic mechanisms whose aim seems to be to disarray, even to destroy, the expressive or representational power of language. They call these mechanisms "demetaphorization," "anti-metaphor," "anti-semantics," or "designification." The recovery of signification is called "cryptonymic analysis" or "decrypting."

Abraham and Torok's terms for indicating the disruptions of language as an expressive medium derive from two of their essays, "The Shell and the Kernel" (1968) and "Mourning *or* Melancholia" (1972) and represent two fields of application for similar ideas. In the first instance, psychoanalytic interpretation is described by Abraham as moving from the collapse of apparent meaning (designification) to nonapparent sources of signification (anasemia).[2] A few years later psychopathologies of secret or intrapsychic crypts are characterized as exhibiting a symptomatology that includes the subversion of meaning, that is, the creation of mechanisms promoting the disintegration of meaning. Cryptonymic analysis in its turn seeks to reveal the processes that inhibit the emergence of signification. Abraham and Torok's discovery of psychic crypts and corresponding forms of hiding in language provide avenues for deciphering the obstructions that prevent linguistic entities from being joined with their potential sources of signification. The authors' interpretations characteristically aim at overcoming the resistance to meaning by explaining it as a symptom of secret and therefore inaccessible traumas.

2. For Abraham's definition of the specificity of psychoanalytic interpretation in terms of anasemia see Editor's Note to Part III.

The theories relative to the blockage of the referential, expressive, metaphoric, or symbolic functions of language form the basis of Abraham and Torok's reassessment of Freud's case of the Wolf Man. Their many references to the Wolf Man in the essays on mourning and crypts become easier to follow when read in conjunction with the systematic account to be found in *The Wolf Man's Magic Word* (1976; English translation 1986). The history of this book's composition shows that Abraham and Torok wrote the essays in the following section at the same time as the opening three chapters of the Wolf Man study. The examination of the Wolf Man's case serves then as an inspiration and as a testing-ground for Abraham and Torok's evolving ideas on secret psychic enclaves or multiple secret "identities." They also use the Wolf Man's case to develop their interpretive techniques for deciphering secrets buried in language.[3]

3. More extensive discussion of the Wolf Man's case can be found in my "Translator's Introduction: Toward A Cryptonymy of Literature" in *The Wolf Man's Magic Word* (Minneapolis: University of Minnesota Press, 1986), pp. li–lx.

FOUR

The Illness of Mourning
and the Fantasy of the
Exquisite Corpse

M. Torok, 1968

A REVELATORY MISUNDERSTANDING

An astonishing exchange of letters between Sigmund Freud and Karl
Abraham brings attentive readers to the origins of my topic and illustrates
its immediately disturbing aspects.[1]

Berlin-Gruenewald, 13.3.22

Dear Professor,

Incorporation of the love-object is very striking in my cases. I can produce very nice material for this concept of yours, demonstrating the process
in all its detail. In this connection I have a small request—for a reprint of
"Mourning and Melancholia," which would be extremely useful to me in
my work. Many thanks in anticipation.

One brief comment on this paper. You, dear Professor, state that you
find nothing in the course of normal mourning which would correspond to
the leap from melancholia to mania. I think, however, I can describe such
a process, without knowing whether this reaction is invariably found. My
impression is that a fair number of people show an increase in libido some
time after a period of mourning. It shows itself in heightened sexual need
and appears to lead relatively often to conception shortly after a death. I
should like to know your opinion and whether you can confirm this observation. The increase of libido some time after "object-loss" would seem to be
a valid addition to the parallel between mourning and melancholia. . . .

Previously published as "Maladie du deuil et fantasme du cadavre exquis," *Revue française de psychanalyse* 32, no. 4 (1968): 715–33; and in *L'Écorce et le noyau* (Paris: Flammarion, 1987), pp. 229–51.

1. *A Psycho-Analytic Dialogue: The Letters of Sigmund Freud and Karl Abraham*, ed.
Hilda C. Abraham and Ernst L. Freud (trans. Bernard Marsh and Hilda C. Abraham)
(London: Hogarth Press 1965), pp. 328–31.

Berggasse 19, Vienna, 30.3.22

Dear Friend,

After more than a fortnight I reread your personal letter, and came across your request for a reprint, which for some reason escaped my attention when I first read it.

I plunge eagerly into the abundance of your scientific insights and intentions; I only wonder why you do not take into account my last suggestion about the nature of mania after melancholia (in "Group Psychology"). Might that be the motivation for my forgetting about "Mourning and Melancholia"? No absurdity is impossible for psychoanalysis. I should like to discuss all these things, particularly with you, but it is impossible to write about them. In the evening I am tired, . . .

Berlin-Gruenewald, 2.5.22

Dear Professor,

. . . Your letter of March 30 is still waiting for a reply, but I have already thanked you for your reprint of "Mourning and Melancholia." I fully understand your forgetting it. Your failure in sending the paper I asked for was meant to indicate that I should first of all study the other source ("Group Psychology"). I am, however, quite familiar with its contents concerning the subject of mania and melancholia but, in spite of going through it once again, I cannot see where I went wrong. I can find no mention anywhere of a parallel reaction after mourning in normal cases which can be compared to the onset of mania (after melancholia). I only know from your remark in "Mourning and Melancholia" that you were aware of something lacking and I referred to this in my observation. The increase of libido after mourning would be fully analogous to the "feast" of the manic, but I have not found this parallel from normal life in that section of "Group Psychology" where this "feast" is discussed. Or have I been so struck by blindness that I am unable to see the actual reference? . . .

Bergasse 19, Vienna, 28.5.22

Dear Friend,

With Eitingon's help I discovered to my amusement that I completely misunderstood you through no fault of yours. You were looking for a normal example of the transition from melancholia to mania, and I was thinking of the explanation of the mechanism.

With many apologies,

This series of misunderstandings cannot be ascribed to pure chance. Karl Abraham senses the fruitfulness of his discovery, he insists, and I understand him. But what to make of the extent of Freud's resistance to a clinical observation? It demonstrates the reluctance we all feel when, in a sacrilegious move, we want to grasp the inmost nature of mourning. It is not surprising that, without encouragement from the professor, Karl Abraham is led to minimize the importance of this subject. He accords it only limited space in his crucial essay of 1924 ("An Outline of the History of the Development of the Libido Based on the Psychoanalysis of Mental Disturbances") and does not come to the theoretical and clinical consequences the problem most assuredly implies.

"NORMAL MANIA" AND THE ILLNESS OF MOURNING

Still, clinical observation brings forward a preliminary fact. All those who admit to having experienced such an "increase in libido" when they lost an object of love, do so with shame, astonishment, hesitation, and in a whisper. "My mother was there, dead. And at a time when people should feel the most intense grief, be doleful and forlorn, at a time when the arms and the legs should give way, when the whole frame should be prostrate, sinking to the floor—I can hardly bring myself to say it—at that moment I had sensations, yes, carnal sensations," says a voice. Another voice says, "I've never understood how something like that could have happened to me; I've never forgiven myself . . . , but a giddy song coursed through my mind and wouldn't leave me. It continued during the entire vigil. I tried on the black veil like a bride preparing for the big day."

These admissions definitely concur with Karl Abraham's ideas. His intuition seems to me fully confirmed by clinical experience. In this essay I will draw the lesson from his preliminary observation by casting new light on all the cases psychoanalysis teaches us to designate as "illness of mourning."

Why are these patients overwhelmed with self-reproach and inhibitions, why are they subject to exhausting ruminations, physical diseases, constant depression, fatigue, and anxiety? Why do they suffer from disinterest in objectal love? What dulls their creativity and makes them sigh nostalgically: "I might if I could . . ."? It is very rare that the connection between their state of mind and the originating event becomes conscious. To effect this realization is the task of analysis. "He pursued me intensely and I wanted to marry him. But an inner voice said to me: 'You would then have to abandon your dead.' This sad and insistent voice would return and for a long time I heeded its call. The world was an immense desert for me." Or this: "I've never forgiven myself for something. The day my father died I had intercourse with my husband. It was the first time I felt desire and satisfaction. Shortly thereafter we separated because . . ."

(here she gives some "good reasons"). This handful of examples characterizes the core around which the illness of mourning is constituted.

The illness of mourning does not result, as might appear, from the
affliction caused by the objectal loss itself, but rather from the feeling of
an irreparable crime: the crime of having been overcome with desire, of
having been surprised by an overflow of libido at the least appropriate
moment, when it would behoove us to be grieved in despair.

These are the clinical facts. A measure of libidinal increase upon the
object's death seems to be a widespread, if not universal phenomenon.
Karl Abraham's intuition leads me to see manic reactions as only one of
the pathologically exaggerated forms of such an increase of libido. (It
should be added that this sudden increase in libido can also lead to the
emergence of a latent neurotic conflict.) How are we to understand the
untoward arrival of this kind of libidinal invasion? A complex set of problems is tied up in this question and I will attempt to highlight some of its
strands. First I will discuss conflictual introjection and the auto-aggressive
reactions that derive from it, in addition to the economical problems they
may engender. Next, I will consider the specific form of repression that
manifests itself in the therapeutic process through a particular content:
incorporation. Finally, and in a more general way, I will try to delimit the
various neurotic trends that might be termed neurosis of transition.
Strickly speaking, the illness of mourning appears to be a restricted form
of this larger category of neurosis.

FERENCZI'S CONCEPT OF THE INTROJECTION
OF DRIVES CONTRASTED WITH THE CONCEPT
OF THE OBJECT'S INCORPORATION

a) Some Transformations of the Concept of Introjection

Whoever approaches the problem of mourning or depression is required
to muddle through a conceptual terrain studded with obstacles, for example "introjection." Ever since Sandor Ferenczi introduced the concept in
1909—first Freud and then Karl Abraham took it up, handing it down to
Melanie Klein and others—the term "introjection" has undergone so
many variations in meaning that its mere mention is enough to arouse in
me the suspicion of confused ideas, not to say verbiage. The initial and
rigorous meaning of this concept must be revived if we are to avoid such
pitfalls. The concept gives shape to the first great discovery Ferenczi

made, being filled with wonder before the phenomenon of psychoanalysis. Only when its initial and precise meaning is restored will the concept of "introjection" reveal its effectiveness in clarifying the clinical facts noted above, as regards both their genesis and evolution.

Freud, Karl Abraham, Melanie Klein, and others are quite willing to consider Ferenczi as the father of the concept of introjection. Nevertheless, it is remarkable that none of these authors attempts an in-depth analysis of the original concept, travestied from the start despite the clarification in Ferenczi's brilliant 1912 article "On the Definition of Introjection." Immediately adopted because of its pithiness, the concept became muddled—departing from its initial sense as an explicative synonym for "transference"—on account of its lexical structure (intro-jection: casting inside) and ended up being given entirely other, even mutually exclusive meanings. The confusion is such that the term "introjection" is often used to denote a mechanism characterized by the impossibility or the refusal to introject, at least in the sense originally intended by Ferenczi.[2]

We know that the study of psychosis and the emphasis placed on the narcissistic forms of the libido between 1913 and 1917 gradually enriched the libido theory (see *The Standard Edition of Freud's Psychological Works*, vol. 14). Freud's views on identification—narcissistic forms of incorporation as opposed to incorporation in the neuroses—continued to gain in complexity and came to constitute the pivotal point in his enonomic understanding of the work of mourning in the 1919 article "Mourning and Melancholia."[3] According to Freud, the trauma of objectal loss leads to a response: incorporation of the object within the ego. The incorporated object, with which the ego would identify partially, makes it possible both to wait while readjusting the internal economy and to redistribute one's investments. Given that it is not possible to liquidate the dead and decree definitively: "they are no more," the bereaved become the dead for themselves and take their time to work through, gradually and step by step, the effects of the separation.

Karl Abraham has established (and Freud recalled this in his study on mourning) that incorporation of the object and separation from it occur in the form of oral-cannibalistic and anal-evacuative processes. Given that they make use of Ferenczi's term "introjection," we might think that neither Freud nor K. Abraham would stray far from Ferenczi's original conception. Yet this initial impression fades as we examine Freud's inter-

---

2. [This paragraph followed the next two in the original and was moved here at Maria Torok's request—Ed.]

3. ["Incorporation" and "introjection" in this historical overview reflect Freud and K. Abraham's use of these terms; Torok's definitions follow in the next two sections.—Ed.]

pretation of the concept. For example, he equates introjection with identification. Moreover, Freud equates introjection with the recovery of investments placed either in a lost object (the ego becomes what it cannot leave) or in an inaccessible ideal object (the ego sets itself the ideal of becoming what it cannot yet be). Both of these processes—the identification with the relinquished object and the rival's so-called "introjection" into the superego, which is also the double requirement for the dissolution of the Oedipus complex—are justified through the loss of love objects in Freud's *Group Psychology and the Analysis of the Ego* and *The Ego and the Id*. In the essay on "Denial" the same theme of introjection, allegedly compensating for a loss or a lack, is found. We will see that completely different ideas inspired Ferenczi's concept.

b) Ferenczi's Text and Its Significance

It will be useful to stop and consider for a moment this basic text, worthy of being read and reconsidered. In any case, it constitutes the keystone of my theoretical elaboration.

> I described introjection as *an extension to the external world of the original autoerotic interests, by including its objects in the ego* [emphasis mine]. I put the emphasis on this "including" and wanted to show thereby that I considered every sort of object love (or transference) both in normal and in neurotic people (and of course also in paranoiacs as far as they are capable of loving) as an extension of the ego, that is as introjection.
>
> In principle, man can love only himself; if he loves an object he takes it into his ego. . . . I used the term "introjection" for all such growing onto, all such including of the loved object in, the ego. As already stated, I conceive the mechanism of all transference onto an object, that is to say all kinds of object love, as an extension of the ego.
>
> I described the excessive proneness to transference of neurotics as unconscious exaggeration of the same mechanism, that is, as addiction to introjection. . . .[4]

What does an analysis of this text teach us? First and foremost, in the sense Ferenczi gave this concept, "introjection" is comprised of three points: (1) the extension of autoerotic interests, (2) the broadening of the ego through the removal of repression, (3) the including of the object in the ego and thereby "an extension to the external world of the [ego's] original autoerotic interests." In the writings of Ferenczi's contemporaries,

---

4. S. Ferenczi, *Final Contributions to the Problems and Methods of Psycho-Analysis* (New York: Brunner/Mazel Publishers, 1980), pp. 316–17.

this initially threefold meaning of introjection is reduced to a single super-ficial aspect: taking possession of the object through *incorporation*, that is, by putting it into the body or the psyche. Yet the difference is consider-able and must be sustained by a clear distinction between the two con-cepts. In defining the illness of mourning more precisely, I want to elimi-nate the misleading synonymy between introjection and incorporation. I will adhere strictly to the proper semantic specificity of each as it manifests itself in clinical work and as should appear clearly in what follows.

Ferenczi's text implies that introjection cannot have as its cause the actual loss of an object of love. No violence is done to his concept by the statement that introjection operates like a genuine instinct. Like transfer-ence (that is, like its mode of action in therapy), introjection is defined as the process of including the Unconscious in the ego through objectal contacts. The loss of the object will halt this process. Introjection does not tend toward compensation, but growth. By broadening and enriching the ego, introjection seeks to introduce into it the unconscious, nameless, or repressed libido. Thus, it is not at all a matter of "introjecting" the object, as is all too commonly stated, but of introjecting the sum total of the drives, and their vicissitudes as occasioned and mediated by the object.

According to Ferenczi, introjection confers on the object, and on the analyst, the role of mediation toward the unconscious. Moving back and forth between "the narcissistic and the objectal realms," between auto- and hetero-eroticism, introjection transforms instinctual promptings into desires and fantasies of desire, making them fit to receive a name and the right to exist and to unfold in the objectal sphere.

c) Incorporation: The Secret Magic Aimed at the Recovery of the Object of Pleasure

Most of the characteristics falsely attributed to introjection in fact apply to the fantasmic mechanism of incorporation. This mechanism does sup-pose the loss of an object in order to take effect; it implies a loss that occurred before the desires concerning the object might have been freed. The loss acts as a prohibition and, whatever form it may take, constitutes an insurmountable obstacle to introjection. The prohibited object is set-tled in the ego in order to compensate for the lost pleasure and the failed introjection. This is incorporation in the strict sense of the term.

Incorporation may operate by means of representations, affects, or bodily states, or use two or three of these means simultaneously. But, whatever the instrument, incorporation is invariably distinct from introjec-tion (a gradual process) because it is instantaneous and magical. The ob-ject of pleasure being absent, incorporation obeys the pleasure principle and functions by way of processes similar to hallucinatory fulfillments.

Furthermore, the recuperative magic of incorporation cannot reveal its nature. Unless there is an openly manic crisis, there are good reasons for it to remain concealed. Let us not forget that incorporation is born of a prohibition it sidesteps but does not actually transgress. The ultimate aim of incorporation is to recover, in secret and through magic, an object that, for one reason or another, evaded its own function: mediating the introjection of desires. Refusing both the object's and reality's verdict, incorporation is an eminently illegal act; it must hide from view along with the desire of introjection it masks; it must hide even from the ego. Secrecy is imperative for survival. Here we see one more difference between incorporation and introjection. True to its spirit, introjection works entirely in the open by dint of its privileged instrument, naming.

The specificity of each of these two movements now appears clearly. While the introjection of desires puts an end to objectal dependency, incorporation of the object creates or reinforces imaginal ties and hence dependency. Installed in place of the lost object, the incorporated object continues to recall the fact that something else was lost: the desires quelled by repression. Like a commemorative monument, the incorporated object betokens the place, the date, and the circumstances in which desires were banished from introjection: they stand like tombs in the life of the ego. Clearly, the mechanisms of introjection and incorporation are at odds. To call these two movements—the introjection of drives and the incorporation of the object—by the same name can hardly contribute to clarity in communication.

d) Incorporation, Its Origin, and Its Telling Nature

There is an archaic level on which the two mechanisms, though subsequently opposed, could still be fused. Let me illustrate this with the early form of the ego which is made up of the oral libido's introjection. This type of process *signals* its meaning to itself by way of a *fantasy* or ingestion. Comprised exclusively of the oral libido's introjection, the ego consists at this stage in the use it makes of ingestion and its variants (salivation, hiccups, vomiting, etc.), in symbolic expressions, such as asking for or refusing food *regardless of the actual state of hunger* or, alternatively, fantasizing the consumption and refusal of food by means of the same mechanism but when the object is absent. The latter corresponds quite precisely to what is usually described as the mechanism of incorporation.

The fantasy of incorporation is the first lie, the effect of the first rudimentary form of language. It is also the first instrument of deception. Satisfying need by offering food does not sate the actual and persistently active hunger for introjection. The offer of food only serves to deceive it.

(A gesture of this type occurs in the manic position too, but in relation to oneself.) Thirsting for introjection despite an insurmountable internal obstacle, the ego tricks itself with a magical procedure in which "eating" (the feast) is paraded as the equivalent of an immediate but purely hallucinatory and illusory "introjection." Manic persons announce with fanfare to their unconscious that they are "eating" (an act signifying the process of introjection and satisfaction for the ego). Yet, this is nothing but empty words and no introjection. When deprived of progressive libidinal nourishment, the ego regresses to this archaic level of magical attainment.

Inasmuch as it is merely a language *signaling* introjection, without actually accomplishing it, the fantasy of incorporation lends itself to a wide-ranging, even opposite contexts. At times it signals the desire for an impossible introjection as in penis envy; at other times its claim is that introjection has already occurred, for example in phallic displays; or else it signals the displacement of introjection, pointing to the oral zone when in fact another zone is meant. Realizing that incorporation is a form of language, which merely *states* the desire to introject, marks an important step forward in psychoanalytic therapy. This language is striking in the vocabulary of dreams. A patient who has never masturbated dreams: "My mother is serving a dish of asparagus and hands me the fork." (I wish she would relinquish her power over my penis and hand it over into my own hand, authorizing me to introject my desire for her.) Another patient dreams: "I am eating and vomiting blood flow and periods." (This recalls a gynecological examination during her puberty at which her father was present.) Any number of examples could be marshalled; they occur daily in clinical work. The same function of language can be found also in the "clinical" study of myths and traditions. Consider Popeye eating spinach; love potions; the fruit of knowledge whose ingestion by the first couple conferred on it genital sexuality; various cannibalistic rites; and the incorporative function of first communions, etc.

All these examples illustrate the point that, unlike lay people, analysts do not understand incorporation as a request to be granted or hunger to be satisifed, but as the disguised language of as yet unborn and unintrojected desires.

FIXATION AND THE ILLNESS OF MOURNING

Having established the difference between Ferenczi's concept of introjection and my own concept of incorporation, it is now time to return to our original problem, Karl Abraham's idea of "normal mania." An increase in libido, leading at times to orgasm, is a reaction to a death. I will now proceęd with a metapsychological reconstruction of this moment, experienced and repressed upon the death of the object. Here we will reach the core of the illness of mourning.

It is clear now that, in the course of its organization and also in transference, the ego makes use of the object (or the analyst) to achieve its libidinal awakening and nourishment. Playing, as it does, the part of mediator between the ego and the unconscious in the introjection of drives, the object's function is not to serve as a complement to instinctual satisfaction. Since it is a pole of the developing ego, the object is the more intensely invested because it carries the promise of introjection. This is manifestly the meaning of the passionate love characteristic of both childhood and transference. Supposedly in possession of all that the ego requires for its own growth, the object long remains its focus of attention. When the process of introjection is complete, the object can descend from the imaginal pedestal where the ego's need for nourishment has placed it. If there is a death, the nature of the bereavement will be a function of the role the object played at the time of the loss. If the desires concerning it were introjected, no breakdown, no illness of mourning or melancholia should be feared. The libido invested in the object will be recovered eventually and the ego, in accordance with Freud's description, will become available once more in order to fix itself on other objects that might be necessary for its libidinal economy. Surely, the work of mourning is a painful process even in these cases, but the ego's integrity guarantees the outcome.

The same is not true in the other case—a rather frequent occurrence—in which the process of introjection was incomplete. Because the unassimilated portion of the drives has congealed into an imago, forever reprojected onto some external object, the incomplete and dependent ego finds itself caught in a self-contradictory obligation. The ego needs to keep alive at all costs that which causes its greatest suffering. Why this obligation? It is understandable if we consider the following. The imago, along with its external embodiment in the object, was set up as the repository of hope; the desires it forbade would be realized one day. Meanwhile, the imago retains the valuable thing whose lack cripples the ego. "My wife took my potency to the grave. She holds my penis there, as though it were in her hand." The imagoic and objectal fixation is cemented precisely by the contradictory and therefore utopian hope that the imago, the warden of repression, would authorize its removal. The object invested with such an imaginal role ought never to die. We sense the disarray into which the object's disappearance throws the ego. Its destiny having been fixation, the ego is henceforth condemned to suffer the illness of mourning.

AN ATTEMPTED RECONSTRUCTION OF THE
METAPSYCHOLOGICAL MOMENT OF LOSS

The initially mysterious increase in libido at the moment of loss becomes understandable in light of the metapsychological analysis of introjection. The increase in libido is a desperate and final attempt at introjection, a sudden amorous fulfillment with the object. Here is how it can be explained.

When patients describe their being overcome with libido (for example, Breuer's Anna O. overcome with "serpents," one of my patients with "fleas," another one with "frivolous" songs), they recount the astonishment they felt at this completely unexpected event. The libido breaks in on them like an unbridled tidal wave, giving no heed to the imago guarding repression. The "surprise" is no doubt a disclaimer: "It's not my fault. It occurred without my being there to intend it." The event is never totally repudiated, however: "It was a dream and yet not a dream." Faced with the imminent threat that it might be too late, the ego regresses to the archaic level of hallucinatory satisfaction. In that realm, as we saw earlier, introjection and incorporation still constitute two aspects of the same mechanism. Not being able to remove repression and thus remaining unfulfilled, the long-contained hope is cornered in a desperate dilemma: deadly renunciation or fallacious triumph. Regression permits the latter, substituting fantasy for the real thing, magic and instantaneous incorporation for the introjective process. The hallucinatory fulfillment exults in orgasm.

Obviously, such a regression to magic does not match the ego's present conformation. In consequence, this fleeting fulfillment is struck with explicit condemnation and immediate repression. The ensuing amnesia concerns the concrete context of the moment in which the regression and the orgasm occurred. Should those ill from mourning consciously recall an orgasm (for which they secondarily blame themselves), its link to a desire for the dying or dead object is always severely censored. The novelty of the illness of mourning in relation to any underlying infantile neurosis is precisely the repression of this particular link. Which is why the relation between the orgasmic moment and the illness of mourning fails to be recognized.

The additional repression placed on the hallucinatory fulfillment of desire is responsible for the particularly intense resistance encountered in the analysis of these cases. The resistance here is comparable to that displayed by patients who, prior to psychoanalysis, have undergone therapy by narcosis. Placed all too abruptly before their desire, without previously having had the chance to deconstruct their imago gradually, these patients awaken in the same situation as those ill from mourning; both carry the buried memory of an instant of illegitimate sexual delight.

In both these cases, repression not only separates, but also has to *preserve* carefully, although in the unconscious, the wish the ego can only represent as an "exquisite corpse" lying somewhere inside it; the ego looks for this exquisite corpse continually in the hope of one day reviving it.

Those patients of mourning who choose psychoanalysis seem to know nothing of their attempt to recapture a precise moment. Everything unfolds as though a mysterious compass led them to the tomb wherein the repressed problem lies.

A character in the verse of Edgar Allan Poe comes to mind here, a character who, unaware of the secret aim of his journey, notwithstanding the admonishments of his Pysche, walks under an ashen sky in a desolate and dank region to his beloved Ulalume's tomb, buried on that very night in the previous year. This poem is psychoanalytical ahead of its time since it symbolizes openly, for the first time in literature, the action of the unconscious. The return of the repressed occurs inescapably through the fatality of acted remembrance. I can say for my part that what drives the Narrator to relive the moment of loss with the blind force of the unconscious is the delight that silenced all prohibition at that supreme moment. The involuntary commemoration a year later exemplifies the revival of the unforgettable moment when the object's death permitted its magical conquest in the rapture of orgasm.

A CLINICAL EXAMPLE

Only in rare cases can the diagnosis of illness of mourning be made quickly. This characterization usually comes at an advanced stage of the analysis when a substantial amount of material has collected around a death.

"Leaving here, I was shaken up. I sobbed. I don't know what I cried over. I feel as if I've just buried my mother. You reminded me of what I said at the beginning: I had to leave that very evening. And that evening she died. She had already been dying for days. I knew, I expected it. I was fleeing. I didn't want to know anything. No, that's not it. Not quite. There is something mysterious. She was dying and I—I'm upset saying it—I had desires, yes, carnal desires actually overcame me."

"What I said at the beginning": Thomas is a young journalist of Alsatian extraction who came to analysis wrenched by anxiety, fatigue, and depression. Gradually, he discovered some regularity in the appearance of his depressive states. They occurred on Thursdays, the day he lost his mother. The analysis showed that this beloved and loving mother contributed a great deal to the formation of an imago: a violent sea [*mer: mère:* mother] that uproots trees, a kind of hard man-woman who withholds money, etc.

The incorporation of the imago, obstructing phallic and genital introjections, took place thus: "When I was a little boy, mom used to wash me in a tub. One day, my penis got really big. She took hold of it abruptly, saying: 'See, if a woman is attacked, she can overpower a man by taking hold of his penis.'" The desire of the little boy and the mother met for an instant then, but for an instant only. The hardly reassuring idea suggested by the erection revealed at once the mother's desire and her superego's aggression toward the penis. This contradiction led to the boy's imaginal incorporation of both the desire and the mother's superego. Fixated on the imago, Thomas never stopped looking for this moment in order to overcome the prohibitive superego, hoping to carry off his mother's and his own desire in a common triumph.

Numerous dreams about rain, flooding, and bathing recall the mother "washing." "A small path. In the middle there was a toilet. I relieved myself. 'How old is the little boy?' asked someone. I wanted to get away. But in front of the door there were some washerwomen. I don't know whether they were taking care of me or not. They were working, laughing and laughing." Thomas said on another occasion: "Your area is completely flooded with water. I like your area of town. I like the antique shops, the little garden in your courtyard." (I like you; wash me as my mother used to like to do.) But as soon as their common desire emerges, the internal mother's superego surfaces to erase it. "A stingy, rude, masculine kind of woman who gives you trouble. Why pay an analyst rather than a plumber?" Yet, Thomas rebels against this imago. He has Chinese men [*chinois: penis—Trans.*] come to Paris in his dreams who spread tar on the ground and make faces with their heads between their legs. "I like people who are assertive, who have their way, saying 'I, me.'" (As for me, I really want my mother to recognize her desire for me.)

The Christmas vacation is drawing closer. Thomas remembers how much he used to like his mother's bed. She would get up and he would slide between the sheets. His rebellion is beginning to bear fruit. Thomas is drawing closer to his desire for his mother just as the internal mother also recognizes her own repression and sexual fear. "I would probably have trouble overseeing a child's sex education. I would be afraid" (like his mother). His depression intensifies. We are two sessions away from the vacation and Thomas says he feels ruined. All he can talk about is his ill health, his anguish, and his failures. But, at the end of the session, he tells me this dream: "A curious image, very clear and distinct, as though suddenly in a spotlight. How could I dream such a thing? I'll tell it because here you have to say everything. Otherwise, I would do my best to forget it. I see her ill on her bed and, despite her age, she appears to be a lustful woman, someone who still has carnal desires. Her eyes are full of . . . , she's out of breath . . . , her thighs are wide open. She is like an old prostitute. Then rails, rails, rails (alluding to the flow occurring at the moment of agony). And while I was watching her, I ruined, ruined, ruined. No! I urinated." Ever since his mother's death Thomas has been ruining himself for having "urinated" that day, for having unearthed their common desire, bringing victory to it by "ruining" his mother's superego. Thomas is astonished when I remind him of this moment. "Yes, I left in a hurry and suddenly. I was seized with intense desire in an incomprehensible way." And now the repressed content revives in the transference: the analyst-mother is leaving and "dies." Thomas says to this old woman in the throes of death: I wish you could be a prostitute for me (and caress my penis in the tub) *since you desire it too.* Shaken after this session, Thomas can finally mourn for his mother and thereby somewhat lighten the load of his imaginal fixation.

THE PAIN OF MOURNING AND THE FANTASY OF THE EXQUISITE CORPSE

The triumphant libidinal intrusion attendant upon objectal loss offers matter for renewed thought about the pain inherent in the work of mourning. Taking up Freud's question as to why the work of mourning is such a painful process, Melanie Klein suggests an answer. Every objectal loss entails a manic sadistic triumph over the object. Such a feeling of triumph seems to be badly tolerated in most cases and the ego allegedly does everything in its power to turn a blind eye to this proof of its ambivalence. The rejection or denial of triumph blocks the work of mourning either temporarily or permanently. The remorse and the guilt felt on account of aggressive fantasies would then explain the pain of mourning. This is so because, according to Melanie Klein, every time a love object is lost, the original situation of objectal loss is revived along with the ego's archaic attitude, namely the depressive position. The latter manifests itself above all in the fear that the child's own sadism might actually have caused the loss of the good and indispensable maternal object. The specific anguish, in this position, of having done the irreparable makes the child lose the prospect of ever being able to restore or reinstate the object permanently in order to guarantee the harmony and cohesion of the internal world.

However rigorous and plausible the Kleinian conception may be, it provides only a partial answer to the question at hand. Neither the dialectic of aggression directed at the "good" object (no doubt found in all patients), nor the repudiated fact of sadistic triumph manages to clarify the true source of the pain of mourning. A distinction is needed here between an internal object and the imago. The former is the fantasmic pole of the introjective process, whereas the latter is precisely all that resisted introjection and that the ego took possession of through other means, namely through the fantasy of incorporation. Melanie Klein seems to have focused, justifiably, on cases in which this type of fixating imago exists. Its dual nature needs to be kept in mind from now on. First of all, this imago was born of a failed introjective relation to an external object, and second, its effect is always to prohibit sexual desire. Clinical experience shows that the imago forms after a satisfaction was initially granted and then withdrawn. The presence of an imago in the subject attests to the fact that a desire became retroactively reprehensible and unspeakable before it could be introjected. The "ayenbite" of remorse no doubt refers to aggression. But psychoanalytic elaboration showed very early on that remorse and rumination arise at the libidinal spring of prohibited sexual desire. No wonder that, despite the suffering it causes, self-torture does not relent, since in it desire concerning the object is both revived and satisfied.

We now see that, upon the death of the object, for an instant hallucinatory regression gratified desire. In cases of fixation the intense pain tied up with the work of mourning concerns this precise moment. Though denying it, the pain testifies to this moment as well as to the objectal fantasy which furnished its content. With every libidinal outburst, with every unconscious revival of the exquisite moment, pleasure takes on the appearance of pain because of repression. The subject of so many sessions, this pain is highly instructive. A genuinely "exquisite" pain, it constitutes a valuable tool for analysis when it is understood in the medical sense of the term, not only because it derives from a desire but also because it points to the place where one needs to operate in order to unearth repression.

Leading us to the tomb where desire lies buried (the pain being a kind of "here lies," an inscription on which the name of the deceased long remains undecipherable), the pain of self-torture is an invitation extended to the analyst to proceed with the exhumation as well as an appropriate directive for this stage of the analysis: "Accuse me."

These kinds of analyses present many special features, but I will mention only one here because it appears constantly and also because it constituted my study's point of departure. The analysis of the ill from mourning often yields a nightmarish dream that patients say brings some relief although it is troubling. The following example captures this type of sometimes recurrent dream. "*I am being accused.* I committed a terrible crime. I ate someone and then buried them. I'm on the site of the crime with someone who is charged with disinterring and examining the remains. This person is accusing me. I don't know who it is I ate and buried. I only know that I myself committed the crime. For this reason I have to spend the rest of my life in prison."

"I ate someone and *then* buried them," a macabre yet palliative dream . . . and a twofold contradiction. Its meaning comes to light when the transference is analyzed. In these dreams the analyst is cast in the role of the accuser. At a time when patients cannot name their desire—so as to recognize it as being legitimately their own—and cannot relive it in the transferential relation, a single avenue remains open: inviting the analyst to don the judge's robes. Let us not be misled by such a request. It is simply a maneuver. Wishing to see the crime proven and the guilty indicted, patients demand that the "crime of repression" ("the burial of the corpse") that followed the satisfaction ("I ate someone") be placed on trial. This particular "crime" explains the feeling of oppression: having to spend one's entire life in prison, locked up in neurotic suffering as a result of repression.

The analyst-judge also acts as a morphologist: they have to reconstruct the event from a few scattered body fragments. Whether they play morphologist or judge, analysts—consulted because of the pain of mourning—are called upon to unmask the "crime" of repression and to identify the victim: the orgasmic moment experienced upon the object's death. That is why, in the dark hours when patients feel they are at an impasse, a dream of this type, though apparently macabre, can bring relief and the hope of finding a way out. Patients ask their analysts: Help me find that moment so that I can come out of the impasse of my interminable mourning.

Thérèse has feelings of sensuality each time she feels she is acting as a "nurse." When asked to visit a bedridden family member or friend, she feels embarrassed ahead of time: "It's going to happen again and I don't know why." And yet she is mysteriously attracted into friendships with people she rightly or wrongly suspects of being ill. Thérèse has been blocked in her work of mourning for over ten years. The suffering and the embarrassment that had led her into analysis turned out to be of the same nature as the "pain of mourning." Analysis has shown a massive repression of the father's death through a scene whose memory she has not stopped wanting to recapture at her ill friends' bedside.

In the course of her analysis Thérèse brought a dream triptych that I also found in other patients of mourning: marriage with an inaccessible man, an indictment for having eaten a corpse, a dentist predicting the exposure of her receding gumline, followed by the total loss of her teeth ("exposure" is an allusion to the father's corpse being dressed for the funeral). The much desired though deeply repressed union in love with her father was consummated hallucinatorily during the last rites. Thérèse's added repression of the moment of magical satisfaction directed her development toward an illness of mourning that endangered both her romantic relationships and her professional pursuits.

THE VICISSITUDES OF TRANSITION AND THE ILLNESS OF MOURNING

In addition to the constantly recurring dream of the "exquisite corpse," we also need to note the existence of another type of dream in illnesses of mourning: dreams about "teeth," about their growth or loss, their mending or their exposure due to a receding gumline (as in Thérèse's case), etc. While dreams about "eating and burying a corpse" characterize the illness of mourning, dreams about "teeth" reach beyond this frame; they are found in nearly all analyses.

What does the language of "teeth" tell? Patients evoke this symbol each time a conflict born of the passage from one stage of introjection to the next is discussed. Teething marks the first great transition, hence its symbolic value in the evocation of transitions in general. Whether it is the oedipal passage, adolescent growth, the attainment of adulthood or progress toward menopause, "teeth" always lend themselves to symbolizing the vicissitudes of libidinal reorganization. "You expect your first period like your teeth," says a patient. For another patient the recurrent dream in which she loses her teeth expresses the loss (in the strong sense of the term) of the oedipal mother when she passes into adolescence.

When dreams about "teeth" appear, they can offer a helpful clue if we know how to take advantage of them for the organization of dispersed material.

A sudden and severe form of adolescent anorexia is set off by a teacher's comment: "You're too big." The boy stops chewing for several months. His passive silence also hides his now adult voice. A dream about "teeth" fortunately throws light on the conflict of adolescent transition and bears fruit in the psychoanalytic process. The dream is a nightmare about "mice who bite" and persecute him. (The boy hears the "biting" comment made by the teacher, the jealous father's substitute image, as follows: "Your penis grew too large when you first ejaculated.") He runs away bewildered from these "beasts with powerful and sharp teeth," is paralyzed and wakes up in anguish.

For those who might ask whether the illness of mourning is an autonomous formation or merely an episode in a prior neurotic problem, the recurrent dreams about teeth, indicating conflicts of transition, authorize an answer. The illness of mourning is a special case of a wider and more inclusive framework of disturbances that generally characterize periods of transition.

Libidinal irruptions occur precisely in moments of transition when the new drive (experienced as pleasant) "cuts through" and forces the ego to reorganize itself and its objectal relations. There really is an intrinsic problem, reminiscent of fixation, in transitional periods. Although mindful of the sweetness of its new drive, the ego is not always ready to accommodate what "the gods give it." The ego remains ambivalent for a more or less lengthy period as regards this newcomer. In cases where the object helps the child ever so slightly to introject the drive, giving it back to the child in objectalized forms, the transition need not degenerate into an insurmountable conflict. Introjection should proceed quite smoothly. If, on the other hand, the object is absent, lacking, or has performed a seduction, the introjection of new drives will be blocked and imaginal fixation will inevitably follow. This is why, as libidinal forces appear, new transitions create a favorable breeding ground for inhibitive developmental disturbances. How is the object who inhibits the ego's growth experienced? Clearly, as someone who is cut off from his or her own desire (as in the case of Thomas's mother). If in addition, the object fleetingly welcomes the child's (that is, its own) desire for an instant *and then rejects it,* the object effectively sets the stage for infantile conflict due to its own conflict. The fixation feeds on the child's unwavering hope that one day the object would once again be *what it was* in the privileged moment. For the child, after all, is not the object comparable to itself, it too being subject to a superego's prohibition, but also, just like the child, an exclusive lover in its heart of hearts?

There is a difference, however, between objectal loss linked to fixation—the loss of a moment of satisfaction and its being buried like a corpse—and the illness of mourning. Loss here consists in the actual death of the object.[5] Paradoxically, the object who is dead because of real death revives momentarily the "exquisite corpse" that together the dead and the survivors had both long before consigned to the grim tomb of repression.

5. In his study "If I Were Dead" (in *De l'art à la mort,* Paris: Gallimard, 1977), Michel de M'Uzan describes the *work of passing away* at the point of death. The dying person experiences an increase in relational appetite in the form of renewed creative impetus. The analysis of people ill from mourning shows the many revivals of these moments in which the respective introjections of both parties converge and the impulse of the survivor coincides with the "last muster" ("let us muster up life") of the dying person; these impulses manifest themselves in an anguished state of confused identity, if not in pain. [This footnote was inserted by Torok in the French edition of *The Shell and the Kernel* in 1978, ten years after she originally published her essay.—Ed.]

FIVE

Mourning *or* Melancholia: Introjection *versus* Incorporation

N. Abraham and M. Torok, 1972

METAPSYCHOLOGICAL REALITY AND FANTASY

Incorporation denotes a fantasy, introjection a process. Here is a useful clarification, sometimes found in Kleinian texts and one that holds no surprises for us. However, we are astonished that Melanie Klein sees fantasy—a product of the ego—as predating the process, which is the product of the entire psyche. On this fundamental point we cannot agree with Kleinian "pan-fantasism." We seek to limit the precise meaning of the concept of fantasy by contrasting it with the entity masked by fantasy. Granting our metapsychological definition of "reality" as everything, whether exogenous or endogenous, that affects the psyche by inflicting a topographical shift on it, "fantasy" can be defined as all those representations, beliefs, or bodily states that gravitate toward the opposite effect, that is, the preservation of the status quo. This definition does not address the contents or the formal characteristics of fantasy, only its function, a preventive and conservative function despite the highly innovative genius of fantasy, its vast field of action, and even despite its definite complacency with respect to desire. In our conception fantasy is essentially narcissistic; it tends to transform the world rather than inflict injury on the subject. That fantasies are often unconscious does not mean they pertain to something outside the subject but rather that they refer to a *secretly perpetuated* topography. Understanding a fantasy entails the identification of the specific topographical change the given fantasy is called upon to resist. Consequently, the primal fantasy would itself repre-

Previously published as "Deuil *ou* mélancolie, introjecter-incorporer," *Nouvelle revue de psychanalyse* 6 (1972): 111–13; and in *L'Écorce et le noyau* (Paris: Flammarion, 1987), pp. 259–75; and as "Introjection-Incorporation: Mourning *or* Melancholia," in Serge Lebovici and Daniel Widlöcher (eds.), *Psychoanalysis in France* (New York: International Universities Press, 1980), pp. 3–16.

sent appropriate measures to keep the original topography intact in the face of danger. In the final analysis, is not metapsychological theory intended to explain how and why fantasy and its corollaries arise? Placing fantasy at the root of the process would seem to suggest a perilous reversal of the entire psychoanalytic method. If on the contrary, by analyzing fantasy, we seek to detect the transformation of the underlying process that is being opposed, we move from the description of phenomena to their transphenomenal basis. Using this characteristic mode of psychoanalytic inquiry, we will find ourselves at just the vantage point where we might be able to read the metapsychological origin of every fantasy as far back as the "origin" of the original fantasy itself.

INCORPORATION: THE FANTASY OF NONINTROJECTION

When it is not truncated or deformed, fantasy can be doubly telling as regards both the subject and the danger to be parried. This is so because fantasy is inseparable from the intrapsychic state of affairs it is supposed to protect as well as from the metapsychological reality that demands a change. Among the various fantasies traceable in this way to their function, some are privileged because their contents illustrate the prevailing conditions of the psychic agencies. Well-known examples of these are the arch-fantasies of the primal scene, castration, and seduction.[1] There is also—but this is much less well known—another type of equally privileged fantasy whose contents illustrate the process whereby the topography is on the verge of being transformed. Such is the fantasy of *incorporation*. Introducing all or part of a love object or a thing into one's own body, possessing, expelling or alternately acquiring, keeping, losing it—here are varieties of fantasy indicating, in the typical forms of possession or feigned dispossession, a basic intrapsychic situation: the situation created by the reality of a loss sustained by the psyche. If accepted and worked through, the loss would require major readjustment. But the fantasy of incorporation merely simulates profound psychic transformation through magic; it does so by implementing literally something that has only figurative meaning. So in order not to have to "swallow" a loss, we fantasize swallowing (or having swallowed) that which has been lost, as if it were some kind of thing. Two interrelated procedures constitute the magic of incorporation: *demetaphorization* (taking literally what is meant figuratively) and *objecti-*

1. J. Laplanche and J. B. Pontalis, *The Language of Psychoanalysis* (New York: W. W. Norton, 1973), p. 331.

vation (pretending that the suffering is not an injury to the subject but instead a loss sustained by the love object). The magical "cure" by incorporation exempts the subject from the painful process of reorganization. When, in the form of imaginary or real nourishment, we ingest the love-object we miss, this means that *we refuse to mourn* and that we shun the consequences of mourning even though our psyche is fully bereaved. Incorporation is the refusal to reclaim as our own the part of ourselves that we placed in what we lost; incorporation is the refusal to acknowledge the full import of the loss, a loss that, if recognized as such, would effectively transform us. In fine, incorporation is the refusal to introject loss. The fantasy of incorporation reveals a gap within the psyche; it points to something that is missing just where introjection should have occurred.

INTROJECTION UNDERSTOOD AS THE COMMUNION OF "EMPTY MOUTHS"

Introjecting (= casting inside) is surely the same thing as incorporating, is it not? Certainly the image is identical, but for reasons that will soon be apparent, it is important to distinguish between them, as we would distinguish between metaphoric and photographic images, between the acquisition of a language as opposed to buying a dictionary, between self-possession gained through psychoanalysis and the fantasy of "incorporating" a "penis."

Sandor Ferenczi, the inventor of both the term and the concept, defined "introjection" as the process of broadening the ego. He ascribed the primary role in this process to transferential love. Yet, however exemplary the psychoanalytic situation might be as its precondition, introjection undoubtedly appears under comparable circumstances soon after birth. Without going into detail, suffice it to say that the initial stages of introjection emerge in infancy when the mouth's emptiness is experienced alongside the mother's simultaneous presence. The emptiness is first experienced in the form of cries and sobs, delayed fullness, then as calling, ways of requesting presence, as language. Further experiences include filling the oral void by producing sound and by exploring the empty cavity with the tongue in response to sounds perceived from the outside. Finally, the early satisfactions of the mouth, as yet filled with the maternal object, are partially and gradually replaced by the novel satisfactions of a mouth now empty of that object but filled with words pertaining to the subject. The transition from a mouth filled with the breast to a mouth filled with words occurs by virtue of the intervening experiences of the empty mouth.

Learning to fill the emptiness of the mouth with words is the initial model for introjection. However, without the constant assistance of a mother endowed with language, introjection could not take place. Not unlike the permanence of Descartes's God, the mother's constancy is the guarantor of the meaning of words. Once this guarantee has been acquired, and only then, can words replace the mother's presence and also give rise to fresh introjections. The absence of objects and the empty mouth are transformed into words; at last, even the experiences related to words are converted into other words. So the wants of the original oral vacancy are remedied by being turned into verbal relationships with the speaking community at large. Introjecting a desire, a pain, a situation means channeling them through language into a communion of empty mouths. This is how the literal ingestion of foods becomes introjection when viewed figuratively. The passage from food to language in the mouth presupposes the successful replacement of the object's presence with the self's cognizance of its absence. Since language acts and makes up for absence by representing, by *giving figurative shape* to presence, it can only be *comprehended* or *shared* in a "community of empty mouths."

INCORPORATION: ONE MOUTH-WORK IN PLACE OF ANOTHER

If all fantasies indicate the refusal to introject and the denial of a gap, we have to wonder why some of them take the privileged form of introducing an object into the body? In other words, why are some fantasies directed at the very metaphor of introjection? Once we put it this way, the question implies part of the answer. Incorporation implements the metaphor of introjection literally when the usually spontaneous process of introjection becomes self-aware, that is, when it undergoes reflexive treatment, as it were. This form of reflexive treatment occurs only if the barely initiated or expected work of introjection encounters a prohibitive obstacle. The obstacle is found in the mouth, in the seat of the phenomena steering introjection. Because our mouth is unable to say certain words and unable to formulate certain sentences, we fantasize, for reasons yet to be determined, that we are actually taking into our mouth the unnamable, the object itself. As the empty mouth calls out in vain to be filled with introjective speech, it reverts to being the food-craving mouth it was prior to the acquisition of speech. Failing to feed itself on words to be exchanged with others, the mouth absorbs in fantasy all or part of a person—the genuine depository of what is now nameless. The crucial move away from introjection (clearly rendered impossible) to incorporation is made when *words* fail to fill the subject's void and hence an imaginary thing is inserted into the mouth in their place. The desperate ploy of filling the mouth with illusory nourishment has the equally illusory effect of eradicating the idea of a void to be filled with words. We may conclude that, in the face of both the urgency and the impossibility of performing one type of mouth-work—speaking to someone about what we have lost—another type of mouth-work is utilized, one that is imaginary and equipped to deny the very existence of the entire problem. Born of the verdict of impracticable introjection, the fantasy of incorporation appears at once as its regressive and reflexive substitute. This means of course that every incorporation has introjection as its nostalgic vocation.

FALSE INCORPORATIONS

Why are the words of introjection suddenly missing? Why the emergency call for them? Once more the questions suggest the answers. *The abrupt loss of a narcissistically indispensable object of love has occurred, yet the loss is of a type that prohibits its being communicated. If this were not so, incorporation would have no reason for being.* Cases of reluctant mourning are well known. Yet they do not inevitably lead to incorporation. We are reminded here of the unforgettable sight of a man, seated alone at a table in a restaurant, ordering two different meals simultaneously; he ate them both as if he were being accompanied by someone else. This man, who was clearly hallucinating the presence of a departed loved one, did not, however, have to resort to incorporation. We can surmise that the shared meal allowed him to keep the dear departed outside his bodily limits and that, even as he was filling his mouth's vacancy, he did not actually have to "absorb" the deceased. "No," he seemed to be saying, "the loved one is not dead, she is still here as before, with her wonted tastes and favorite dishes." The waiter seemed to be aware of the situation and was helping the man choose the *other* dish; perhaps he knew the habits of the deceased. . . . Nothing of the sort would ever happen in cases of incorporation. Once an incorporation has occurred, no one at all should be apprized of it. The very fact of *having had a loss* would be denied in incorporation. The imaginary meal, eaten in the company of the deceased, may be seen as a protection against the danger of incorporation. Such a meal is reminiscent of the wake, which must have a similar purpose, namely the communion of the survivors through the partaking of food. The communion here means: instead of the deceased we are absorbing our mutual presence in the form of digestible food. We will bury the deceased in the ground rather than in ourselves. Necrophagia, always, a collective practice, is also distinct from incorporation. Even though it might well be born of fantasy, necrophagia constitutes a form of language because it is a group activity. By acting out the fantasy of incorporation, the actual eating of the corpse symbolizes both the impossibility of introjecting the loss and the fact that the loss has already occurred. Eating the corpse results in the exorcism of the survivors' potential tendency for psychic incorporation after a death. Necrophagia is therefore not at all a variety of incorporation but a preventive measure of *anti-incorporation.*

THE INTRAPSYCHIC TOMB

Even when denied introjection, not every narcissistic loss is fated to incorporation. *Incorporation results from those losses that for some reason cannot be acknowledged as such.* In these special cases the impossibility of introjection is so profound that even our refusal to mourn is prohibited from being given a language, that we are debarred from providing any indication whatsoever that we are inconsolable. Without the escape-route of somehow conveying our refusal to mourn, we are reduced to a radical denial of the loss, to pretending that we had absolutely nothing to lose. There can be no thought of speaking to someone else about our grief under these circumstances. The words that cannot be uttered, the scenes that cannot be recalled, the tears that cannot be shed—everything will be swallowed along with the trauma that led to the loss. Swallowed and preserved. Inexpressible mourning erects a secret tomb inside the subject. Reconstituted from the memories of words, scenes, and affects, the objectal correlative of the loss is buried alive in the crypt as a full-fledged person, complete with its own topography. The crypt also includes the actual or supposed traumas that made introjection impracticable. A whole world of unconscious fantasy is created, one that leads its own separate and concealed existence. Sometimes in the dead of the night, when libidinal fulfillments have their way, the ghost of the crypt comes back to haunt the cemetery guard, giving him strange and incomprehensible signals, making him perform bizarre acts, or subjecting him to unexpected sensations.

One of us has analyzed a boy who "carried" inside him his sister, two years older than he. This sister, who died when the boy was eight, had "seduced" him. Several years of analytic relationship and a providential slip of the tongue—in which the boy gave as his own the age his sister would have been, had she lived—led to the reconstruction of the boy's internal situation and also revealed the motivation behind his kleptomania.

"Yes," he said, explaining his thefts, "at fourteen she would have needed a bra." This boy's crypt sheltered the girl "alive" as he unconsciously followed her maturation. This example shows why the introjection of the loss was impossible and why incorporation of the object became for the boy the only viable means of narcissistic reparation. His prohibited and shameful sexual games did not admit of any form of verbal communication. Only the incorporation of, and subsequent identification with, the girl allowed the boy to safeguard his topography marked by the seduction. The carrier of a shared secret, he became, after his sister's death, the carrier of a crypt. To underscore the continuity of these two psychic states, we have chosen the term *cryptophoria*. To have a fantasy of incorporation is to have no other choice but to perpetuate a clandestine pleasure by transforming it, after it has been lost, into an *intrapsychic secret*.

INCORPORATION AS ANTIMETAPHOR

The foregoing represents our hypothesis. Its clinical import is that every time an incorporation is uncovered, it can be attributed to the undisclosable grief that befalls an ego already partitioned on account of a previous objectal experience tainted with shame. The crypt perpetuates the dividing walls by its very nature. No crypt arises without a shared secret's having already split the subject's topography. In the realm of shame and secrecy, however, we need to determine *who* it is that ought to blush, *who* is to hide. Is it the subject for having been guilty of crimes, of shameful or unseemly acts? That supposition will not help lay the foundation for a single crypt. Crypts are constructed only when the shameful secret is the love object's doing and when that object also functions for the subject as an ego ideal. It is therefore the *object's* secret that needs to be kept, *his* shame covered up. Yet the love object's mourning does not proceed in the usual way with the help of words used figuratively. This is so because if the metaphors that were used to shame the object somehow reemerged in the course of mourning, the ensuing loss of the ego ideal, their guarantor, would nullify them in their role as metaphors. The cryptophoric subject's solution, then, is to annul the humiliation by secretly or openly adopting the literal meaning of the words causing the humiliation. "Introjection" regresses here to the level of "inserting in the mouth, swallowing, eating." As for the debased love object, he will be "fecalized," that is, actually rendered excremental. The refusal to introject the loss of the ideal will be expressed in the most extreme cases by defying the humiliation itself through various manifestations of the fantasy of eating excrement: unkempt outward appearance, filth, coprolalia, and the like. The above makes clear that *the crucial aspect of these fantasies of incorporation is not their reference to a cannibalistic stage of development, but rather their annulment of figurative language.* To save their ideal object, cryptophores undermine anyone who would shame their object. They neutralize, as it were, the material instruments of humiliation, the metaphors of dejection and excrement, by pretending that these disgraceful metaphors are edible, even appetizing. If we are determined to see a form of language in the processes governing this type of fantasy, we will need a new figure of speech in our traditional inventory, namely the figure of the active destruction of representation. We propose to call this figure *antimetaphor.* Let us make clear that it is not simply a matter of reverting to the literal meaning of words, but of using them in such a way—whether in speech or deed—that their very capacity for figurative representation is destroyed. Coprophagy is the prime example of such an act and an instance of this type of language use can be found in obscenities encouraging incest. But the most antimetaphorical of all is incorporation itself. *Incorporation entails the fantasmic destruction of the act by means of which metaphors become possible: the act of putting the original oral void into words, in fine, the act of introjection.*

FANTASY VERSUS INTRAPSYCHIC REALITY

Demetaphorization is not primary; its cause is the intrapsychic immurement of an experience endangering the topography. The role of confinement, imprisonment, and (in extreme cases) entombment is to objectify the fantasy of incorporation. Contriving ways to exclude even while holding fast from within, the fantasy of incorporation is deluded as regards its effectiveness. Clearly, incorporation is nothing more than a reassuring fantasy for the ego. The psychic reality is radically different. The unspeakable words and sentences, linked as they are to memories of great libidinal and narcissistic value, cannot accept their exclusion. From their hideaway in the imaginary crypt—into which fantasy had thrust them to hibernate lifeless, anesthetized, and designified—the unspeakable words never cease their subversive action.

We suspect that, in a recently completed essay, we have uncovered the existence of such an untellable word in the Wolf Man's psyche: the Russian verb *teret,* meaning "to rub." In our view, the traumatic events the Wolf Man experienced crystallized around this word when he was less than four years old; the events were related to the incestuous fondling by which the Wolf Man's father had received gratification from his daughter, the boy's elder sister by two years. We have described how, through its varied disguises, this word condensed the Wolf Man's entire libidinal life as well as his sublimating activities.[2] We may add at present that this same word also played a role some sixteen years later in the schizophrenic suicide of the sister in question. The young woman died from the consequences of a delirious act that we consider suicidal only because of its fatal effects: she drank a bottle of liquid mercury. Now, the Russian word for mercury is *rtut*, which is the phonetic inversion of a somewhat guttural rendition of *teret* (as in the glottal pronunciation *t.r.t*). It is as if, with this delirious and tragic act, the daughter had wanted to rehabilitate her ideal object's spurned desire. She did so by eating, by proclaiming that it was "fine to eat" the word that had become excremental to others and was now objectified in a toxic substance (mercury). Let us note in passing, because it makes our position clear, that though tempting for some, it would be a grave misjudgment to interpret the young woman's ingestion of mercury as a disguised wish to perform fellatio. It was the word, the demetaphorized and objectified word that had to be swallowed in a display of coprophagic bravado.

The examples just cited illustrate another crucial aspect of the fantasy of incorporation (whose ineffectual counter-cathecting role was indicated earlier). Incorporation might at first sight resemble a hysterical type of repression, complete with the return of the repressed and having even a sexual element. Yet appearances here are false. Certainly, in the example drawn from the Wolf Man's material there are hallucinatory wish-fulfillments on the part of both the brother and the sister. Nonetheless, there is also a major qualification. The fulfillments are not representative of the subjects experiencing them but of their incorporated object of love, here their father. Both the brother and sister identify with their father by means of the spurned word denoting him. The boy achieves orgasm, in his father's place, as it were, by disguising the word in question (*teret:* to rub) in the visual image of a woman scrubbing the floor. Perhaps for oedipal reasons, the girl does not do quite as well. Nevertheless, she too acts as if she were her father; she gives the father an erection just as the boy does through his own fantasy of the charwoman. The basic difference here between incorporation and hysterical repression is that the father,

---

2. "Le mot magique de l'Homme aux loups: Incorporation, hystérie interne, cryptonymie," *Revue française de psychanalyse,* no. 1 (1971); since then chapters 1 and 2 of *The Wolf Man's Magic Word: A Cryptonymy* (Minneapolis: University of Minnesota Press, 1986).

rather than the children themselves, is the genuine subject of the children's acts. Through their acts, the father is the one claiming the right to affirm his spurned desire. This means that because of their identification, both children (the boy through fetishism, the girl with her delirious action) are trying at all costs to reinstate their father as their ego ideal. The children's acts (sexual in the one case and only apparently so in the other) have the narcissistic mission of bolstering the ego ideal. In short, the symptoms of incorporation are a medium through which the spurned ego ideal seeks acceptance. We can conclude therefore that the primary aim of the fantasy life born of incorporation is to repair—in the realm of the imaginary, of course—the injury that really occurred and really affected the ideal object. The fantasy of incorporation reveals a utopian wish that the memory of the affliction had never existed or, on a deeper level, that the affliction had had nothing to inflict.

INCLUSION TOPOGRAPHY

The effects of incorporation are extremely difficult to diagnose. Many an analysis of cryptophores is conducted as though the patients were hysterical or hysterophobic. A curious and troubling process sometimes occurs when patients behave as if they were truly hysterophobic (it is amazing that they can do this). Such patients end their therapy without ever touching on their basic problem. A lot remains to be said about these *as if analyses*[3] and their effects on incorporation. But these analytic misapprehensions are not surprising, since incorporation is indeed a cryptic phenomenon, as regards both its genesis and its function. Incorporation often hides behind "normalcy," takes flight in "personality traits" or "perversions," and appears openly only in delirium, in the mental state Freud called narcissistic neurosis, that is, manic-depressive psychosis. Yet the inherently cryptic nature of incorporation is perhaps not sufficient to explain the lack of recognition from which it has suffered. Since Freud's essay on "Mourning and Melancholia" nothing has emerged that would increase our understanding of the meaning of the fantasy life bound up with incorporation and so-called manic-depressive psychosis. Sections of Freud's correspondence with Karl Abraham hint at the nature of the problem. In the exchange K. Abraham suggested that melancholia might be linked to issues of instinct (such as guilt associated with cannibalistic and anal-sadistic desires blocking the process of an archaic mourning). To

---

3. [The phrase "as if analyses" appears in English in the original.—Ed.]

this Freud responded that the instinctual factors might well be important but are too general, as would be an explanation based on the Oedipus complex or castration anxiety. He called to his friend's attention the topographic, dynamic, and economic considerations that might help define the problem.[4] Let us note that for our part, we understand the instinctual factors to be composed primarily of fantasies. It is certainly regrettable that K. Abraham's insights were not pursued to their potentially fruitful conclusion. Actually, the opposite occurred. At the same time, K. Abraham's own disinclination to use a metapsychological perspective whenever his conceptions appeared adequate without it was responsible for the subsequent development of Kleinian theory, a rigorous, generous, and in some respects even grandiose theory, but one that proved unable to transcend a descriptive system of drives dependent on the universal centrality of fantasy.

In Freud's conception, melancholia hovers between love and hate amid archaic unconscious representations that are unable to reach consciousness. The issue in this struggle seems to be whether or not one should keep investing the love object despite disappointments, ill treatment, and ultimately, despite the loss of the love object. This type of ambivalent unconscious situation as regards the object might well derive from predispositions acquired during infancy, but does not in our view define melancholia. After a careful rereading of Freud's beautiful and difficult essay, we are struck by the recurrent image of an open wound that is said to attract the whole of the counter-cathecting libido. This is precisely, we think, the wound the melancholic attempts to hide, wall in, and encrypt. Furthermore, we posit that this activity does not occur in the unconscious, but in the system where the wound itself is located, namely in the preconscious-conscious system. For the melancholic, it is in this psychic system that an intratopographic process must take place. The process recreates in a single psychic area, system, or agency, the correlate of the entire topography, isolating the wound and separating it (with a multitude of counter-investments) from the rest of the psyche and especially from the memory of what had been torn from it. Such a creation is only justified when reality must be denied along with the narcissistic and libidinal import of the loss. We propose to call this supplemental topography *inclusion* and one of us has earlier called its effect *preservative repression*. The derivatives of the fantasy of incorporation are related to the secret life of inclusion topography.[5]

---

4. *A Psychoanalytic Dialogue: The Letters of Sigmund Freud and Karl Abraham.*

5. [Two sentences from the original French text were omitted here at Maria Torok's request.—Ed.]

MELANCHOLIA: FROM "MOURNING" TO SUICIDE

In the light of our hypothesis of incorporation, is it possible to interpret the struggle of "love and hate" in a subject who, according to Freud, *has in fact been* disappointed in and mistreated by the love object? We find it crucial to affirm the prior existence of a love totally free of ambivalence, to insist on the undisclosable character of this love, and finally to show that a real and therefore traumatic cause had put an end to it. The system of counter-investments—using the themes of hate, disappointment, and mistreatment supposedly endured on account of the object—results from some traumatic affliction and from the utter impossibility of mourning. Hence the fantasized aggression is not in fact primary; it merely extends the genuine aggression the object actually suffered *earlier* in the form of death, disgrace, or removal—this being the involuntary cause of the separation. Inclusion does not occur unless the subject is convinced of the object's total innocence. In the opposite case, when a narcissistic disappointment did originate with the object, schizophrenia would set in, implying the destruction of both the object and the subject. It is not so with melancholics. Their undisclosable idyll was pure and devoid of aggression. It did not end because of infidelity but owing to hostile external forces. This is why melancholics cherish the memory as their most precious possession, even though it must be concealed by a crypt built with the bricks of hate and aggression. It should be remarked that as long as the crypt holds, there is no melancholia. It erupts when the walls are shaken, often as a result of the loss of some secondary love-object who had buttressed them. Faced with the danger of seeing the crypt crumble, the whole of the ego becomes one with the crypt, showing the concealed object of love in its own guise. Threatened with the imminent loss of its internal support—the kernal of its being—the ego will fuse with the included object, imagining that the object is bereft of its partner. Consequently, the ego begins the public display of an interminable process of mourning. The subject heralds the love-object's sadness, his gaping wound, his universal guilt—without ever revealing, of course, the unspeakable secret, well worth the entire universe. The only means left by which the subject can covertly revive the secret paradise taken from him is to stage the grief attributed to the object who lost him. Freud is surprised that melancholics show no shame at all at the horrible things for which they blame themselves. Now we can understand it: the more suffering and degradation the object undergoes (meaning: the more he pines for the subject he lost), the prouder the subject can be: "he endures all this because of me." Being a melancholic, I stage and let everyone else see the full extent of my love object's grief over having lost me.

Melancholics seem to inflict pain on themselves, but in fact they lend their own flesh to their phantom object of love.[6] Freud saw in this self-inflicted pain an aggressiveness against the love-object which has been shifted onto the melancholics themselves. Yet is it worthwhile to wonder whether melancholics really love their phantom object? It matters very little since the phantom object is simply "crazy" about the melancholic: the phantom is ready to do anything for him. Melancholics embody their phantom object in everything that the phantom, frantic with grief, endured "for them." If there is any aggression at all, it is shared between the love object and the melancholic subject in being directed at the external world at large in the form of withdrawal and retreat from libidinal investments.

Needless to say, the phantom object haunts the process of counter-transference as well and this fact represents a real danger in psychoanalytic therapy. Analysts may unwittingly target the phantom object, not realizing that for the melancholic the phantom (the incorporated object) is the only partner. Assigning aggression to the love object, the analyst actually speaks out *against* the melancholic's most precious and most carefully concealed treasure. And yet, we analysts are meant to recognize the love object behind all the disguises of hate and aggression. The realization that the one is pleased by the other's grief over him; the recognition not of the hate but of the love felt by the object for the subject; the acceptance ultimately of the narcissistic bliss at having received the object's love despite dangerous transgressions—this is what melancholics expect from psychoanalysis. When they obtain this acknowledgment, the inclusion can gradually give way to genuine mourning and the fantasies of incorporation can be transferred into introjections. But if this acknowledgment fails to occur, the original gaping wound will revive and will transform the analyst's comments on aggression into fresh narcissistic injuries. The best response to these injuries might well be a manic reaction. Once the object is under attack, mania parades the omnipotence of love: "See how force-fully he defends me, how marvelously he pleads our cause; he never tires of 'socking it to them': he doesn't mince his words, nothing frightens him, he has no rest . . . ; isn't his passion admirable?" Triumph, scorn, fury, defiance in the face of shame, these are some of the titles in the manic repertory. Admittedly, not much analytic progress is made under these circumstances, but at least the patient's life is safe. Unfortunately, melancholic "mourning" is often the subject's last chance at narcissistic restoration. This becomes clearer if we consider that the bereaved object is

6. ["Phantom object of love" is used here in the medical sense of "phantom limb syndrome," a condition in which amputees continue to experience pain in the missing limb. Abraham went on to use the term "phantom" in a very different sense in "Notes on the Phantom."—Ed.]

envisioned as having *not yet entirely lost* the partner for whom he is, as it were, mourning in anticipation. So, when the subject learns from the analyst, in a repetition of the initial trauma, that his secret lover *must* be attacked, he has no choice but to push his fantasy of mourning to its ultimate conclusion: "If my beloved is to lose me forever, he will not survive this loss." This certainty restores peace of mind to the subject, a picture of what recovery might look like. The cure will be complete the day when the "object" makes the supreme sacrifice. . . .

SIX

"The Lost Object—Me": Notes on Endocryptic Identification

N. Abraham and M. Torok, 1975

The soul that in life did not its divine right
Acquire, has not, even in Hades, repose.
Hölderlin, To the Fates

THE HAUNTED ANALYST . . .

So speaks the poet. Yes. The "divine right," the work born of the rediscovery of oneself, comes into being only if one asserts one's value, only if one succeeds in being acknowledged. Recognized, acknowledged by oneself to oneself before the whole universe. Sometimes the "whole universe" is represented by the psychoanalyst. Before the analyst the "divine right" is created or gradually unveiled. Would that analysts could understand it, accept it, rejoice in it as we rejoice in poetry! But how many are the roads leading there and how many the traps along the way. Do analysts have an ear for *all* "poems" and for *all* "poets"? Surely not. But those whose message they failed to hear, those whose deficient, mutilated text they have listened to time after time—the riddles with no key—those who left their analysts without yielding up the distinctive *oeuvre* of their lives, these people return forever as the ghosts of their unfulfilled destiny and as the haunting phantoms of the analyst's deficiency.

Who among us is not battling with specters that implore Heaven and demand of us their due, while we are beholden to them for our own

Previously published as "L' 'objet perdu—moi': Notations sur l'identification endocryptique," *Revue française de psychanalyse* 39, no. 3 (1975): 411–26; and in *L'Écorce et le noyau* (Paris: Flammarion, 1987), pp. 295–317; as "Poetics of Psychoanalysis: The 'Lost Object—Me,'" trans. N. Rand, *Sub-Stance* 43 (1984): 3–18; and as "The 'Lost Object—Me': Notes on Endocryptic Identification," trans. N. Rand, *Psychoanalytic Inquiry* 4, no. 2 (1984): 221–42.

salvation? Just think of Freud and his Wolf Man. From 1910 well into Freud's extreme old age, the case of this enigmatic Russian—bewitched by some secret—never stopped haunting him, drawing from him theory upon theory because he could not discover the key to the poem. This too was our situation before the enigma of the great poetics, not of a single individual but of an entire and extended family, rightly or wrongly called by the collective name "manic-depressive psychosis." It has been a long while since the two of us joined forces to establish its semantics and to formulate its prosody. Let us bring to you, after a very long and groping search, inspired by our many ghosts, a few examples and outlines drawn from our clinical practice. It would be presumptuous indeed to allege that we have reached our goal. Yet it would be false modesty to deny our suspicion that we are finally entering an open road.

We begin by giving a brief summary of our most recent efforts and leave for later the delineation of some errant "shadows" they have helped set free.

... AND THE CRYPT ON THE COUCH

The image of the phantom does not come to us accidentally as a term for the analyst's torment.[1] This image points to an occasion of torment for

1. This image of the "phantom"—meant at first to indicate a rift (inflicted upon the listening analyst by some secret of the patient that could not be revealed) which creates a formation in the unconscious of the listener—lent itself to a variety of theoretical elaborations. The analyst, attuned to the dictates of the couch, is surely, in some respects, comparable to a child maturing on the psychic nourishment received from his parents. Should a child have parents "with secrets," parents whose speech is not exactly complementary to their unstated repressions, the child will receive from them a gap in the unconscious, an unknown, unrecognized knowledge—a *nescience*—subjected to a form of "repression" before the fact.

The buried speech of the parent will be (a) dead (gap) without a burial place in the child. This unknown phantom returns from the unconscious to haunt its host and may lead to phobias, madness, and obsessions. Its effect can persist through several generations and determine the fate of an entire family line.

Could this be the "mysterious" primary repression hypothesized by Freud? It is too early to provide an answer. All the same, the clinical impact of the *phantom* is becoming clearer. In this text (March 1973), the image of the phantom simply represents a specific malaise of the analyst; it has since been transposed into a metapsychological concept, a matter for new research and renewed analytic listening. It has been further expanded in a seminar, held since February 1974 at the Paris Psychoanalytic Institute by Nicolas Abraham, on Dual Unity and one of its consequences: the *metapsychological phantom* (see "Notes du séminaire sur l'Unité Duelle et le Fantôme," in *L'écorce et le noyau* [Paris: Aubier-Flammarion, 1978;

patients as well—a memory they buried *without legal burial place.* The memory is of an idyll, experienced with a valued object and yet for some reason unspeakable. It is memory entombed in a fast and secure place, awaiting resurrection. Between the idyllic moment and its subsequent forgetting (we have called the latter "preservative repression"),[2] there was the metapsychological traumatism of a loss or, more precisely, the "loss" that resulted from a traumatism. This segment of an ever so painfully lived Reality—untellable and therefore inaccessible to the gradual, assimilative work of mourning—causes a genuinely covert shift in the entire psyche. The shift itself is covert, since both the fact that the idyll was real and that it was later lost must be disguised and denied. This leads to the establishment of a sealed-off psychic place, a crypt in the ego. Created by a self-governing mechanism we call *inclusion,* the crypt is comparable to the formation of a cocoon around the chrysalis.[3] Inclusion or crypt is a form of anti-introjection, a mechanism whereby the assimilation of both the illegitimate idyll and its loss is precluded.

LIVING IN A CRYPT

The "shadow of the object" strays endlessly about the crypt until it is finally reincarnated in the person of the subject. Far from displaying itself, this kind of identification is destined to remain concealed. We consider it useful to complement Freud's metapsychological formula, in "Mourning and Melancholia"—which shows "the ego in the guise of the object"—by its opposite, in order to signal an initial clinical finding: *the "object," in its turn, carries the ego as its mask,* that is, either the ego itself or some other façade. This one is an imaginary and covert identification, a crypto-fantasy that, being untellable, cannot be shown in the light of day. The identification concerns not so much the object who may no longer exist, but essentially the "mourning" that this "object" might allegedly carry out because of having lost the subject; the subject, consequently, appears to be painfully missed by the "object." Clearly, an identifying empathy of

---

will be included in the second volume of the American edition], pp. 393–425). Further applications can be found in the following articles: Nicolas Abraham, "Notes on the Phantom"; and Maria Torok, "Story of Fear" [See also Abraham's interpretation of Shakespeare's *Hamlet* with his addition of a sixth act: "The Phantom of Hamlet or the Sixth Act," all three in this volume].

2. See "The Topography of Reality," in this volume.

3. See our article "Mourning *or* Melancholia: Introjection *versus* Incorporation" [in this volume].

this type could not say its name, let alone divulge its aim. Accordingly, it hides behind a mask, even in the so-called "periodic states" of manic-depressive psychosis. The mechanism consists of exchanging one's own identity for a fantasmic identification with the "life"—beyond the grave— of an object of love, lost as a result of some metapsychological traumatism. Lacking a better term, we will call this mechanism *endocryptic identification.*

A fantasy of identifying empathy! What does it mean? Consider the fantasy first. We hold that fantasy is never the simple translation of a psychic process; quite the opposite, it is the illusory and painstakingly reiterated proof that no process whatever has or should take place. Only in this sense can fantasy, as we see it, refer to a metapsychological state of affairs. Having established this, we can clarify the status of the identification now recognized as endocryptic. To state that endocryptic identification is the work of fantasy alone means that its content amounts to maintaining the illusion of the topographical *status quo,* as it had been prior to the covert transformation. As for the *inclusion* itself, it is not fantasy. Inclusion attests to a painful reality, forever *denied:* the "gaping wound" of the topography. It is therefore crucial to establish the following. The melancholic's complaints translate a fantasy—the imaginary sufferings of the endocryptic object—a fantasy that only serves to mask the real suffering, this one unavowed, caused by a wound the subject does not know how to heal.

That is in short our argument. Clearly the poetics born of the crypt gives rise to as many poems as there are individual *cryptophores.* A great many creations of a decidedly nonmelancholic appearance also turn out to come from the same school. "Melancholy," in fact, seems to occupy a rather limited area of the potential uses authorized by the concept of intrapsychic crypt and endocryptic identification. In point of fact, these concepts were familiar to us long before we found them appropriate to circumscribe manic-depressive psychosis. For years we have been talking about "preservative repression," "unutterable libidinal experiences," and "covert identification." Now that the nature of melancholic identification is at last clearly expressed, quite a few other equally enigmatic modes of being have crystallized for us around the same ideas. In addition to the manic-depressive, let us mention two other forms of being, commonly called "fetishism" and "neurosis of failure." It seems to us that these inventions of the mind also rest on some "gaping wound," opened long ago within the ego and disguised by a fantasmic and secret construction in place of the very thing from which, through the loss, the ego was severed. In all cases, the goal of this type of construction is to disguise the wound because it is unspeakable, because to state it openly would prove fatal to the entire topography. Individual cases differ only as to the shape of the wound and the particular form of the arrangement invented so as to reveal nothing.[4]

SOME MODEL CRYPTS

"Victor" and "Gilles," or How to Keep?

"I'll bash your head against the wall; that'll cure you of loving me." This sentence, never uttered but put into action, was an ending. It was preceded by another sentence that did not have to be said either: "I'll bash your head against the wall if you tell anyone what we did together." No more was needed to cut off speech. To say everything once and for all, only one recurring theme was left: contrition-failure, failure-contrition. "No, I should not have!" "I can't control myself!" Words laboriously illustrated by deeds.

Victor is middle-aged. "I am neurotically unsuccessful," he says right away. "Yet, I'm like any other man, married, with children, and a powerful job. Yes, power, giving orders! . . . that's what I'd like most. But I can't bring myself to act on it. Something always makes me side with my subordinates. I am always on the verge of getting into a fight with my superiors. It ends in dismissal." He is aware of it and contrite, but the analyst is perplexed. Acts and words occur before her eyes, and she obviously understands nothing.

From the start, the battle with repression is missing, the neurotic compromise that certifies the existence of an "I." Above all, the transference onto the analyst is lacking. In its absence, what is said seems empty of any present content: timeless words directed at no one. The present, if it exists—and we are justified in doubting that it does—is the indefinitely reiterated account of day-to-day failures and the regret over having sunk so low. No accusations, no projection; everything is taken on almost too conscientiously. Boredom sets in, stagnation. . . .

If the analyst thinks for a moment that she should feel affected, that she is going to be involved in some repeated experience, in some affective recollection, she is greatly mistaken. Whatever she does know, she did not learn from associations, but by drawing her own conclusions. At this rate, she would have been better off becoming a detective. For, how on earth could a "boat ride" at age eleven, with an elder brother of seventeen, have caused an almost fatal illness for the patient the following day? There

---

4. [The order of the following case studies was altered for the purposes of this translation at Maria Torok's request; several other minor changes were also made as a result.—Ed.]

are complaints about his wife who, according to him, is jealous, shrewish, possessive, frustrating. Another question: if she is this way, how could he have stood her for so long? Yet, he seems to desire her intensely on occasion, his potency never letting him down. "When I see her in the bathroom in certain positions, I *cannot hold back*. Why doesn't she tolerate the least bit of interest on my part for anyone else, man or woman? She is jealous even of the reading I do. Does she expect me to succeed professionally? No sooner do I achieve something than she despises it. She wants me to be hers, totally and only hers. During intercourse she readily accepts all positions, except the one I want most."

Does Victor enjoy suffering? humiliation? Nothing in the analytic relationship leads one to believe this. Does he perhaps say all of this, after an oedipal fashion, to pacify his father? If this were the case, the analyst would have no reason to fret. And then there is the brother: "He was so mean and so stupid. When he got engaged, he gave me such a thrashing, I had to stay in bed for three days—which, by the way, kept me from taking part in the festivities."

The detective surfaces then. Was the patient possibly in love with his brother to the point of provoking him, out of frustration, at the moment he was being unfaithful? The analyst, however, is not supposed to have the faintest idea about anything. . . . Then, one fine day comes the account of one of the numerous car accidents Victor has had, an accident which almost cost the life of a young friend who was with him. "I only had a concussion, but after the coma I could no longer find my young friend. Dazed and confused, I sleepwalked from house to house in the village where I had been taken in, asking: 'Where is the little one? Where is little Viki?'" Finally! The detective can be dismissed. The analyst reassumes her function. With hindsight she finally hears, behind the dreary everyday of failures and regrets, the sounds of the love Victor attributes within himself to his brother Gilles. And he himself *is* this older brother, even in the coma. That much is now clear. Strange paradox of action. The elder one searches for the younger one. In real life was it not the reverse? Gilles, the elder, had "jilted" Viki, first to act macho, then to marry a woman. Gilles, once his guardian angel in school, his pride in front of everyone, this handsome fellow, virile and muscular; Gilles, the delight of their mother, who could be tough with their father; Gilles the pure, the ultimate, with a temper worthy of Jupiter. Yes, Victor *was* this ideal brother *in secret;* he was this brother while driving with his young friend; he continued to be him, even in the coma and the subsequent daze, as he desperately searched for his young friend after having regained consciousness. According to his fantasy, the little one lived on in the big one whom Victor has become, as remorse, as a lack.

But why the accident? This lack of attention on a deserted road? . . .

There lies the question mark of Victor's whole life. He *is* Gilles, sure enough, that much we now know, but he is Gilles in order to upset him and to defeat him all the time: that is what "Gilles," his lover, deserves for having rejected him.

Our understanding is at long last open. What appears now and later on is *"Gilles in love and contrite, remorseful* at not being able to stop loving and then at being unfaithful." Meanwhile, Victor deserts himself by taking up residence in a Xanthippe-like woman, his nagging and quarrelsome wife. She will say to "Gilles," the big brother, all that "Victor," the little one, has on his mind. As far as "Gilles" is concerned, "Gilles" his lover, Victor recoups him as well by *becoming* "Gilles" for "Victor." . . . Yet, it is a shaky solution. He contemplates divorce. But how could he go through with a divorce if, with his wife gone, he would have to give up Victor, whom she embodies? Day by day, he and she thus jointly defeat "Gilles" *and his ego ideal*—the recognized cause of their traumatic separation. Does he expect to get ahead in business? We are going to thwart him. He wants to look at women? He's going to have a hard time. Blocked in all acts of life, "Gilles" remains, "Gilles" will not leave. His wings clipped, he will not fly from the hiding place Victor has set up for him. One day the analyst announces: "Victor does not want Gilles to make it, to go out with women; he straps him down, he wants to keep him for himself." This moment marks a turning point. Recollections ensue, then the contours of transference.

Why did it take years to unmask "Gilles" in Victor's guise? For the simple reason that there is no cryptic identification that does not emanate from a crypt, an inclusion, or from an *unspeakable scene*. The scene took place, we learn bit by bit, during a boat ride. This ride recalls once more the image of an impassable wall: "I'll bash your head against the wall if you say a word," says the analyst. It is not yet Victor who recounts the scene but "Gilles," with reserve, embellishments, and omissions. In the boat, between his legs, leaning back on his penis, is little Victor. The day after his account there is no longer a serious illness, as there was after the event, but a dream. "He is disemboweling a chicken while pulling on its esophagus and windpipe [*trachée-artère*]. But the chicken won't relinquish life [*n'arrive pas à mourir*]. It becomes his little daughter. He wants desperately to take her life [*lui donner la mort*] so she will no longer suffer. No use." Yes, Gilles can "wind up" (ejaculate, windpipe) [*cracher par terre*, spit on the ground; *trachée-artère*, windpipe], but little Victor has to swallow (esophagus) his orgasm. His own penis is really only a "little girl" whose "life" (love) [*la mort: l'amour*] cannot yet be had. This was the situation when Victor's orgasm was taken abroad by Gilles—right up to the latter's return immediately preceding his marriage. Only at age sixteen and a half, after having received his brother's thrashing, did the aggression of despair finally set off the process of puberty in Victor. Being unable to dislodge "Gilles" (whom he has become) from his twofold and incompatible position of being both his lover and his ego ideal, Victor spends his life attacking him by attacking himself, by thwarting him—*in his own* endeavors prescribed by their shared ego ideal. Similarly, the ostensible spitefulness he has felt against his wife for not wanting to perform *coitus a tergo* is in fact "Gilles's" belligerence. As for Victor, he can only gloat over it in his heart of hearts. "It serves him right, that betrayer, who used to love me so much and then left me." "Gilles" fantasizes about wild orgies, . . . but alas, they don't work out. "Fortunately," hoots little Victor up his sleeve.

We now understand that, were it not for the aggression directed at the elder brother, Victor would remain crestfallen in his identification with a fantasmic object, who is supposedly in mourning for him. The fact that this did not happen was due to a special situation. In Victor's case, another conflictual element is present in addition to his fantasmic identification with his elder brother; this element works as a neurosis would. His brother's ego ideal and his own are one and the same for Victor. It was precisely this ideal inherent in Gilles that once separated them, and which explains why every attempt to realize this shared ideal brings with it a large measure of aggressivity directed against the ideal. Hence the illusion, but only the illusion, of a masochistic or self-destructive neurosis. Hence also the relative ease of a pseudoanalytic dialogue. Indeed, there is obviously a conflict, but it is not where if first appears to be.

The Afflicted Dead

The following case is quite different. No conflict is visible between the cryptophoric subject and the object of the crypt. The two of them are accomplices in secretly hating the outsiders who long ago separated them. Together they should live and die.

At the time of her suicide attempt, she had just given birth. It was a miracle that she could be saved. A few years spent in a sanatorium, then came a lengthy and unwieldy analysis. Themes of self-deprecation, worthlessness, void, internal rotting, refusal to get medical care; all of this alternated with periods of bravado, contempt, feelings of superiority filling the universe. A psychiatrist might describe her in this way. As for the analyst, being unable to understand, he too is reduced to much the same thing. Listening to her, he fixes on an enigma: when the little girl was still too young to go to school, her "irresponsible father" deserted the family for some obscure reason and was gone forever. Is he still alive? This question remains without an answer to this day.

The analysis begins in an atmosphere of elation. Here the patient finds again the "warmth of the fire" that had fed her bygone dreams. "*Someone* is happy and full of hope." If only the analyst had heard it this way from the start! He would have been spared having to grope for several years, not fruitlessly to be sure, but yet running the risk of serious errors. "*Someone* is happy." Is it really the young woman or somebody else? Her father, perhaps. . . . This is how we would formulate the question today. Short of this, the analyst is disoriented. He looks for the transference, or at least for the role he is meant to play. To no avail. He does not yet suspect that it is possible to disguise under one's own traits a fantasy person endowed with entirely fictitious greatness and torments. No wonder than that afterward the analyst's words bounce off like peanuts thrown against a wall, without making the least difference. The dreams are monotonous: cuts, dislocations, scattered limbs. Are the ideas tormenting the patient ideas of castration? Or is she cut off from her father? Or castrated by her mother? Or filled with hatred of some people or the analyst? It might appear so. Still . . . nothing budges. Whose are these *scattered limbs?* Does the patient have to recover a lost object in her own name, an object that might be projected onto the analyst, or one that the oedipal mother, for instance, might have taken away from her? . . . Very much the stuff of fairy tales with no other effect, all in all, than the benefit of a stable and secure relation. But then, whose are these *scattered limbs?* The turning point comes, illuminated by other cases, as soon as the hypothesis of mourning arises—a cryptic mourning, however, fantasized as the incessant affliction of *an other.* Retroactively, it is easier to clarify the meaning of the patient's attitudes, repeatedly alternating between depression and vigor. How in fact could she have transferred onto the analyst the feelings of a little girl looking for her father, when, in fact, she *lived entirely* on the concealed fantasy that she *was* herself her father, weeping over her, suffering because he is bereft of her; the father who, forever disconsolate, accuses himself of the worst of crimes, since he had to be subjected to the punishment of losing her; being her father who, taking on giant proportions and equipped with every guile, flies, in "manic" moments, to his beloved darling, being absolutely confident that nothing will stop him. In these exalted moments, she runs from dealer to dealer, trying to add a precious doll to her collection: her father thirsting after her is looking for her, is going to find her. Once she finds the "little specimen," her eagerness to acquire it knows no bounds and pushes her into nearly criminal acts. This must be the force of love.

In sum, she *was* her "father," but *without* giving any sign of it in her demeanor, which remained most feminine, or in her professional pursuits. Still, if the analyst had known about the mechanism of endocryptic identification, he would have understood it quickly. When quite small, the patient would daydream: "Someone was charged with child murder and I realized finally that the defendant was myself." Was it not the lost father who, in the little girl's fantasies, endured the mother's accusations? The analyst's office is called funereal. To be understood: it is a lifeless abode for the beloved girl, long dead for her father's desire. One day, she walks past an "escalator" with her child (her father was seen near an escalator for the last time): a sudden impression that the child is going to be "devoured" by the machine. "I felt my arms fall crushed." This is what it was like for her father to lose *his* little lover. Yes, all these statements could have guided the analyst, had he not been sacrificing to prejudices such as that of the "I."

In endocryptic identification, the "I" is understood as the lost object's fantasied ego. On the couch, even more than in life, the "I" stages the words, gestures, and feelings—in short, the entire imaginary lot—of the lover who mourns for his forever "dead" object. As the patient recounts her experience of the escalator for the nth time (where her arms fell crushed), the analyst finally states that all the "fallen arms" and "scattered limbs" of her dreams and fantasies represent her father's inconsolable suffering: his arms are as if cut off, not having his little girl to carry.

From then on, the incorporated father becomes "decorporated" onto the analyst, so to speak. Witness this dream: "A quack doctor cuts off one of his arms when he loses his daughter." "As a sign of mourning," says the analyst, the "quack."

This is the end of the endocryptic identification. As confirmation the young woman sketches a drawing hastily on the back of an album, a relic of her father. The drawing is entitled "Aida." Here, the characters of the drama find their places. Aida is the imprisoned daughter dying of starvation. A living corpse, she waits for her former lover to come and deliver her. This reworking of identities occurs inside the crypt still, but the edifice is swaying. Soon enough it will give way to a genuine recollection: "It's shameful, it's disgusting," shouts the neighbor in unison with the mother. "These women are tearing her father away from the child." No need to fill in the blank between the shame inflicted on the father and his subsequent disappearance. Henceforth the crypt is unlocked, the battle for the father approaches in the open. From this moment on, the infantile conflict reappears as it was before the loss, before the entombment.

The Wolf Man's Secret

Recently we felt that it was necessary to violate with impious hands the hypothetical "grave" the Wolf Man carried within him. We did so in order to uncover—behind the utterable memory of the Wolf Man's seduction by his sister—the memory of an earlier, secret seduction to which his sister herself must have been subjected by their father. To be sure, the Wolf Man was only vicariously a melancholic. His crypt did not in fact contain *his own* illegitimate object (as would be the case with a genuine "melancholic"), but someone else's: his father's daughter. The Wolf Man's wound does not seem to be—as Freud was inclined to think—the loss of his own object, the sister, but that he was unable to participate in the initial scene of seduction (which, we believe, was narrated and relived with him by his sister), and could not tell anyone about it, so as to legitimize it. The disappointment at not having been the one seduced by his father might make him resemble hysterics (in the Freudian sense) who are never quite seduced enough; the impossibility of exposing his disappointment without bringing down the whole world around him apparently forced him to transform his vindictive tendencies into an intrapsychic secret. Otherwise, he might have lost his other wish as well—the wish of supplanting his sister in the initial scene. The solution he later found to squaring this circle, as we established it, was—let us admit—quite ingenious.[5] With the ideas related to the account so marvelously illustrated by his sister, he managed to create a crypt in his ego. In the crypt, he also carefully preserved the words taken from the account, words which proved truly magical since they were good both for making statements and for producing pleasure. Thus preserved, the words were readily available. To use them, all he had to do was apply them innocently in a different sense and construct—by means of astute homonyms—quite another scene, not in the least resembling the encrypted one. This new scene, though altogether different, was no less effective in producing pleasure. One of the words seems to have been the Russian verb *teret,* first used to mean "to rub" (the penis is understood) and then applied, for the requirements of his case, in the altered sense of: "to polish," "to shine." The woman rubbing the penis became, in the new scene translated from the old one, a woman polishing the floor. Thus a fetishistic image was created from a fetish word whose initial meaning had been forgotten: shine-gleam-glisten.

The Man of Milk and His Fetish

All of us analysts must have had a Wolf Man or other similar cases on the couch. Let us briefly draw on one from our practice. A middle-aged man

5. See N. Abraham and M. Torok, *The Wolf Man's Magic Word: A Cryptonymy* (Minneapolis: University of Minnesota Press, 1986; original French edition 1976), part 2, pp. 27–40. That chapter is a contribution to the psychoanalysis of dreams and phobia. It elaborates the secret content of the Wolf Man's "crypt" and the manner in which it returns in his famous nightmare. The chapter was originally a lecture given in Paris on 15 January 1974 to commemorate the centenary of Sandor Ferenczi's birth.

has had a lengthy analysis with a colleague: some improvement. Has feelings of inadequacy, not always justified. A persistent fear of impotence, mostly unfounded. Married, the father of a large family. He is consistent and effective in his professional life, but has difficulty playing his role in public and asserting himself in accordance with the demands of his position. What is "wrong" is "in the head" and sometimes "in the body."

Listening to him, one wonders how solid common sense can coexist with cranky fantasies devoid of any apparent link to a tension in his own psychic topography. The same is true of his sometimes fantastical feelings that are out of place and never fail to surprise him, though they have been habitual with him since childhood. A few themes recur over the years in the flood of enigmas he pours out while on the couch. It takes some time to understand that he speaks and lives someone else's words and affects. Whose? As will be established later, they are those of his encrypted father. It is now possible to grasp the theme of the cemetery, apparently visible to the analyst through the window, but not within view of the patient. For good reason, since the patient himself lives in this tomb. A lethargic beauty is waiting in a glass coffin, always expecting to be awakened by a magical kiss. Why is the patient dead, if indeed he is dead? Because he is a monster. "Here comes the monster," people say when he comes forward with a wish. But what kind of wish? Who will find out? He has a strange mytho-maniac theme: Once upon a time in South America he was a front-wheel drive champion [*traction avant,* literally: front-pull drive—*Trans.*]. He doesn't understand it. Is he mad to be so convinced of the truth of his own fantastic account? "Am I mad?" and then he says, "a goatherd, goatherds, milking, goat's milk." (*Traction* [pulling] refers to drawing milk [*traite: traction:* pulling] and goat's milk in French [*lait de chèvre*] refers homophonically to *leche,* the word for milk in South America, thinks the analyst.)

This confirmed a hypothesis the analyst had formulated several months earlier: the father's physical and mental demise and the older sister's psychosis have something to do with each other. This relationship is in *pulling the teat* [*traction sur le pis*]. "Punch, the puppet," the patient says, "I could never stand him. He jerks and jumps about. I especially hate the pasty paint smeared all over his head and that white stuff dripping down" (*leche* . . .). These must have been the words the sister had used in telling him about her "scandalous encounter" with their father's penis. Presumably, this took place on a South American farm during a family trip. A recurring dream: a game of billiards, one billiard ball hits another, the second one a third on the rebound. Yes, that is it precisely. He is hit on the rebound. And when he wants to play with himself, one name— *Letitia* [*lait,* milk]—is enough: he falls in love with and marries a woman on whom he often performs cunnilingus (*leche* [*lécher:* lick]). The magic word *leche* (i.e., sperm), the outcome of the "front-pull" on the penis, had led to a sexual practice which is apparently the opposite of its original model. Cunnilingus constitutes a dreamlike staging of the secret magic word *leche*.

The analyst only learned about this toward the end when he also learned about another key, the one explaining the way in which the endo-cryptic identification with the father became manifest. First, the patient subjected the analyst to lengthy and insidious testing. (Would the analyst be able to hear everything? Would he feel sympathy for the father who considered himself a monster? Could he listen without spurning the fa-ther, without condemning him to death, so as not to repeat what the father had done to himself?) The patient finally revealed that his father had gone nearly blind by refusing medical care and that, to end it all, he had slashed his wrists. Many things are clear now: for example, the pa-tient's recurring experience of losing his sight in large areas of his visual field—manifestly not because of scotoma or negative hallucination, as one might have thought, but as a result of his identification with his father's blindness—precisely when coming to the analyst's office. . . . This was a case of the patient's empathetic identification with the fantasied remorse of his "guilty" father. It also caused the patient's truly unjustified panic at having scratched his wrists while doing odd jobs. The effect of the same empathy was that (unaccountably for himself and, for a long time, for the analyst) he experienced "affects" that were not his own. Now we under-stand that they were in fact his father's affects, his ruminations, his re-morse, his fantasies, his desires—all imagined or surmised by the son. The patient's long walks led him invariably to the same spot. Once there, an internal dialogue, always the same, emerged in him: "Is there some-body here?"—"No, there's nobody. . . . We're alone." At a clearing, he had the impression of being a character in a fairy tale: *Sleeping Beauty.*

One day, anxious before entering the door to the analyst's office, he had the sudden impression that there was someone inside. This is the meaning of the fantasy he was acting out: *father* (the patient) *is going to see his daughter* (the analyst). A recollection came: the sister gone mad showed her clenched fist while her other hand moved up and down. The father could not stand it. Beside himself, he shook her. Shortly afterward, she was institutionalized. "What did your father feel then?" asked the analyst. Then, for the first time after a very long period of analysis, the patient burst out in tears. "My father must have been so awfully misera-ble," he said in his own name this time. Officially, he has revealed nothing, but he understands that his drama is known. The father could not stand his daughter's gesture, whose tragic and ironic meaning he alone was supposed to understand: she replayed the secret scene, clenching the father's penis in her hand while he caressed her. It is now clear why the patient thinks his mother is so "cold." Yes, his father (who he believes himself to be) deserves a wife who behaves like an "ice statue" toward him. He brought another dream for confirmation. "A gang of shady characters [toute une faune]. There was going to be a brawl. I was stifling, I was stifling." Father is a goat [faune], but the scandal has to be stifled. If the scandal is stifled inside, shut up in a crypt, only the word of the desire returns with an altered meaning: the word thing, the sole survivor of a topographic catastrophe. A silent witness to the unspeakable leche(r), lick—yes—and all can continue to live.

FETISH: THE SYMBOL OF WHAT CANNOT BE SYMBOLIZED

Many points of this type of analysis seem instructive with respect to certain received ideas. If, according to Freud, a fetish is to be understood as a penis attributed to the mother who in reality is devoid or deprived of it, then the meaning of this deprivation can be made more precise: the lack of the penis is actually linked to the son's and the mother's parallel fate, since both of them are excluded from an illegitimate libidinal scene. The "fetish" and its counterpart, "the mother's penis," are invented to compensate for the mother's lack of pleasure and the son's loss of his ideal, even though the topographical status quo is being maintained, so that the son should not have to renounce his own pleasure. In fact, were it necessary to accept "castration" (which we define as the lack of sexual pleasure due to an irreparable exclusion from the libidinal scene), lethal aggressiveness would be unleashed, pushing the young subject (now inseparable from the wronged mother) into revealing and thus annihilating the illegitimate scene, along with its participants. But by the same token, what has secretly become his own libidinal ideal, his own raison de vivre, would also be annihilated. How to find a way out of this impasse? Through the creation of an internal or narcissistic public, so to speak, for one's own "hysteria" (which varies according to age), a kind of self-to-self "hysteria." In this case, all that survives of the relationship to others is the dynamic repression, not of the desire for pleasure, but of the desire to speak out. Apart from this relational residue, everything can work in seclusion; for the fetish to be effective, there need be no witnesses, except to test its opacity. The analyst who "will never understand" has no other apparent function than to bring to the fore the constant temptation to speak out while permitting the cryptophore to verify, day in day out, that the crypt itself remains unscathed.

Let us return to the split in the ego that Freud finally posited in 1938 to provide an explanation for cases like the Wolf Man's. These belated yet new findings need only one final complement in our view. The split manifests itself, according to Freud, in a "double tendency" which feeds the patient's words during analysis in such cases. There is a conformist tendency that lacks adequate affective charge and an enigmatic tendency that translates, in a cryptic manner, the identification with one of the participants in the scene. This second tendency—as we saw in our patient's case (the Man of Milk)—is entirely parallel to and independent of the first, and, when it eludes rationalization, is usually expressed in incomprehensible terms or in the description of "feelings" that are being experienced as inappropriate. We would speak of melancholia if this were the case of a fantasmic empathy with someone who is bereaved by the loss of the subject (i.e., his beloved). But, in our patient's case, the subject was simply a witness and excluded from the idyll. Since the idyll, now his libidinal ideal, was not his own to be exposed or put to use, the subject created a symbol, the alloseme of the *word* of his desire, made into a thing and dramatized: the fetish word, strictly speaking. What creates the symbol here is not related to prohibition, as in a neurosis, but to the intrinsic impossibility of having recourse to it. The impossibility itself bears no name and, therefore, becomes one with the word indicating the impossible desire. This is the structure of the symbol *leche*. As for cunnilingus, the fetishistic act, it is not symbolic in this case, but instead works as a veritable *symbol-cover*. The magic word (i.e., the genuine symbol), the subject's authentic and full creation, remains concealed by the fetish. The triple complement of such a hidden symbol (the desire to participate in the illegitimate scene, the desire of aggressive intrusion, and the desire to speak out) is not at all the latent counterpart of some manifest discourse, since this discourse is, in turn, concealed *behind* acts, dreams, and symptoms disguising the symbol which originates in a different world, a world that cannot be symbolized. The analyst's work is not to condone the concealment, but rather to draw forth the word of desire, to recognize it as a symbol precisely—as an exceptional work of crisis and for this reason the more valuable—as *the symbol of what cannot be symbolized.*

The splitting of the ego Freud noted thus gains in precision. The enigmatic trend issues from the crypt or the inclusion just like the magic word itself. As for the conformist trend, it results from the wish to conceal the symbol, the product of the crypt, and includes, however paradoxical this may seem, the description and the transformations of the fetishistic act as well as everyday trivialities.

Returning to the Wolf Man, we had no idea until later that he had been attracted, not only by the squatting position of the floor scrubber, but also, through some semantic contagion, by the sight of a "shining nose." For confirmation, it will suffice to read carefully Freud's essay *On Fetishism* (1927). It is easy to guess that with this "shine on the nose" the

Wolf Man is alluding to the word *teret* ("to rub," "to shine")—the very symbol of his interred desire. The ailments of this same nose—pimples, holes, blackheads—symbolize the desire to break into the scene, while the choice of the nose as their place (the nose betrays lies) tells of the desire to speak out. This is a good example of the covert and threefold purpose of the fetish-work, which was fated to remain obscure. Only after having been deciphered, understood, and appreciated can it restore to its creator his own "divine right"—hiding under enigmas, yet demanding the light of day.

VARIETIES OF ENDOCRYPTIC IDENTIFICATION

Both the Wolf Man and the Man of Milk created their crypts not because they knew of an illegitimate sexual scene, but to overcome a double impossibility: they could neither transform the scene into a disclosable ideal nor expose it for fear of destroying their libidinal ideal. This kind of contradiction is not characteristic of neurosis. The impossibility of speaking inhibits the development of a neurosis, as it were. An apparent renunciation replaces the betrayal of the libidinal ideal and any wishes for revenge. Preservative repression saves the consensus, while the fetish, a most ingenious conceit, reduces the danger of a "cosmic cataclysm" to a harmless oddity capable of reviving desire.

There is another form of crypt, the crypt of the blameless and guiltless object who left the subject after the idyll for a good reason, or as it were, in spite of himself. This object has been totally good, absolutely perfect, and no one should suspect its secret love. Rather than lead to an impossible mourning, the loss of such an object—*always regarded as innocent of desertion*—produces an endocryptic identification free of any aggression, at least as far as the partners themselves are concerned (if not the outside world). This is the crypt psychiatrists might call "melancholic."

Altogether different is the fate of those who personally benefited from an unutterable favor. Not being able to put their loss into words, or to communicate it to others and resign themselves through grief, they choose to deny everything—the loss as well as the love. There is no alternative but to deny everything, shut everything up in themselves, the pleasure and the suffering.

The variety of such cases is infinite. There are those who, at the time of the loss, suffered a disappointment in their object of love, in its sincerity or value. Their crypt is under double lock and, due to a tragic split, they desperately try to destroy what is dearest to them. These people are deprived of even the hope of ever being acknowledged.

In some cases, a trend of covert aggression, directed against the object, survives in the deserted partner alongside the endocryptic identification. This creates a useful arrangement for the purposes of analysis, because the presence of the patient's own aggression directed at the object—at first disguised in a "failure syndome"—facilitates the opening of the crypt.

UNLOCKING THE CRYPT: BEFORE AND AFTER

We have sketched three very different cases of inclusion. In all three, we were disoriented by the unnoticed action of a covert identification that led to apparently unintelligible words and behavior—apparently unintelligible to psychoanalytic listening. Only after showing our receptiveness to this mode of being can the inclusion slowly give way to real mourning, namely introjection. Three successive movements can be distinguished in this lengthy process.

The first movement coincides with the onset of the analytic relationship. Without abandoning their endocryptic identification, the subjects secretly project the *child* partner of their crypt onto the analyst. *Secretly,* it is important to emphasize; in the manifest analytic relationship none of this must show. The partners' faithfulness to each other shows only in the regularity of the sessions and a certain degree of animation. This first segment is followed by a very long period of seeming stagnation, but it is in fact used surreptitiously by patients to study the listening capabilities of their analysts, i.e., their prejudices (and not their desire, as would be the case in objectal neuroses). During this whole phase, the patients' regular return to the couch has the same libidinal significance for them as the regularity of their physiological functions: breathing, bowel movements, menstruation. These are symbolic recurrences of the interred experience. The diseases affecting these functions (asthma, colitis, painful periods or their cessation, involution, etc.), if they communicate anything at all, speak *to the subject only and not to others* (as would be the case, for example, in conversion hysteria). The illness tells the subject: "The return is here, but it is an illness." This return is the mirror image of what happens on the couch—when coming to the sessions and speaking are considered as suffering or torture by the patient. By means of this translation into words, that is, through the expression of pain, the self-to-self affliction can enjoy a respite as soon as the analysis begins.

The second movement takes place when the secret projection of the child onto the analyst gives way to the equally secretive "decorporation" of the cryptic object. The impulse for this change may be quite contingent.

But, above all, it is the task of interpretation to lay open, at the right time, the endocryptic identification. The false "I" will then be reconverted into the third person, while patients are given to understand that it is possible to evoke the prodigal love of their objects without subjecting them to shame or losing them morally—the more so since the transgression itself implies an authentic and privileged encounter with the depths of the object's psyche that the patient will henceforth attempt to understand.

The great danger during this second phase is that, on opening the crypt, the object may be implicitly or explicitly condemned by the analyst; what is required instead is the capacity to mourn the object, that is, the capacity to acquire for oneself the libidinal resources the object had hitherto retained. Saying in this context, "You want to *seduce* me," or "You're making a *seducer* out of me," or "It's time to forget all that" does not feel like a trivial comment to patients, but like an irreversible verdict, capable of upsetting everything. If, on the contrary, rather than shaming the object, the narcissistic value (for *both* partners) of the entombed experience is acknowledged—with the crypt unlocked, its treasure laid out in the open and recognized as the unalienable property of the subject—the third and last movement will be set in motion, by way of a new impetus, with the task of overtly undertaking the final battle with the oedipal party—the last hurdle on the way to fructifying the interred treasure.

At the close of this all too rapid overview of some effects of inclusion and of endocryptic identification in particular, let us express the hope that these concepts will lighten the very difficult task of listening to some patients. We also hope that we have increased their chances of being heard and that the treasures which lie buried in crypts will become the delight of their owner and can be made to work to the benefit of us all.

SEVEN

The Topography of Reality: Sketching a Metapsychology of Secrets

N. Abraham and M. Torok, 1971

I n these remarks we have chosen to put aside the various meanings of the term "reality," whether they are derived from law, philosophy, or even the sciences. All these meanings, taken independently, would in fact be foreign to our own science, psychoanalysis. Yet, the notion of reality is one we encounter daily in our practice, albeit in a disguised, even unrecognizable form. For us, as analysts, it is this very masking and denial which, more than anything else, attests to the presence of that which has the status of reality for our patients—a reality, needless to say, to be avoided. In consequence, we analysts can speak of "reality" only insofar as the patient's very refusal of it designates it as such. *In this sense and in this sense only can "reality" claim to become a metapsychological concept.* Reality can then be defined as what is rejected, masked, denied precisely as "reality"; it is that which *is*, all the more so since it must not be known; in short, Reality is defined as a *secret*. The metapsychological concept of Reality refers to the place, in the psychic apparatus, where the secret is buried.[1]

Of course, the opposition between apparent and hidden, manifest and latent desire and its disguises, has been a major theme of psychoanalysis since its inception. This type of opposition does not, however, necessarily lead to the idea of a secret or of a "reality" intended to be secret.

Previously published as "La topique réalitaire: Notations sur une métapsychologie du secret," *Revue française de psychanalyse* 35, no. 5–6 (1971): 277–82; and in *L'Écorce et le noyau* (Paris: Flammarion, 1987), pp. 252–58; and as "The Topography of Reality: Toward a Metapsychology of Secrets," trans. N. Rand, *Oxford Literary Review* 11, no. 2 (1990): 38–44.

1. When considered as a metapsychological concept, the word "reality" needs to be capitalized, especially since all other forms of reality presuppose and derive from it. The metapsychological Reality of the secret is a counterpart to the reality of the outside world; the negation of the one entails the refusal of the other.

Only representations or desires are repressed. These return as symptoms, as so many "materializations" of *words,* of the very words that repressed them. In fact, the hysteric does not get so far as to intend a reality—and thus possesses no secrets—at least not in the metapsychological sense. It cannot be said that what the hysteric represses had a name, a prior existence as speech, at the moment of repression and that, as a consequence, the function of repression would be to hide a secret. The hysteric's desire and attendant representations are merely the offshoots of words that do not in fact voice desire or pleasure, but their prohibition. To call desire by the very name of its prohibition is the law of hysteria's transparent opacity. And that is fundamentally what we all do.

Unless we also carry one—or many secrets. . . . What does it mean to be a *cryptophore?* How does such a condition occur? Just as desire is born along with prohibition, Reality too, at least in the metapsychological sense, is born of the necessity of remaining concealed, unspoken. This means that, at the moment of its birth, Reality is comparable to an offense, a crime. The crime's name is not identical with prohibition, as is the case in the desire of the hysteric. Its name is genuinely affirmative, therefore unutterable, like the name of God or of orgasmic delight.

All secrets are shared at the start. Hence the "crime" under consideration cannot be a solitary one, since it was turned into a secret. The "crime" points to an accomplice, the locus of undue enjoyment, as well as to others who are excluded and, by dint of this same enjoyment, eliminated. In the absence of a concept of infringement, the "crime" would entail no secret.

How can one rid oneself of a crime burdened with the weight of Reality? When the secret is too heavy to bear, accepting the exquisite defeat of unburdening might seem to be enough. The tension having become unbearable, you would simply go to the police and give yourself up. "To spill the beans and come clean," what a relief! the dream of all cryptophores. In point of fact, do they not go to see the analyst in order to give themselves up? Yet once they are there, they are forced to recognize that even this desperate relief is denied them. From the first attempt on, they cannot carry out their endeavor. How indeed could one put the unnameable into words? If cryptophores were to do so, they would die of it, thunderstruck; the whole world would be swallowed up in this cataclysm, the police and the analyst's couch included. If they were tempted to speak, it was surely not to destroy the universe, but the better to protect it, even at the risk of turning it into a prison. So, after some hesitation, cryptophores will make a different choice, the only one left to them: they will turn the policeman-analyst into an analyst-accomplice and will relive with him, between the words, that which has no place in words. It is understandable that, under these circumstances, Reality—a crime committed—will sooner or later appear during analysis. That will be the beginning of the end. In the meantime, the secret's covert presence weighs all the more heavily on the therapy. The crypt is there with its fine lock, but where is the key to open it?

The crypt marks a definite place in the topography. It is neither the dynamic unconscious nor the ego of introjections. Rather, it is an enclave between the two, a kind of artificial unconscious, lodged in the very midst of the ego. Such a tomb has the effect of sealing up the semipermeable walls of the dynamic unconscious. Nothing at all must filter to the outside world. The ego is given the task of a cemetery guard. It stands fast there, keeping an eye on the comings and goings of the members of its immediate family who—for various reasons—might claim access to the tomb. When the ego lets in some curious or injured parties, or detectives, it carefully provides them with false leads and fake graves. Those who have visiting privileges will be variously maneuvered and manipulated. They too will be kept constantly inside the ego. Clearly, the career of this guard of the tomb—who has to adapt to a varied crowd—is made of guile, ingenuity, and diplomacy. Its motto is: there is always someone smarter than you.

To use less metaphorical language we shall call the tomb and its lock *preservative repression,* setting it off from the *constitutive repression* that is particularly apparent in hysteria and generally called dynamic repression. The essential difference between the two types of repression is that in hysteria, the desire, born of prohibition, seeks a way out through detours and finds it through symbolic fulfillment; whereas for the cryptophore, an already fulfilled desire lies buried—equally incapable of rising or of disintegrating. Nothing can undo the consummation of the desire or efface its memory. This past is present in the subject as a *block of reality;* it is referred to as such in denials and disavowals. This reality cannot quite die, nor can it hope to revive. A parade of internal characters prevents it from doing so. In analysis we deal with them much more than with the subject. And it is a long-term endeavor—as we all know—to induce these internal characters to be kind, to permit the door of the tomb to open.

What if the "crime," the secret content we choose to call Reality, were nothing but fantasy? Or, at the very least, a case of faulty recognition after the fact of an innocent past? Many analysts maintain one or the other of these views to the great satisfaction or to the great displeasure of the parties involved. We shall not linger over the discussion of the fantasmic or realistic origins of the tomb and of its unnameable content.

In either case, the tomb's content is unique in that it cannot appear in the light of day as speech. And yet, it is precisely a matter of words. Without question, in the depths of the crypt unspeakable words buried alive are held fast, like owls in ceaseless vigil. The fact of reality consists in these words whose covert existence is certified by their manifest absence. What confers reality on them is that they are stripped of their customary communicative function. Why? Undoubtedly because, unlike the words of the hysteric—which point to desire by way of prohibition— these words have somehow acquired the value of positive existence. Thus they have become a *mortal danger for the underlying constitutive hysterical repression*. The tomb's function is to protect hysterical repression. In other words, the constitutive repression was threatened by what is buried. In what way?—you may ask. In such a way that the words of prohibition have lost their prohibitive effect. A disaster struck the words of the subject, causing them to be withdrawn from circulation. And this truly happened. The accomplishment of desire prior to its being buried is proven precisely by the fact that the words pointing to it acquired their sense of positive existence (which does not preclude the possibility that this mutation might have taken place subsequently) and were in consequence removed from daylight. The existence of the tomb is sufficient proof of a *real* event implicating the representatives of the prohibitive psychic agencies as accomplices in the fulfillment of a desire unduly completed to the point of orgasmic delight. Otherwise, the desire could be exposed (as in hysterical accusations). Our insistence that the event termed *real* is being viewed exclusively in the metapsychological sense cannot be overemphasized.

Returning to the paper that inspired us—and let us note in passing how impressed we were by its richness and scope—we think that the title "Psychoanalysis and Reality" requires as its complement the term *secret*. The objective and active existence of a secret can be posited as the very criterion of Reality when the latter is considered as *a metapsychological concept*. In light of the implication of infringement in its conceptual core, it will hardly be surprising to find that Reality—a result of denial—at least potentially implies a lawsuit, with its attendant cast of characters: defendant, judge, defense attorney, prosecutor, and the corpus delicti. These are, at any rate, the roles successively attributed to the analyst. S/he has to be able to reject them all—these are the technical implications of the concept of metapsychological Reality—in order for the true process to begin, a process which consists of *making Reality acceptable* to all parties involved, including the subject. This means eliminating the metapsychological weight of a Reality that owes its existence to its being repudiated. The trap for the analyst, burdened by the seduction theory or its contrary, is to move on the same legal ground as the cryptophore. The result is an unavoidable lawsuit that all parties will paradoxically and inevitably lose. The subject is convicted from the start along with his/her object of pleasure. Analysts will inevitably suffer conviction in turn, since they can only fail in the other roles given them: judge, prosecutor, lawyer, defendant, corpus delicti. Judicial error will ensue as well as the crypt's consolidation through acquittal.

What can be done? Deny the reality of the trauma by turning it into mere fantasy? Would this not in fact confer on it, by dint of its very negation, an additional and absolutely insurmountable status of reality? That would once more seal off all the avenues leading toward a resolution. Might it not be better deliberately to take up the cudgels against the legal and judicial apparatus the patients bring with them?

The "real"—so frequently invoked by patients as regards the coercive nature of the external world—will vanish in the same movement as the rejection of the judicial realm, itself a side effect of the "real." At this stage, only potential speculation about legislation itself, about its relativity and necessity, will survive. A defendant, judge, prosecutor, or defense attorney turned legislator?—is that in fact the way to eliminate the secret's Reality? Would this not mean going one better on the previously cited motto, turning it into: there is always someone much smarter than you?

It would seem that we need to overcome yet another obstacle. But the mere presentiment of this obstacle is dizzying. In the history of psychoanalysis the epistemological alternatives to eliminating the Reality of the "crime"—either branding it as fantasy or dispelling the judicial realm by proclaiming its relativity or arbitrariness—both seem to derive from the same vertigo. It is the vertigo created by the threat that the constitutive repression might be unexpectedly removed; in other words, it is vertigo at the possibility of madness. Both of these theoretical orientations, equally founded on the negation of metapsychological Reality, repudiate themselves in the end, fettering the spirit that psychoanalysis ought to foster. These are also attitudes that contribute to the birth of madness or to reinforcing the tomb's supporting walls.

On the other hand, this heavy architecture will gradually be shaken and will disappear in the course of the patient's prolonged presence on the couch, since it will appear bit by bit that, for lack of a lawsuit, the walls of denial have become obsolete. By means of the prohibition against not telling, the distinctive feature of the analytic situation, the unutterable will change its sign. It will turn into an actively and dynamically repressed desire *not to tell*, forging its paths, detours, and myriad ways of being symbolized. At that moment, and only then, will Reality become desire.

EIGHT

Self-to-Self Affliction: Notes of a Conversation on "Psychosomatics"

N. Abraham and M. Torok, 1973

W e have just seen the meaning of the initial phase of psychoanalysis for "endocryptic" patients. We noted that their regular return to the analytic couch had the same libidinal significance for them as the regularity of their physiological functions (such as breathing, bowel movements, menstruation, etc.). If they ever manage to acquire the power of expression, the various diseases befalling these functions will speak only to the subjects concerned, not to others. The illnesses are to be translated: "Just as I keep returning to you (my analyst), so I keep hoping to retrieve the encrypted experience" or "The lover will recover the beloved." Such a translation into words can bring relief in cases of *self-to-self affliction* (asthma, colitis, etc.). The hidden side of the vast majority of the so-called "psychosomatic" illnesses is actually the return— by way of pain, sickness, and physiological calamity—of "the dead who are in mourning." This is so because the melancholic fantasy—the fantasy of empathy with "the lost object who is bereft of me"—is taboo. The so-called psychosomatic subjects are incapable of producing the endocryptic melancholic fantasy of their object's mourning them; they also cannot fantasize (indirect though this activity may be) about the object's tears, laments, self-reproach, etc. For some reason, they also have to cut away the object's own melancholic fantasy, since admitting this fantasy even unconsciously would lead to the revival of the self-destructive narcissistic trauma of separation. On the other hand, it is safe to assume that psychosomatics have no particular reason to persecute their love objects after a paranoid fashion (= persecution of one's own melancholic crypt as "projected" onto the outside world). Hence "psychosomatics" are positioned

Previously published as "La maladie de soi-à-soi: Note de conversation sur la 'psychosomatique,' in *L'Écorce et le noyau* (Paris: Flammarion, 1987), pp. 318–21.

jected" onto the outside world). Hence "psychosomatics" are positioned half-way between "melancholia" and "paranoia." The potential for paranoia does persist in people who are not authorized to mourn in the name of their lost object; at times these psychosomatic patients have "bouts" of paranoia.

What happens when endocryptic subjects are denied the melancholic fantasy? When they have no way of indirectly evoking the contents of their crypt? The only resolution available to them is to *use their own body in a quasi-hysterical fashion, thereby avoiding the fantasy of endocryptic identification.* Such people may put themselves in somebody else's place to the point of developing an ulcer, for example. In this way no melancholic fantasy need manifest itself in the form of affects or words. Other kinds of fantasy are not necessarily absent in these patients, of course, only the melancholic one. The illnesses are a case of "internal conversion." The affliction that "occurs fatefully," like a disaster, is simply a self-to-self hysteria.

Yet who actually is sick? The dead. Of what? They are sick of it: they cannot "stomach" the trauma of their loss of the subject. The deceased person is incorporated by the subject in this way: "I carry in me someone who is dead and who cannot digest the fact of having lost me." (We might add that the loss was not caused by infidelity but by a trauma that befell the love object; this should certainly save the self-regard of many a person suffering from ulcers.)

Instead of the repressed melancholic fantasy of "the deceased who is grief-stricken at having lost his object of love," i.e., instead of the crypt's actual contents (or after opening the crypt: endocryptic identification), what we see is a process of *necroplasia.* For example: the capillaries retreat and no longer irrigate the stomach; the insufficient blood circulation results in ulceration. Vaso-constriction "manufactures" the "dead" inside (the ulcer). The dead person "weeps" a complaint through the disease: "I have nothing to eat" (= to love); "I get nothing but acid, bitterness, and causticity" (= nothing sweet). The person suffering from an ulcer (necrosis) is bearing a love-object who, unable to digest the loss of his beloved subject, must die. The person bearing the necrosis has had to swallow both the loss and the unspeakable circumstances that led to it. In short, necrosis seems to coincide with an unproduced fantasy of empathy concerning the subject who is now supposedly dead in the eyes of the object.

The reasons for the specific location of the necrosis need to be elucidated in each case.

A man suffering from ulcers has an accident in which he loses a finger, and is by the same token cured of his ulcers. The loss of his finger mimics the loss of his love-object, but now he (the subject) can mourn that loss since he carries the symbol of the loss *for the whole world to see*. This man need no longer be consumed by his (unspeakable) grief for his love object. Both the grief and the loss are now brought to completion. The sense of self-mutilation to which this man has been subjected (when he lost his finger) has modified the particulars of his problem. Now it is a matter of the self-mutilation, a sign of grief, of his lost object who had loved him. Through his involuntary mutilation the patient has been exorcised. The repression of the (forbidden) melancholic fantasy about the object's grief for him is no longer necessary. The loss has "taken place."

In all such cases the illness is a *self-to-self affliction*. It does not aim at any *expressive* communication with others, as occurs, for example, in hysteria.

When it is not a matter of hysterical conversion, "psychosomatic" illness appears to derive from an *internal conversion*. This type of conversion may be viewed as a particular instance of "peripherization" (see this heading in "A Glossary of Hermann's Theme Clusters").[1] The melancholic crypt is pushed to the periphery of the psychic apparatus: the body. The illness replaces the words of the deceased: "I grieve; I am sick with sorrow; I no longer eat." The controversy raging among psychosomaticians (some of whom assert that the illness takes the place of the person's entire fantasy life) and the Kleinians (who assert that the illness represents the vengeful mother, among other fantasies) becomes moot. Internal conversion—that is, *the self-to-self affliction—does not aim at the production of symptoms that might be visible on the outside or might indicate the need to exorcise a state of being; the illness functions as the subject's own internal substitute for the impossible endocryptic fantasy of empathy with the love object.* The true import of the symptoms resulting from such an internal conversion is often quite different from what we might suppose. The precipitation of uric acid in gout and other related ailments does not in fact aim at producing pain; instead, a number of conversional shifts have occurred in the person's physiology, so that the symptoms at hand are no more than the secondary consequences of these shifts and are in no way expressive of them.

Other cases of "psychosomatic" illness, for example asthma, may represent the work of the phantom in the unconscious as when a "stifling" and secret problem in the father's life reappears through the asthma of his son.

---

1. [A section in Abraham's "Introducing the 'Filial Instinct'"; it will appear in volume 2 of this work.—Ed.]

Part V

Secrets and Posterity:
The Theory of the
Transgenerational Phantom

Editor's Note Written and/or published in 1975, the essays in this section represent the final segment of Abraham and Torok's twenty years of collaboration. The concept of the transgenerational phantom, discovered and outlined for publication by Abraham in "Notes on the Phantom" (1975), is foreshadowed in much previous work, especially Torok's "The Meaning of 'Penis Envy' in Women" (1964), "The Illness of Mourning or the Fantasy of the Exquisite Corpse" (1968), and Abraham's "Introducing *The Filial Instinct*" (1972, to appear in volume 2 of this work). Abraham and Torok use the term "phantom" in a different though related context in the first paragraph of "'The Lost Object—Me'" (1973); at its time of publication in 1975, the authors added an explanatory footnote, indicating the subsequent development of the theory of the phantom. Abraham devoted a seminar to the phantom at the Paris Psychoanalytic Institute in 1974–75; the preliminary notes for nine sessions were published in 1978 as "The Seminar on Dual Unity and the Phantom" (to appear in volume 2 of this work). In the 1980s Torok extended Abraham's theory of the phantom beyond her initial contribution in the "Story of Fear" (1975), in order to outline the psychoanalysis of theoretical discourse in "Melanie Klein or Melanie Mell? The Vicissitudes of a Traumatic Name" (1982; to appear in volume 2 of this work) as well as in "What is Occult in Occultism? Between Sigmund Freud and Sergei Pankeiev—Wolf Man" (1983), reprinted as a postscript to the American edition of Abraham and Torok's *The Wolf Man's Magic Word* (1986). Rand and Torok introduced the first English-language publication of Abraham's "Notes on the Phantom" with an essay, "The Secret of Psychoanalysis: History Reads Theory," that sees the concept of the phantom as a way of analyzing the history of the psychoanalytic movement.[1]

The concept of the phantom moves the focus of psychoanalytic inquiry beyond the individual being analyzed because it postulates that some people unwittingly inherit the secret psychic substance of their ancestors' lives. The "phantom" represents a radical reorientation of Freudian and post-Freudian theories of psychopathology, since here symptoms do not spring from the individual's own life experiences but from someone else's psychic conflicts, traumas, or secrets. Psychoanalysis in general defines personal identity by including in it the constant interruptions produced by the unconscious. Following Freud, the continuance of self acquires a paradoxical and discontinuous "unity," to be characterized as a form of shifting coherence attained despite disruptions. Abraham's theory of the phantom enlarges upon Freud's metapsychology by suggesting that the unsettling disruptions in the psychic life of one person can adversely and unconsciously affect someone else. Abraham likens the foreign presence to ventriloquism and calls it a "phantom," a "haunting," or a "phantomatic haunting." The concept of the phantom redraws the boundaries of psychopathology and extends the realm of possibilities for its cure by suggesting the existence within an individual of a collective psychology comprised of several generations, so that the analyst must listen for the voices of one generation in the unconscious of another.

The terms "phantom," "ghosts," and "revenants," as used by Abraham and Torok, derive from folklore. Giving psychological substance to age-old beliefs, Abraham seeks to broaden the scope of knowledge by introducing elements of irrational or nonrational imagination into the realm of rational understand-

---

1. *Critical Inquiry* 13, no. 2 (Winter 1987): 278–86.

ing. Thus the psychoanalytic idea of the phantom concurs, on the level of description, with Roman, Old-Norse, Germanic, and other lore, according to which only certain categories of the dead return to torment the living: those who were denied the rite of burial or died an unnatural, abnormal death, were criminals or outcasts, or suffered injustice in their lifetime. In Abraham's view, the dead do not return, but their lives' unfinished business is unconsciously handed down to their descendants. The peoples of antiquity and the Christian Middle Ages performed complicated funeral rites to insure a peaceful passage into the afterworld and to prevent the return of the dead. The cult of ancestors remains a common form of religion or tradition in some parts of the world today. One could say metaphorically that Abraham calls for a psychoanalytic cult of ancestors and a psychoanalytic form of honoring the dead with rightful burial. But in the psychoanalytic realm, laying the dead to rest and cultivating our ancestors implies uncovering their shameful secrets, understanding their nameless and undisclosed suffering. We should engage in this unveiling and understanding of the former existence of the dead not because we may want to appease them or prevent them from perpetrating their nocturnal pranks, but because, unsuspected, the dead continue to lead a devastating psychic half-life in us.

An illustration of the theory of the phantom may be found in Abraham's "The Phantom of Hamlet or the Sixth Act" (written in 1975, published in 1978), a fictive sequel in decasyllabic verse to Shakespeare's tragedy. Here Abraham interprets Shakespeare's play by casting new light on the old problem of Hamlet's indecision when faced with the task of avenging his father's murder. This had previously been the subject of psychoanalytic commentary by Freud in *The Interpretation of Dreams* (1900) and Ernest Jones in *Hamlet and Oedipus* (1949). Both Freud and Jones attributed Hamlet's puzzling behavior to his unresolved Oedipus complex in relation to his dead father. Freud argued that Hamlet could not take revenge on his father's assassin because of his unconscious gratitude toward the person who accomplished the act he himself desired to perform. Using his theory of the phantom, Abraham suggests that the ghost, not Hamlet, is the primary object of interpretation. Hamlet is not tormented by conflicts or desires of his own making but by the consequences of a shameful secret his father took to the grave. Hamlet's indecision is the result of events which happened to someone else. In a more general sense, this conception offers a complement or alternative to interpretive methods relying on Freud's ideas of sexually motivated individual complexes or fantasies. Abraham's interpretation of *Hamlet* adds the possibility of relating people and fictional characters to the (concealed) lives of their forebears. The concept of the phantom brings the idea and importance of family history, in particular the secret history of families, to the forefront of psychoanalysis.[2]

While it is a distinct clinical and theoretical entity, the idea of the phantom is also a direct extension of Abraham and Torok's previous work on secrets and crypts (Part IV of this volume). The phantom represents the interpersonal and transgenerational consequences of silence. The concept of the crypt designates a secret psychic configuration arising from an individual's own life experiences; the idea of the phantom concerns itself with the unwitting reception of someone else's secret. Though manifest in one individual's psyche, the phantom eventually leads to the psychoanalysis *in absentia* of several generations (parents, grandparents, uncles, et al.) through the symptoms of a descendant.

The concept of the phantom may be contrasted with Freud's gradually evolving ideas about "archaic heritage," the inheritance of the actual primeval experiences of humankind. Often called by Freud "the phylogenetic derivation of the neuroses," "archaic heritage" is said to result from real ancestral occurrences—such as the observation of parental coitus, seduction, castration, parricide—that determine both the constitutional (as opposed to the individual) factor in the individual's disposition toward psychopathology and the uniform if not universal content of many neurotic fantasies and complexes. Clearly, for Freud as well as Abraham, the issue is the process of transmission which assures the survival of the memory traces derived from the experiences of earlier generations. However, Freud seeks to discover "mental antiquities," which, in the form

2. For a discussion of Abraham's work, see Nicholas Rand, "Family Romance or Family History? Psychoanalysis and Dramatic Invention in N. Abraham's *The Phantom of Hamlet*," *Diacritics* 18, no. 4 (Winter 1988): 20–30. Torok and I edited a posthumous volume of Abraham's early essays of literary analysis *Rythmes: De l'oeuvre, de la traduction et de la psychanalyse* (Paris: Flammarion, 1985). I translated one essay from that volume, as "Psychoanalytic Esthetics: Time, Rhythm, and the Unconscious" (1962) *Diacritics* 16, no. 3 (Fall 1986): 3–15, as well as the editors' "Postface." The entire volume is forthcoming in English at Stanford University Press.

of innate and invariable psychic matter, preserve the earliest periods of the beginnings of the human race in the individual of today. Abraham studies the unwitting transmission of secrets by one generation to another and sees the phantom as a function of the individual life experiences of the person who transmits it to his or her descendants. Such a transmission may occur at any given time in human history.

The idea of the phantom has implications beyond the study of individual psychology or even familial psychology. Aspects of this concept have the potential to illuminate the genesis of social institutions and may provide a new perspective for inquiring into the psychological roots of cultural patterns and political ideology. For example, a phantom can help account for the periodic return of political ideologies rendered shameful with the military defeat of their proponents. A case in point is the neo-Nazi movements of the 1980s and 1990s in Germany and elsewhere, which appeal, often inexplicably, to adolescents who obviously had no direct contact with wartime Nazi reality. The concept of the phantom gives one a basis for positing the unwitting transmission of shameful family history as the hidden motivating force that blindly drives some youths into movements modeled on the once openly glorified violence of their grandparents. Abraham and Torok's work enables us to understand how the falsification, ignorance, or disregard of the past—whether institutionalized by a totalitarian state (as in former East Germany) or practiced by parents and grandparents—is the breeding ground of the phantomatic return of shameful secrets on the level of individuals, families, the community, and possibly even entire nations.

NINE

Notes on the Phantom:
A Complement to
Freud's Metapsychology

N. Abraham, 1975

The belief that the spirits of the dead can return to haunt the living exists either as an accepted tenet or as a marginal conviction in all civilizations, ancient or modern. More often than not, the dead do not return to rejoin the living but rather to lead them into some dreadful snare, entrapping them with disastrous consequences. To be sure, all the departed may return, but some are destined to haunt: the dead who were shamed during their lifetime or those who took unspeakable secrets to the grave. From the brucolacs, the errant spirits of outcasts in ancient Greece, to the ghost of Hamlet's vengeful father, and on down to the rapping spirits of modern times, the theme of the dead—who, having suffered repression by their family or society, cannot enjoy, even in death, a state of authenticity—appears to be omnipresent (whether overtly expressed or disguised) on the fringes of religions and, failing that, in rational systems. It is a fact that the "phantom," whatever its form, is nothing but an invention of the living. Yes, an invention in the sense that the phantom is meant to objectify, even if under the guise of individual or collective hallucinations, the gap produced in us by the concealment of some part of a love object's life. The phantom is therefore also a metapsychological fact: what haunts are not the dead, but the gaps left within us by the secrets of others.

Since the phantom is not related to the loss of an object of love, it cannot be considered the effect of unsuccessful mourning, as would be the

Previously published as "Notules sur le fantôme," *Études freudiennes* 9–10 (1975): 109–15; and in *L'Écorce et le noyau* (Paris: Flammarion, 1987), pp. 426–33; and as "Notes on the Phantom: A Complement to Freud's Metapsychology," trans. N. Rand, *Critical Inquiry* 13, no. 2 (1987): 287–92; and in Françoise Meltzer (ed.), *The Trials of Psychoanalysis* (Chicago: University of Chicago Press, 1987), pp. 75–80. (The subtitle has been added by Nicholas Rand for the purposes of this translation.)

case with melancholics or with all those who carry a tomb in themselves. It is the children's or descendants' lot to objectify these buried tombs through diverse species of ghosts. What comes back to haunt are the tombs of others. The phantoms of folklore merely objectify a metaphor active in the unconscious: the burial of an unspeakable fact *within the love-object.*

Here we are in the realm of clinical psychoanalysis and still shrouded in obscurity, an obscurity, however, that the nocturnal being of phantoms (if only in the metapsychological sense) can, paradoxically, be called upon to clarify.

A resourceful and enthusiastic young scientist is filled with energy for his work, the comparative study of the morphology and microchemistry of human spermatozoa. During his lengthy analysis with a woman, he found a new hobby for his spare time, studying the genealogy of the high- and middle-rank nobility in Europe and its armorial variations. Given the identity of illegitimate children, he can on request trace anyone's origins to prestigious forebears. When I saw him after a break in his long years of analysis, he immediately insulted me in a fit of persecution: I was of low birth; I despised aristocrats and the nobility. Devoid of religious sentiment, I was a liberal conspiring against everything on which the nobility prides itself. I was indifferent to my origins; neither did I care that his be known and publicized. Instead, I was doing everything I could to destroy him since he laid claim to a world other than my own. A moment's hesitation. Then, he apologized for his excessive language. He did not really mean what he had just said so vehemently. His own father is a free-thinker. He hates genealogical inquiries. A man is worth what he is on his own. Why delve into the past? This, however, did not stop his father from marrying an aristocrat. And his grandfather? "Well, he died long before World War I when my father was still quite small. Grandmother always stayed with us. She had many children after my father, who was the eldest." The eldest of how many children? "I don't even know. There must have been a good dozen. They were mostly boys; all of them became important people. Do I know them? No, I never met them"; (confused) "oh, you know, it was all on account of my father's beliefs. . . . The family on his side deserted us. I am also the eldest and my name is the same as my father's middle name. In fact, it is also one of the Christian names of an uncle who must be the youngest of the boys. My first analysis? It was a wonderful analysis, very successful, except for the end. From time to time I would speak about myself with another very well known analyst, a man. He made a crucial remark that I immediately reported to my analyst. After that everything went along beautifully, except for the one thing which made me seem worthless and ridiculous to everybody: *my analyst refused to admit that I was the child she had had with her prestigious colleague.* Then I became very anxious and left her. My parents? They are very fond of each other, they never fight. They help each other. My father is very busy in his plant. He puts herbal teas into airtight packages bearing the names of various eighteenth-century courtesans. He has won medals at various exhibitions."

Who could have failed to grasp in this speech what our subject does not know and must be covered with the veil of modesty: the fact that his father is a bastard who bears his mother's maiden name. An insignificant fact in itself, had it not led to a secret pain in the father and to his constructing an entire family romance about his aristocratic origins along with some efficiently repressed ill feelings toward his "whore" mother. The father's unconscious is focused on one thought: if my mother had not concealed the name of the illustrious lover whose son I am, I would not have to hide the degrading fact that I am an illegitimate child. How could this thought, alive in the father's unconscious, become transferred into the unconscious of his eldest son, everybody's favorite, and remain so active there as to provoke fits? Yes, viewed from any and every angle, the patient appears possessed not by his own unconscious but by someone else's. The father's family romance was a repressed fantasy: the initially restrained and finally delirious preoccupation of the patient seems to be the effect of being haunted by a phantom, itself due to the tomb enclosed within his father's psyche. The patient's delirium embodies this phantom and stages the verbal stirrings of a secret buried alive in the father's unconscious.

This is one case among several dozen others I have come to know. Can I begin to theorize? I am jotting down ideas as they come. The grand synthesis, if it is called for, will have to wait. . . . Perhaps I can say this much in the meantime. The phantom is a formation of the unconscious that has never been conscious—for good reason. It passes—in a way yet to be determined—from the parent's unconscious into the child's. Clearly, the phantom has a function different from dynamic repression. The phantom's periodic and compulsive return lies beyond the scope of symptom-formation in the sense of a return of the repressed; it works like a ventriloquist, like a stranger within the subject's own mental topography. The imaginings issuing from the presence of a stranger have nothing to do with fantasy strictly speaking. They neither preserve a topographical status quo nor announce a shift in it. Instead, by their gratuitousness in relation to the subject, they create the impression of surrealistic flights of fancy or of *oulipo*-like verbal feats.[1]

1. [OuLiPo (Ouvroir de Littérature Potentielle = Workshop for Potential Literature) is a research group of experimental writing founded in 1960 by Raymond Queneau and François de Lionnais. The aim of the group is to invent "artificial" formal constraints (not

174 / Secrets and Posterity

Thus, the phantom cannot even be recognized by the subject as evident in an "aha" experience and, during analysis, can only give rise to constructions with all their attendant uncertainties. The phantom may nevertheless be deconstructed by analytic construction, though this occurs without the patients' having the impression that they were in fact the subject of the analysis. It is clear that, in contrast to other types of cases, this work requires a genuine partnership between patient and analyst, the more so since the construction arrived at in this way bears no direct relation to the patient's own topography but concerns someone else's. The special difficulty of these analyses lies in the patient's horror at violating a parent's or a family's guarded secret, even though the secret's text and content are inscribed within the patient's own unconscious. The horror of transgression, in the strict sense of the term, is compounded by the risk of undermining the fictitious yet necessary integrity of the parental figure in question.

Let me offer, among others, one idea to explain the birth of a phantom. The phantom counteracts libidinal introjection; that is, it obstructs our perception of words as implicitly referring to their unconscious portion. In point of fact, the words used by the phantom to carry out its return (and which the child sensed in the parent) do not refer to a source of speech in the parent. Instead, they point to a gap, they refer to the unspeakable. In the parent's topography, these words play the crucial role of having to some extent stripped speech of its libidinal grounding. The phantom is summoned therefore, at the opportune moment, when it is recognized that a gap was transmitted to the subject with the result of barring him or her from the specific introjections he or she would seek at present. The presence of the phantom indicates the effects, on the descendants, of something that had inflicted narcissistic injury or even catastrophe on the parents.

The difference between *the stranger incorporated* through suggestion and *the dead returning to haunt* does not necessarily come to the fore at first, precisely because both act as foreign bodies lodged within the subject. In classical analysis, an attempt is made to uncover the roots in a parental wish. While incorporation, which behaves like a post-hypnotic suggestion, may recede before appropriate forms of classical analysis, the phantom remains beyond the reach of the tools of classical analysis. The phantom will vanish only when its radically heterogeneous nature with respect to the subject is recognized, a subject to whom it at no time has

---

unlike the traditional sonnet form or acrostics, for example) and to demonstrate that by applying them systematically, the potential scope of linguistic creation can be expanded. As in Queneau's *Cent mille milliards de poèmes*, semantic coherence is virtually never pursued.—Ed.]

any direct reference. In no way can the subject relate to the phantom as his or her own repressed experience, not even as an experience by incorporation. *The phantom which returns to haunt bears witness to the existence of the dead buried within the other.*

A surprising fact gradually emerges: the work of the phantom coincides in every respect with Freud's description of the death instinct. First of all, it has no energy of its own; it cannot be "abreacted," merely designated. Second, it pursues its work of disarray in silence. Let us note that the phantom is sustained by secreted words, invisible gnomes whose aim is to wreak havoc, from within the unconscious, in the coherence of logical progression. Finally, it gives rise to endless repetition and, more often than not, eludes rationalization.

At best, phantom words of this kind can be invested with libido and determine the choice of hobbies, leisure activities, or professional pursuits. One carrier of a phantom became a nature lover on weekends, acting out the fate of his mother's beloved. The loved one had been denounced by the grandmother (an unspeakable and secret fact) and, having been sent to "break rocks" [*casser les cailloux* = do forced labor—*Trans.*], he later died in the gas chamber. What does our man do on weekends? A lover of geology, he "breaks rocks," catches butterflies, and proceeds to kill them in a can of cyanide.

Cases like this rarely provide sufficient material to "construct" the phantom purely on the basis of information gleaned from the patient. At times, the patient's surroundings quite accidently reveal the nature of the missing pieces. Once we listen for the possibility of detecting a phantom, after having eliminated other explanations, it is usually possible to formulate some likely, if general, hypothesis. To take the example above, even without knowledge of the antecedents, one ends up noticing that the subject is possessed by a question of "forced labor." And though the story is entirely foreign to the subject himself, it does influence his habits and actions while, at the same time, running counter to his own desires. Often enough, patients need only feel that the analytic construction does not endanger their own topography; they need only sense, apart from any form of transference, an alliance with the analyst in order to eject a *bizarre foreign body*—and not the content of repression Freud called a *familiar stranger*. In this way, "the phantom effect" (in the form of acting out as well as other specific symptoms) will gradually fade. When the analyst offers a comment like *"Somebody* is breaking rocks," the patient no doubt notices the analyst's frame of mind and sees that the latter refrains from implicating the subject. The analyst implicitly signals the emergence of the stranger and thereby masters it.

Only in such cases can one reject the analytic stance that is typically, albeit here incongruously, bent on tracing the information received to instincts or to the Oedipus complex. This would result in the patients' displaced acceptance of the phantom as part of their own libidinal life which could, in turn, lead to bizarre and even delirious acts.

In general, "phantomogenic" words become travesties and can be acted out or expressed in phobias of all kinds (such as impulse phobia), obsessions, restricted phantasmagorias or ones that take over the entire field of the subject's mental activities. In all cases, these words undo the system of relationships that, in an oedipal fashion, the libido is trying in vain to establish. The oedipal conflict is rather more acute in these cases than in others and can lead to the complacent use of the phantom as a guard against the Oedipus complex. This occurs sometimes at the close of the treatment when the phantom has already been successfully exorcised.

It is crucial to emphasize that the words giving sustenance to the phantom return to haunt from the unconscious. These are often the very words that rule an entire family's history and function as the tokens of its pitiable articulations.

Extending the idea of the phantom, it is reasonable to maintain that the "phantom effect" progressively fades during its transmission from one generation to the next and that, finally, it disappears. Yet, this is not at all the case when shared or complementary phantoms find a way of being established as social practices along the lines of *staged words* (as in the examples above). We must not lose sight of the fact that to stage a word— whether metaphorically, as an alloseme, or as a cryptonym—constitutes an attempt at exorcism, an attempt, that is, to relieve the unconscious by placing the effects of the phantom in the social realm.

TEN

Story of Fear: The Symptoms of Phobia—the Return of the Repressed or the Return of the Phantom?

M. Torok, 1975

They say that children are phobic by nature. Freud attributes this to the child's oedipal nature. The paradoxes of infantile libidinal desire force the child to seek repression. Yet ill-controlled repression fails to quell anxiety. In cases where the unabandoned libidinal desire returned victorious, the most dangerous of situations would materialize in its wake: namely castration, that is, the destruction of the very desire seeking victory. Hence, according to Freud, a solid fear (no matter how unreasoned, yet nameable, circumscribed, in addition to being easily managed in society, and regardless of whether the phobia is temporary or more permanent) seems to be a safety valve against the threat of pervasive anxiety. Certainly, the symptom has disadvantages unforeseen by its bearer; however, reason suggests that the advantages must outweigh the disadvantages.

We are in 1908. Phobia defends the ego against the indistinct threat of the return of the repressed. The threat itself appears to emerge along the oedipal path. Working through the Oedipus complex and castration, by means of affective transference, bringing to light the words of the desire as well as the prohibition, thereby freeing them both of anxiety—this is the alleged task of analysis. Psychoanalysis claims to effect the progressive enrichment of the ego by giving it access to its own repressed libidinal stock. Little Hans was supposed to have been rid of his uncomfortable symptom by an analysis of this type, which also seems to have

Previously published as "Histoire de peur, le symptôme phobique: Retour de refoulé ou retour du fantôme," *Études freudiennes* 9–10 (1975): 229–38; and in *L'Écorce et le noyau* (Paris: Flammarion, 1987), pp. 434–46.

permitted him to recover his charming optimism, a much appreciated character trait.

It is hard to deny that whenever analysts encounter any form of phobic suffering—be it the fear of streets, depths, rats, wolves, moths . . . —this is the conception they tend to use. What is the desire being repressed? Who hides behind the image of the wolf? the horse? And yes, who is doing the castrating? If successful, analysts will say, "This was a case of superficial phobia"; when less successful, "This one differs from other phobias; it is not the genital kind, rather pregenital, born of deep-seated, non-neurotic anxiety."

A nontraditional phobia of this sort came Freud's way as well some time after he finished writing the case history of little Hans. Everybody knows the mysterious old man who signs his paintings and memoirs as the Wolf Man, this famous patient of Freud's who at the age of five had the unusual phobia of seeing in an open book a picture of a wolf standing on its hind legs. For Freud the standing wolf, like Little Hans's horse, had to coincide with a displaced image of the castrating father. As soon as the unconscious was willing to provide the image of the father, rising up against the boy's oedipal desire, Sergei was supposed to have been in good enough condition to return to his native steppes. But we know that this did not happen. The dynamics of Wolf Man's phobia, as well as the meaning of his nightmare about wolves, did not fit the simple scheme of the fear of oedipal castration.

Freud realized this quickly and attempted to adapt his theory to a resistant case. He outlined a novel situation of anxiety, the primal scene and the vicissitudes of the wish to be penetrated by the father. In this so-called "passive" or "feminine" position, the boy might have an altogether unique fear, the fear of losing his penis during his intercourse with his father. The new point of view certainly seemed better suited to the case. Yet the Wolf Man's subsequent relapses showed clearly that he never really gave Freud the key to the illness that had started with his phobia.

Why was little Hans cured? Why not Sergei? Freud returned to this question periodically during his entire career, testing a variety of answers. Several of his works contain suggestions: *Inhibitions, Symptoms, and Anxiety*, "On Fetishism," even *An Outline of Psychoanalysis*, as well as Freud's final reflections on "The Splitting of the Ego in the Process of Defence." There are at least three references to the path Freud had glimpsed but failed to follow in deepening his theory of phobia. First there is the reference, in metapsychological terms, to the fact that a form of communication exists between the unconsciouses of two persons.

It is a very remarkable thing that the *Unconscious* of one human being can react upon that of another, without passing through the *Conscious*. This deserves closer examination, especially with a view to finding out whether preconscious activity can be excluded as playing a part in it; but, descriptively speaking, the fact is incontestable.[1]

Clearly, Freud is not talking here about mystical phenomena having to do with telepathy, but most likely about the beginnings of a form of conscious communication that nevertheless makes its way through the unconscious only, without managing to return into the realm of consciousness. This occurs most probably when the messages require repression either because they are of an unspeakable nature or for other reasons. The second reference, contained in *Inhibitions, Symptoms, and Anxiety,* describes phobic symptoms as anxiety signals, in short as a form of language, a manner of speaking the presence of danger. The phobic symptom's stated object does not coincide with the genuine object of the primary fear to which the displaced symptom actually refers. Hence it would have been possible to conclude that phobic symptoms neither match the compromise symptoms of hysteria, nor resolve any type of economical problem.

Finally, there is a passage in Lou Andreas Salome's *The Freud Journal:*

> The day after the congress, September 9 [1913], with Freud in the Hofgarten. The long conversation (in confidence) on these rare instances of thought transference which certainly torment him. This is a point which he hopes need never again be touched in his lifetime; I hope the contrary. In a recent case the situation goes like this: . . . the mother had indeed abreacted that which had retained its intensity in the daughter, quite as though it were her own, far beyond her own experience.[2]

The date, 1913, is important. Freud had been conducting the Wolf Man's analysis for the past three years. It is certainly surprising to see that, rather than the strange Russian, a woman patient should lead Freud to the unexplored idea of a person showing signs of the most intense emotion during a psychoanalytic session and yet being entirely absent as far as her own person is concerned. This means that when people say "I," they might in fact be referring to something quite different from their own identity as recorded in their identification papers. Further, they might not even be referring to another person with whom they identify. It means that some people are completely detached from their own libidinal roots and only produce puppet emotions. Instead of the girl, says Lou Andreas

1. Freud, "The Unconscious," *S.E.* 14: 194.

2. Lou Andreas Salome, *The Freud Journal,* trans. Stanley A. Leavy (London: Quartet Books, 1987), pp. 169–70.

Salome, it is the mother who "abreacts." I would say that in the patient's place, a *phantom,* to use Nicolas Abraham's recently introduced term, is acting, a phantom is speaking.[3] Before we can hope to gain access to the patient's own conflicts, the phantom must vanish and, while waiting for that to happen, we need to replace the traditional question—what kind of repression is returning in the guise of the symptom?—with another: what is the nature of the phantom returning to haunt? How can the phantom be weakened so as to make it restore the unhappy subject's own speech—whether or not it ultimately refers to repression—that had been victimized by the haunting?

Was there an internal obstacle within Freud that might have kept him from advancing on the path he clearly glimpsed? The question is quite complex and I, for my part, am hardly competent to broach it.

Leaving aside Freud as a person, let me recall in this connection the harmful effects of one of the most tenacious psychoanalytic prejudices, one that survived even Freud's own above-mentioned observation in 1913: the prejudice of the "I." It consists in hearing the first person singular whenever somebody says "I." Yet, when faced in particular with phobia, we are hard put to find the identity of this "I" who is claiming to be fearful. Can we take for granted that, at the tender age when these symptoms usually appear for the first time, the "I" really means the legal identity of the subject? "I am afraid of . . ." might be better rendered as: "There is a fear of. . . ." This also has the advantage of moving the emphasis from the actual fear to its verbal and pantomimed expression.[4]

If we now set aside the prejudice concerning the "I," what of the phobic symptom itself? More often than not, even advanced forms of rationalization will not allow us to discover in the fearsome thing even the smallest trace of what really inspires the fear. Why shriek in fear when somebody wants to show you a picture you could just as easily shut your eyes to? A symbolic allusion to another object of fear must be involved, an object that is the more unknown for not being derived from the child's own desires or drives but from another place: the father's or the mother's unconscious, in which are inscribed the parents' unspoken fears, their apprehensions, the reasons for their enslavement, their hidden faults. Inscribed there is also the fact that parents are not at all the gods of coherence and consistency, courage, and power that their young offspring would wish. I could say more simply that phobic children communicate a *story*

---

3. Cf. Abraham's "Notes on the Phantom" [in this volume].

4. Fits of phobia often occur with a slight delay in relation to normal reactions. This is clearly the sign of a secondary type of expressivity.

of fear in their symptoms: either a fear whose actual victims are their parents or, alternatively, a fear that the parents themselves had inherited and now transmit willy-nilly to their own reluctant offspring.

In 1967 I presented some thoughts on a rather widespread "story" of fear in our culture to a group of colleagues: the "fear of wolves." Why the wolf? Why is this animal chosen to provoke the idea of fear in children? What inspires us to invent stories about wolves for them? I concluded that this type of phobia often referred to a grandparent through the mother's own unconscious fear of her mother. She fears that her mother might castrate her in the sense that she would prevent her from becoming a mother in turn. This unconscious fear, as frequent as the childish fear of wolves, suggests that the "wolf" is chosen precisely for its implicit reference to the grandmother. Are not wolves the only mammals apart from grandmothers, of course, that can assume the task of raising children? At that time, the link I proposed, joining phobia to grandparents, was mere intuition. Since then, Abraham's recently elaborated *theory of the phantom* has shed new light on the problem of phobia as well as many others.

In general terms, the "phantom" is a formation in the dynamic unconscious that is found there not because of the subject's own repression but on account *of a direct empathy with the unconscious or the rejected psychic matter of a parental object.* Consequently, the phantom is not at all the product of the subject's self-creation by means of the interplay between repressions and introjections. The phantom is alien to the subject who harbors it. Moreover, the diverse manifestations of the phantom, which we call *haunting,* are not directly related to instinctual life and are not to be confused with the return of the repressed. On the contrary, the phantom would much more likely take the form of an impediment to the subject's instinctual life (and this is in fact the easiest way there is to detect phantoms), an impediment cloaked in the very prohibition that, under normal circumstances, regulates and gives concrete shape to instinctual promptings.

The alien nature of the phantom resembles the indirect characteristics of phobia. For, although the phobic subjects actually speak and behave with the help of their own psychic apparatus, their phobias come from elsewhere. Phobia's *stated intention of speaking* amounts to no more than the impenetrable opacity of its genuine speech. However, the opacity does yield when specific phantoms are invoked; hence the concept of the phantom appears to be a key in understanding phobias.

Phobia-inducing phantoms haunt in order to move the haunted persons to expose a concealed and unspoken parental fear. This type of phantom produces a sleeplike state during the visitation and replays the fearful scene according to the laws of dream-work (staged visualization, distortion, etc.). The waking dream imitates the very fact and effect of the parental repressions or else it stages the parents' concealment of something. It should be added, however, that phobic haunting also exhibits a measure of loyalty toward the parents, since it confines the genuine object of fear to the child's unconscious.

I would now like to test the concept of the phobic phantom on the classic case of little Hans. We know that he developed a very serious phobia of "horses" under circumstances minutely described by Freud with the help of the child's father. It was a phobia that disappeared after a single interview with Freud, a conversation in which, as is well known, Freud explained his oedipal interpretation to the child: the "horse" represents the father, as displaced onto an animal, and the phobia itself represents an intense fear of castration as related to the child's desire for his mother. Granted, but even as we understand this, questions arise.

First, what justifies the choice of a "horse" rather than a "knife," a "locomotive," or a "vicious dog"? Is this choice mere chance? Another question: if the hypothesis of castration has any foundation at all, why does little Hans not show the least fear of his parents or later of Freud himself? Would simple displacement have been enough to protect him from such a fear? That would be miraculous indeed. How are we to understand the obviously dynamic effect, temporarily soothing for his phobia as well, of his learning about the sexual life of adults, in particular his discovery that his mother had no "weenie"? One would expect this revelation to have intensified his castration anxieties. My provisional answer to all these questions will be that the form of the cure does not necessarily contain the reason behind the symptoms' formation. A person cured with an oedipal interpretation need not have been sick with the Oedipus complex.

The situation in which little Hans was raised, especially as regards the close ties between his parents and Freud, both before and during his phobia, would suggest that one of the difficulties Hans encountered was precisely the fact that he was denied the oedipal conflict and therefore also escaped the pretty blueprint, decked out with the fear of castration, that Freud eventually suggested to him with the well-known therapeutic success. I have every reason to believe that the odedipal conflict was simply *imported from the outside* through Freud's interpretation rather than resolved in the young subject. On the other hand, we will see shortly that the artificial introduction of the oedipal conflict inadvertently helped to drive out a troublesome "phantom."

This is apparent in several elements. The absent yet omnipresent person in Hans's life was none other than Freud himself. Two facts provide sufficient corroboration: (1) prior to her marriage, Hans's mother had been in analysis with Freud; (2) ever since he was two years old, little Hans's actions were reported by his father to Freud at the latter's behest. Far from being fully autonomous in their union, the parents appear to have been polarized by Freud and were consequently ill suited to respond to their child's need of oedipal self-elaboration. The child had no choice but to thrash about between the two poles assigned to him: to be an object of pleasure as well as an object of fear in relation to an absent third party, as mediated by both his father and mother respectively. Hans was an object of pleasure in his father's relationship to Freud, and an object of fear in his mother's relationship, most likely, to her own mother, a relationship that was probably transferred onto her former analyst, who must have functioned as a substitute for her mother fixation. The precise moment of the outbreak of little Hans's phobia bears witness to this maternal aspect of the situation. It appears at just the moment Freud enters the scene. The event is well known: Hans's "weenie" provides the occasion. Washing him, his mother refused to "put her finger" on it, calling the gesture requested by the child "dirty."

The child is anything but deaf. He seems to be hearing a phantomatic voice repeating an earlier order, which had been given to his mother, not to put her "finger" in an unseemly place. Strangely enough, it must be noted, the voice does not say "hand" but "finger." The child is unable to formulate this—anyhow, would he dare?—but it is not at all a matter of his "weenie" but her genitals, his mother's, the other person in the dialogue who is forbidden to touch herself down there. Did the Professor forbid her to do so? At this point, the mother is simply a frustrated and contrite little girl, obeying a very strict adult. A mother can of course state her disapproval of masturbation rather harmlessly, but then she herself cannot appear to be a passive victim. By merely stating her disapproval, she lends herself to becoming invested as an ego ideal by the child. However, if along with their prohibition, parents also convey their own fear of the genitals to their children, they will clearly have missed their vocation of being both an ego ideal to be matched and an obstacle to be overcome. Hans's mother seems unable to adopt these roles because she rehearses on her son the prohibition to which she herself had been subjected previously.

The child's response is instantaneous. He stages a story of fear for his castrated mother, the very fear that makes her tremble before another person Hans does not yet know, a phantom.

Why is this phantom called a "horse" (*Pferd*), you may wonder? And why does this "horse" have something black around its mouth (*Mund*)? After what I have said so far, I feel compelled to conclude that the child is saying in effect: "We need to fear Freud (*Pferd*). There is something obscure about Sigmund (*Mund*). He retains mama's pleasure (*Freude*)."[5] You have to go see Freud in order to retrieve mama's pleasure. Sure enough, little Hans, who so loudly stages mother's fear of Freud (Freud: *Pferd*), is not afraid really of him at all and, when the time comes, will speak to him as to an equal. Dramatizing his parents' fears does not mean that the little boy also needs to fear Freud. Rather the contrary.

Our hero may be disappointed in a mother whose sexuality is not her own; he is equally disappointed in his father, whose mouth is full of the Professor's words, especially when speaking about the "weenie." Hans's masturbatory pleasures (*Freude*) are constantly being interpreted in the Professor's name as the cause of the child's phobia. The more reason for the little patient to intensify his phobic symptoms, thereby exposing both of his parents' enslavement.

Everything little Hans ever says is recorded stenographically and communicated by his father to the Professor with a foreordained name, since he wields father's pleasure (*Freude*) as well. Most certainly it is the Professor who forbids daddy to be "dirty," which of course in no way prevents Hans from devoting himself to masturbation all the more and even admitting to it for the benefit of this invasive though absent person who is supposed to prohibit everyone from doing it. By his admission, the child defies his parents. You may be afraid of the Professor, but I certainly am not. Of course, the Professor does not mean the same thing for the two parents. For the mother he is an object of fixation, somebody who prohibits, whereas for the father he is primarily an object of desire, an ideal object. Daddy is not afraid of touching Hans's "weenie" to help him do his job. Daddy gives Hans the type of satisfaction he himself would like to receive from the Professor for reporting on Hans. At any rate, both of Hans's parents behave with their shared phantom like very reasonable children, fearing that if they disobey him, he will have a fit (*krawall-machen*) like the "horse" in the phobia. In a variation on his symptom, Hans shows his parents that it would behoove them "to throw a fit" for Freud in order to free themselves from his influence.

Little Hans has really nothing to fear from Freud. For quite some time now, he has been "playing Freud" with his friends (*Freunde*), both real and imaginary. And when at long last he finds himself in Freud's office, face to face with the person who up to then had been his "phantom," he is far from afraid of him and quite unimpressed by his glory; he speaks to Freud as to an old acquaintance, as to a person whom he had

---

5. Cf. Barbro Sylwan, "C'est pour mieux t'écouter mon enfant," *Études freudiennes* 7–8 (1975): 121–32.

for a long while imagined meeting through his parents; Freud is a person he can talk to as to his equal while he can see his father as being the Professor's son.

Yet surprisingly, the little "grandfather" Hans seems to think he is in relation to this father is quickly put back in his place as the child of his adult parents. The Professor quite unexpectedly shows him his Oedipus complex of a little boy and his fear of being castrated by his father. The "horse" is simply his father and the little boy's fear is nothing more than his fear of having to confront his father if he, the child, attempted to get close to Mother. *Si non e vero, e ben trovato.* . . . The child-father has now been reestablished in his dignity and God Freud vanishes into the thin air of his own theories. No further need of the Professor since from now on father exercises his full moral authority. . . . Freud's happy maneuver struck two birds with one stone. Readers of the case history will note that after the visit, the father rather miraculously acquires a measure of autonomy that allows him to behave as a more effective analyst of his son.

The case history does not say what effect this shift had on the mother, but all indications are that it could only have been beneficial. For little Hans, the phantom has vanished and he now has his parents for his very own and with them he can accomplish the introjective play of desires and prohibitions.

The happy end of little Hans's case contrasts with the relative lack of success in the Wolf Man's case. Granted, administering the Oedipus complex had some passing beneficial effect on him as well. But I will venture to say, it was not a genuinely psychoanalytic effect. Why not? The reason may be found, if we follow Nicolas Abraham's hypothesis, in the fundamental difference between the two stories of fear and their respective stagings.[6] Hans played out, for the benefit of his parents, their own fear of being castrated by Freud. In his phobia the Wolf Man staged his parents' fear that an undue libidinal act might be discovered if the child revealed it. "Fantomizing" that which we know with the obligatory provision of lack of knowledge (nescience) can also lead to phobic manifestations. In this, the Wolf Man's case, the Oedipus complex and castration were clearly limited in their helpfulness. The fear transmitted to the Wolf Man by his mother does not even concern her own psychic apparatus, but his father's, who objectified his own crypt in a *real event*. This event had little if anything to do with the son's Oedipus complex as it seems to stem from the father's melancholic mental condition. Here the oedipal interpretation can only function as a prosthetic substitute and will not resolve the genuine conflict.

6. Cf. *The Wolf Man's Magic Word* (Minneapolis: University of Minnesota Press, 1986), ch. 3.

The fact that, more than half a century after Freud's account of these two cases, I should have arrived at views somewhat different from his (and accounting for a greater number of facts) shows that psychoanalysis is neither dogmatic nor the art of mindless application. This fact proves that, by making use of its rigorous methods, psychoanalysis can progress on the path of theory as well as practice, as a living and constantly renewable science.

ELEVEN

The Phantom of Hamlet
or The Sixth Act
preceded by
The Intermission of "Truth"

N. Abraham, 1975

The Intermission of "Truth"

. . . if thou hast uphoarded in thy life
Extorted treasure in the womb of earth,
For which, they say, you spirits oft walk in death,
Speak of it.

Hamlet I.1.136–9

. . . *aurais-tu, vif, enfoui*
Quelque indû trésor au terrestre ventre
—Raison que, morts, les esprits se promènent—
Parles-en!

Hamlet I.1.136–9

The final scene of the *Tragedy of Hamlet* does not close the dramatic action, it simply cuts it off. Sophocles' *Oedipus the King* "purified" the soul, as Freud has shown, by directly uncovering the unconscious. Not so Shakespeare's play. Quite the reverse. The action, laced with visions and intrigues, simulation and madness, grinds to a halt stripped of protagonists. As the curtain falls, only corpses and riddles are left, silent like the night of Elsinore. Having lost all hope of seeing the mystery unraveled, the spectator remains bewildered.

This play, staged more often than any other, initiates an unconscious process, keeps it alive, yet fails to put it to rest. The state of mind that is

Previously published as "Le fantôme d'Hamlet ou le VIᵉ Acte, précédé par l'Entre'Acte de la 'Vérité,'" in *L'Écorce et le noyau* (Paris: Flammarion, 1987), pp. 447–68; and as "The Phantom of Hamlet or the Sixth Act, Preceded by the Intermission of Truth," trans. N. Rand, *Diacritics* 18, no. 4 (1988): 2–19.

provokẹd endures long after the play has ended; it forces itself upon us like an inescapable necessity emanating from some unknown source. Psychoanalysts experience similar kinds of uneasiness, occasioned in particular by those visitors to the analytic couch who, unbeknown to themselves, carry the concealed shame of their families. These people are prey to strange and incongruous words or acts, transferred from events unknown to them, events whose initiator was *an other*.

The great majority of the tragedy's characters do in fact appear driven by some stranger within them. Hamlet, his mother, Claudius, and Ophelia all end up victims of an evil spell, puppets of a phantom. Thus, it occurs to me that entire libraries of enigmas in literature would yield up their key, were we but to reconsider the "supernatural element" responsible for them: to be precise, the appearance of a Specter.

". . . if thou hast uphoarded in thy life/Extorted treasure in the womb of earth/For which, they say, you spirits oft walk in death—/Speak of it. . . ." Yes, the shameful and therefore concealed secret always does return to haunt. To exorcise it one must *express it in words*. But how are we to accomplish this when the phantoms inhabiting our minds do so without our knowledge, embodying the unspeakable secret of . . . *an other?* This other, of course, is a love object. Produced by the secret, the gaps and impediment in our communication with the love object create a twofold and contrary effect: the prohibition of knowledge coupled with an unconscious investigation. As a result "haunted" individuals are caught between two inclinations. They must at all costs maintain their ignorance of a loved one's secret; hence the semblance of unawareness (nescience) concerning it. At the same time they must eliminate the state of secrecy; hence the reconstruction of the secret in the form of unconscious knowledge. This twofold movement is manifest in symptoms and gives rise to "gratuitous" or uncalled for acts and words, creating eerie effects: hallucinations and delirium, showing and hiding that which, in the depths of the unconscious, dwells as the living-dead knowledge of *someone else's secret*. So it is with the "phantom" of Hamlet.

The appearance of the Father's ghost at the start of the play objectifies the son's awareness-unawareness. Awareness-unawareness of what? Of his own uneasiness due to a circumstance not to be doubted: the late King must have taken a secret with him to the grave. Does the ghost appear in order to lift the state of unawareness? If that were the case, the ghost's objectification would have no more object than Hamlet's own dubious "madness of doubt." A ghost returns to haunt with the intent of lying: its would-be "revelations" are false by nature.

This is what spectators and critics alike have, for nearly four hundred years, failed to consider. The "secret" revealed by Hamlet's "phantom," and which includes a demand for vengeance, is merely a subterfuge. It masks another secret, this one genuine and truthful, but resulting from an infamy which the father, unbeknown to his son, has on his conscience. That is an almost a priori hypothesis. The true mainspring of the dramatic action would thus relate to our inmost and inexpressible conviction that the ghost's revelations are lies and that Hamlet's fits of indecision tussle with both a fallacious "truth" forced upon him and a "true" truth his unconscious has long since guessed. The hero's search is distorted and authenticated by the same token. Shakespeare's superlative skill consists in holding back one aspect of the conflict played out between a "true" truth and a lie. He has thereby created in poetry the unconscious dimension that so many have enjoyed without being able to identify it.

The tragedy's aim may now be stated more clearly: it is to spur the public to react unconsciously to the enigmas that remain and to backtrack toward an equally unstated yet no less imperative goal: breaking down the "phantom" and eradicating its effect, the uneasy state of knowledge-nonknowledge responsible for the unconscious conflict and incongruous repetitions. The aim, in other words, is to cancel the secret buried in the unconscious and to display it *in its initial openness*. But how can the secret be exposed if the guilt and shame attached to it persist? Their exorcism leads necessarily not to the punishment, real or imagined, of the other, but to a higher wisdom about oneself and the world of humans at large.

The same can be said of the "truth" revealed on the analytic couch. Naturally, in reinstating the "truth," we implicitly challenge other lies, all of them originating in one ultimate "Truth." One senses that this Truth, the final cause of so many lies, is supremely *abominable* and as such is intolerable to the gaze. Nonetheless, thanks to this idea, a measure of wisdom is acquired. The dissipation of even a single phantom cannot but indirectly touch the clandestine core of the ultimate abomination. Consequently, its offspring will be modified; some of its partial "truths" will acquire the right to exist openly. These truths emerge as differences of degree in "virtue," and hence, conversely, in abomination.

The specific question for us remains: How are we to reduce the phantom? Though no ready formula is available, the way is implied in the very nature of what returns to haunt, in the nature of the thing "phantomized" during the preceding generation, "phantomized" because it was unspeakable in words, because it had to be wrapped in silence. Reducing the "phantom" entails reducing the sin attached to someone else's secret and stating it in acceptable terms so as to defy, circumvent, or domesticate the phantom's (and our) resistances, its (and our) refusals, gaining acceptance for a higher degree of "truth."

It would no doubt be most instructive to probe some of the historical and political aspects of the two versions (1601 and 1603) we have of the play. But would scholarship of this kind do more than supply additional content for the play's continuing relevance? It seems to me that the riddle of our centuries-long fascination with *Hamlet* must be credited to the endurance of the "phantom effect" in us and to the constancy of our irreverent desire to reduce it by reobjectifying the unconscious, by tracing it back to its origin.

Are we the public, now nearly four hundred years old, finally in a position to articulate in words what for our forebears in literary criticism has remained a series of rationalizations? Since Freud, the problem at least has been raised. We have come to understand that in his play Shakespeare bequeathed to us an unstated and unrevealed unconscious process that has endured for centuries. We are prepared to pursue what Freud began and investigate a possible outcome of the drama, a conclusion suspended at the final slaughter. Unmistakably, this is a case requiring a fresh psychoanalysis of the hero.

A new "segment" of analysis for Hamlet after his analysis with Freud and Ernest Jones is a necessary complement. The fact of the Oedipus complex and the symptomatic consequences of its defective workings have been aptly diagnosed. But not what would have made them operative and fruitful. Would Hamlet have been "cured" on Freud's couch? Nothing permits us to affirm otherwise. But my enterprise here is much more ambitious. I seek to "cure" the *public* of a covert neurosis the *Tragedy of Hamlet* has, for centuries, inflicted upon it. The only solution is to continue beyond the combination of dead ends that (might have) buried everything. It was necessary to kill, to die for nothing so that an external and sympathetic eye could make the phantom appear in the light of day, so that, once known, understood, and exorcised, the phantom should go from our unconscious, vanish into the reality whence it had come, disappear into a bygone and vanquished world.

Having reflected on all these things, I realized that this analysis might result in another play—nearly as dramatic—directed by the desire to resuscitate the "dead" ghost, to "cure" him, to allow him finally to cease being a phantom: to die happy, in the end, at having been understood, in his *surmounted* truth.

I am convinced that the dissipation of a single "phantom" is capable ultimately of modifying the structure of the grand abominable Truth— postulated though nonexistent—that nevertheless does, in its constantly changing forms, govern the universe. Each time a small victory is won over Death for Love. What follows is inspired by that hope.

April 1974 and March–July 1975

The Phantom of Hamlet
or
The Sixth Act

SCENE 1

FORTINBRAS, HORATIO

FORTINBRAS
    Foul stench of poison, merged with mist of blood:
    A vanished dynasty before me lies,
    A bygone era, turned prey to suicide.
    The land of Elsinore, swept clean and fresh
    By Norway, will before long dry its tears;
    With pledge of tribute to my uncle's Norway,
    Will reconstruct its ramparts and its dikes
    To check therewith the swelling of its grief.
    I will put Hamlet back upon his throne,
    Despite his death, as rightful and just heir.
    To me, his successor, this Prince bequeathed
    You, Horatio, his faithful witness,
    His bosom friend, his heart's most inward ear,
    Alert to secrets th' mind prefers to shun.
    Before I set this crown upon my head,
    I plead we may as one expose to view,
    Amid the shapes which to our eyes appear,
    The unseen web iniquity has cast.

HORATIO
    I beg, my lord, forgive me that I weep.
    To peer at souls does sorely ill befit
    The sorrow their departure in us breeds.
    Though truth delights us when she naked shows,
    Before the public eye she cloaks herself.
    So said my late sweet prince. One day, he spiced
    His play of wit with antic prophecy,
    As though the future he could read in dreams:
    Before another thousand years have passed
    A learned doctor in Vienna will
    Unlock dark treasures deep within our souls.
    Then others, spurred on by his blazing light,

191

Will contemplate our trouble-coiled century,
Inventing all: the hidden shame and crimes
Our forebears wrought, unknown albeit known,
Absurd and baneful phantoms of the mind
Who, unrestrained, make havoc of our world.

FORTINBRAS

    Let heaven help me mind your prudent words.
    This distant master will enlighten me.

HORATIO

    Your manner, my gentle lord, proclaims it so.
    When using words like "phantom," did Prince Hamlet
    Foreglimpse his Father's spectre? Unhappy days!
    Six heads struck down, among them three were royal.
    What horror he had seen I cannot know
    But, like the bodies carried from this room,
    King Hamlet also died by poison's sting.

[FORTINBRAS *takes up the Cup and notices, next to it, the Pearl of the Union.*]

HORATIO

    Here lies th' Union, prime jewel of the crown,
    Envenomed; today Claudius let it fly
    In Hamlet's cup, dissembling his sure death
    With show of high regard.

FORTINBRAS

    Of ruby wine and poison, then, was born
    This Union . . . or what remains to us. . . .

HORATIO

    The Prince pried loose this chalice from my hand
    When, trailing him in death, I longed to drink.
    Let go, he cried, and hurled it to the floor.
    The Pearl of th' Union fell and rolled away. . . .

FORTINBRAS

    The truth is opened by his final act,
    At journey's end the honest fact will out.
    This Union's realm of poisoned blood was born.

SCENE 2

THE GHOST, FORTINBRAS, HORATIO

FORTINBRAS

A ghost. Well-timed! He surely must be part of this.

HORATIO

My lord, you see the very image of old King Hamlet. Such was the
armor he wore in combat with your father.

FORTINBRAS

Why, noontide's not the hour when spirits walk. Confound it! He
must be sorely pressed to disregard the law of wandering ghosts.

THE GHOST

Valiant Fortinbras, the hour spurs me on. Before you set the crown
upon your head, my urgent duty bids me warn you 'gainst my son.
You must learn that Hamlet had neither courage nor heart. He
failed to act and stopped before revenge most fitting for his father's
brutal murder. He stood and watched while the royal bed of
Denmark became a couch for rank incest. Mark my words. The
usurper poured poison from a vial into my ear and curdled my
blood. This poison still infects the Union. Never replace it in
your crown. Reclaim for your uncle the provinces I gained in fair
combat; let not our people be slaves to bygone wars and time-worn
disputes.

HORATIO

Too great is my amazement; I am perplexed, mighty King, to see
you walking still, to hear you speak so ill of Hamlet, your son, who,
paying with his own strong spirit, did all to lay your wandering self
to rest. The venomous "serpent" that stung your life the Prince has
slain. And your Gertrude took her life, imbibing the wine of incest.

FORTINBRAS

Yes, what else prevents your rest, old King, that you would steal
upon the day to tell us "secrets" we already know? What need have
I of your wisdom to disrupt the Union and cede its provinces to
Norway? The truth is, Ghost, alarmed by my talk, you have
returned. "This Union's realm of poisoned blood was born"—those
words plagued you and so you came to distract and trouble me.

HORATIO (*aside*)

Poison and blood: what is this intuition?

FORTINBRAS

What say you, Ghost? Poison poured from "a vial" or, rather, was it "violation" poured into your ear? No doubt, this poison was the violation of some secret, so much is understood. Your serpent brother whispered in your sleep-drowned ear that *he knew*. Your blood first boiled in your veins, then congealed; your smooth body smothered under the loathsome crust of your shames. Ever since, your soul walks on and cuts off those who know. You wreak havoc and pile corpses. But I, Fortinbras, have guessed your secret, though it may cost my life. The Union . . . the Duel.

[THE GHOST *turns white and trembles.*]

FORTINBRAS

Yes, who kept this secret? Who could have sold it to Claudius so that, with a mere word poured into your ear, he could strike you dead with shame and remorse?

[THE GHOST *turns livid and nearly falls over. A salute of guns is fired as ordered by* FORTINBRAS *in honor of the late Prince* HAMLET.]

SCENE 3

[MESSENGER]

MESSENGER

A miracle! Yes, a heaven-sent miracle. Scarcely were the salutes fired when young Prince Hamlet arose from the clasp of death. The dumbfounded multitude, seeing the sign, exulted: "Long live Hamlet, long live King Hamlet!" Yet our prince exclaimed, "No, no, leave me, I am dead," leapt up, parted the crowd, and ran toward the river where Ophelia had met her end. The guards struggled to restrain him. Now, he is borne hither, restored to life.

SCENE 4

HORATIO

Happy hour! I revive.

FORTINBRAS

And I as loyal kin cede the crown and return the throne.

THE GHOST [*coming back to himself*]
>To silence a ghost, an outrage! I nearly missed my aim. Knowing
>that the poisoned point had hardly scratched my feckless son, I
>rushed here to tell you what Hamlet truly was: weak as water,
>infirm of purpose, a threat to our dear fatherland. Come what may,
>do not allow the crown to fall to its lawful heir. Let my son take
>refuge in the country, willing or unwilling. Get him to a madhouse
>or abroad under close arrest. Keep the throne, valiant Fortinbras,
>return the disputed provinces to Norway—this is my will.

HORATIO
>You deserve the fire and brimstone of Hell, unfeeling father.
>Vanish!

FORTINBRAS
>Stop, Horatio. Do not repel him. Think of us, the living. We do not
>stand to gain by burning souls or ghosts. Far better that he stay to
>speak, and depart blessed.

SCENE 5

[HAMLET *enters propped up on a stretcher; he does not see* THE GHOST.]

HAMLET, HORATIO, FORTINBRAS, THE GHOST

HAMLET
>To be or not to be. . . . Derisive fate.
>He that is not, is—he that is, is not.
>Am I alive? Am I a pilgrim phantom?
>My soul's unrest has surely bought the peace
>That filial respect bestowed upon you,
>My father, as was due. What myriad
>Misfortunes have I caused for your shade's rest,
>For your redemption. How many corpses,
>Among them mine, were strewn about the floor,
>The empty throne. No matter, since today
>Infamy's washed away, foulness is dead.
>And yet, that incestuous beast, Claudius,
>My spineless uncle, your insidious foe,
>Forever he has won the day.
>With me your line is ended. Tell me, Father,

Whom will I coax and wheedle, bereft of son
Or kin, to avenge my craven murder?
There is no living soul to urge the truth.
Poor Prince, they'll say with gloom. Mercy on him!
He was mad—his father had driven him mad.
He eyed th' crown, th' Queen, and fair Ophelia . . .
Or was plain mad.
No, Hamlet was a decent sort, learned
In grammar, keen-witted. But truth be told,
None fancied him a king, and for a reason.
No smoke without a fire, he was traitor
To mankind, a pervert, wild, ranting beast,
A deadly serpent, stung by the poisoned
Product of his own thought-contorted mind.
No more! Let him die, provided he's not
Already dead. Words are rotten to the core.
For me there is but silence . . . to tell you
That your actions are just, in your own truth.
My truth? Little do I care. My every move
Was hollow, stripped of sense. Empty of vice,
Virtue or worth, my actions only wrought
Their own swift destruction. They were nothing.
Father, what's become of me, your single hope?
To die, to live? These words do not ring true
When there's no sense left in them.

[*Notices* THE GHOST]
Old skeleton. What do I see before me? Do the dead too have
visions? Dead, surely I am. Or might I be alive? No matter! My
dear ghost, your good cheer has but one equal, the irony of our
people exulting over my dead body: "Long live King Hamlet!" Did
they acclaim you so, father? I thought I quit this world for your
sake, so that you should have no more concerns here on earth. And
now, in the twinkling of an eye, we have changed places. From the
shores of my nothingness I will have lived to see this, too. Speak
my dearest father. Why do you not keep company with the blessed?
Did I not gain your redemption, forteiting my own, leaving our
Denmark an orphan?

FORTINBRAS
Denmark an orphan? Not so, Hamlet, while you live. Though she
remains without rule so long as your father's suffering soul does not
unfold its tale. Question him, Denmark's fate hangs upon it.

HAMLET [*notices him*]

> Are you Fortinbras, the son of the king this ghost of a ghost did once upon a time so valiantly send to his account, according to contract sanctioned by law and the codes of chivalry?

[THE GHOST *begins to tremble.*]

HORATIO (*aside*)

> What's this stench?

FORTINBRAS

> Look at him, he's trembling.

HAMLET

> For his land, Fortinbras, delivered into your hands and will.

FORTINBRAS

> No, Hamlet. A ghost who trembles fears the truth. Deception is his nature, for he makes you fancy that you see him. He spins stories of his doom, of crimes committed, injustice suffered; he makes you answer for his own disgrace and, in the end, you suppose him innocent before eternity. His shame is yours, you think. You think, to know would be death. Yet, wishing to tread in darkness nearly cost you your life. Trap him, he must answer.

HAMLET

> Dead as I am, I yet behold a ghost
> With Fortinbras, who claims I am alive
> And lawful heir to all my father's lands.
> Are jests like these to supply a prelude
> To my reception through the gates of heaven?
> A new affliction stirs my lifeless soul.
> I longed to clasp Ophelia in my arms
> Amid the stream and fancied that her mother
> In childbirth succumbed to watery death.
> Ophelia, our fate is intertwined;
> My own birth, too, meant someone else's death.

FORTINBRAS

> Of the man who had begotten you?

HAMLET

> Yes, if my mother had been wed to Fortinbras. A gravedigger told me I was born the day King Hamlet overcame old Fortinbras. But no, your notions are absurd. My own father too would have had to die were I to be an orphan like Ophelia, daughter to Polonius . . .

HORATIO

. . . the counsellor young Hamlet killed. Once prisoner and apothecary at the court of Fortinbras, he was set free. And the villain then sold his soothing potions to the enemy, bringing him promise of courage, ruse, and decisive victory.

FORTINBRAS

Hamlet, twice your fate was blackened by Poland.

HAMLET

Ophelia with her father's strange mad weeds
Did trophies and fantastic garlands make,
Onto the weeping brook's bed lay herself
To rest, in the waters that had giv'n her life
And seen her mother's death. On wings of love
Let me depart this life, Ophelia.

FORTINBRAS

And drown in the waters of your birth. Did Gertrude not lose the husband of her heart the day you were born?

THE GHOST

Stop there. I will render myself to the eternal torment of fire rather than endure this shame.

FORTINBRAS

You shall yet be saved, kind Ghost.

HAMLET

Her heart's husband, say you? Could this have been your own father? At times the Queen cast her dream-filled eyes on me, calling me Orphelius. For her it must have been the truth.

THE GHOST

Since all must be told, I'll reveal it all.
Alas, it was most true, alas it was.
Despairing of my cause, I did accept
My rival's challenge. His skill and valor
Left me but little hope. My life was worthless,
Yet in triumph I thought my manliness and
Sacrifice would beguile your mother's heart.
I vanquished him. But no elation met
The victor. Gertrude darted looks of hate.
I was despised, the slayer of her love.
Still, is it criminal to best a foe
In a fair test of arms? I did not think

To stay the swiftest rapier of the North,
Yet, God willing in the fray, I presumed
To win in love, as well. But love is far
Stronger than God. I ne'er again enjoyed
Gertrude's heart or flesh. Her child fulfilled her,
As if it did inherit her dead love's
And hero's soul. My life was but my crown,
No more, for thirty long, languishing years.

HAMLET [*exaggerated*]
My dear father, the pains you have endured
On my account. Much pain I suffered, too.
My mother's waves of affection for me,
Her unwholesome chimeras landed her
In a trap and to your prowess left her blind.

FORTINBRAS
As you wish, Hamlet, be yet more a toy of his deceptions. Your
noble feelings do you justice. But you, Spirit, you would have
vanished long ago, had you not more lies in store for us. Does it
matter to spirits what mortals think of them? Their power over us
is the insidious poison of their speech; their existence is pure
falsehood. We must contradict them as rejoinder to their venom.
But let us now expose the other side of these tales. The story opens
with a wager. With a wager it nearly ended. . . . Of the two duels,
fought thirty years apart, the second must include the first. Hamlet
was skilled but Laertes won. . . .

THE GHOST
It was not my fault. . . .

FORTINBRAS
Do not interrupt the flow of my thought! A memory must have
inspired him to anoint his sword with poison.

HAMLET [*vehemently, and speaking in the voice of* THE GHOST]
Enough, the trail is false. Was it not all
Claudius's doing? He alone could lead
Astray Laertes, free from all contriving,
With the promise of making him a prince.
They both have died. Let the rest be silence.

FORTINBRAS
Filial piety blinds you, Hamlet. No matter what the aim, Polonius
concocted the poison. The source of Laertes' renown as swordsman,
equal only to the late Fortinbras, must have been the unction

prepared by his father and smeared on his sword. Yes, the idea of
a wager on your head, like the one that long ago had struck my
father down, did come from Claudius, I grant you that. Still, a
wager combined with poison, this means of action, could only have
sprung from. . . .

THE GHOST
Fortinbras, enough! Your mind's overthrown,
Your base dishonesty is clear to all.
Enough said, enough insinuated.
To Hamlet the throne of Denmark belongs.
He, my son, is the only rightful heir.

FORTINBRAS
Old liar. Shall I tell you wherefore he has come? His urgent duty
was to provoke me against his son, unworthy, as he said, of the
crown and his succession.

HAMLET
Is this true Fortinbras?

FORTINBRAS
Horatio is my witness. Knowing that Hamlet would revive, he
rushed here, despite the uncongenial hour for ghosts, to remove his
son from the throne.

HAMLET
It baffles me. This illusion bears my late father's fair and warlike
aspect, but none of his courage or excellence.

FORTINBRAS
Yet who else if not he, when you were roused from eternal sleep
and the crowd acclaimed you "Long live King Hamlet!" whispered
to your tongue the senseless cry "Leave me, I am dead," and kept
you from replying "Long live Denmark!" as you should have?
Hamlet, your generous soul does not wish to know that you are
hateful to your father. Your soul keeps watch against the poison of
your forebears. They schemed, connived, and slaughtered in vain.
Your candor, seconded by your keen wits, shut your eyes to the
true model of your purity. No, it was not your father, Hamlet, but
the man Gertrude loved, a hero all the more for being dead, his
virtue shining more pristine and true seen through the eyes of
a woman. Claudius, whom your father mistakenly called an

incestuous, adulterate beast, simply tipped the scales by putting his own poison in the balance.

HAMLET
You dare insult the dead. Speak more clearly!

THE GHOST
Not another word! Hamlet! Hamlet! My son! Duel with him. Your father begs you.

FORTINBRAS
But do not forget to anoint his sword with a few drops of Hebenon.

[THE GHOST *grows unsteady.*]

HORATIO [*aside*]
Ah, that odor, I now understand. Curdled by poison, the blood of Fortinbras on Hamlet's sword reeked of this vile stench . . . thirty years ago.

FORTINBRAS
He wants more carnage, don't you see? Falsehood at bay craves murder lest the truth be known.

HAMLET
What truth? Is there a truth?

FORTINBRAS
You carry the truth within your soul. The spirit returns to haunt the witnesses and to entrap them in fatal snares.

HAMLET
Even at the cost of his own salvation?

FORTINBRAS
He would rather burn in hell than be disgraced. That is what saves him. He is a weak and cowardly ghost who yet proclaims his honor. You know how he died? Of too much honesty. A coward, yes, but still not a villain. Claudius whispered in his ear that he knew the secret of the pearl, the secret behind the Union of our lands; he told him that he knew what hateful weapon he had used to extort his unmanly victory. When he heard, whispered in his ear, the truth his accomplice should have sealed in eternal silence, when his ears were violated by his secret, his blood ran cold, chilled by his own poison. To die of shame is to expiate a crime. This prevails over all else, including his final cry: "Accursed be treacherous Polonius."

HAMLET
Ophelia's father. . . .

FORTINBRAS
As you say. And former confidant to old Fortinbras.

HAMLET
Polonius was the instigator then. He led my father into crime by
selling him the poison that changed the combat into murder and
made murder seem a duel. I did no wrong by slaying him. But had
I pierced the secret first, she would now be queen. Ophelia would
have surely absolved me for slaying a fiend by accident, though he
was her father. She suspected . . . as her final action proved. The
garland of venomous plants, the wreath of poison was a clear
allusion to Old Hamlet's crime, suggested by her father. Her
madness points to his guilt and grants my wish. Thank you kindly,
Fortinbras, for curing her beyond the grave, for winning back her
heart.

FORTINBRAS
Only our ghost is left to be dispatched to heaven, since hell has
rejected him. Now that your shame is understood, kind ghost, and
everyone knows your secret, you may take your rightful place in the
company of good men. Had you not challenged my father, you
might now be in hell. What more keeps you here?

[THE GHOST *does not move.*]

HORATIO
There is a fault in your reasoning and that's what keeps him here.
I'll vouch in his favor that the challenge came from Fortinbras of
Norway and not from him. And since his opponent's valor was well
known, his honor and pride forbade his drawing back. He saw it as
piratical extortion. Norway feigned venturing all his lands, while for
Hamlet the wager meant a single province.

FORTINBRAS
In a king that is rash.

HAMLET
Unless he is sure to win. Who knows whether Polonius . . .

FORTINBRAS
Damned Polonius! Who knows whether he did not in fact sell his
poison . . .

HAMLET

> Separately to both. Otherwise, would the one risk making such a
> challenge? And would the other accept?

FORTINBRAS

> I cede to your reasoning, Hamlet. My father is roasting in hell. We
> are quits and rid of both.

THE GHOST

> I suspected as much. I overturned his sleds on the ice; Fortinbras
> took him prisoner. And he tricked us both. Thank you! Thank you,
> all, adieu! [*He vanishes.*]

SCENE 6

FORTINBRAS, HAMLET, HORATIO

HAMLET [*ironic*]

> Forever blessed be the name of him
> Who skillfully prevailed on equal terms.

FORTINBRAS [*saddened*]

> Farewell my father's cherished memory.
> Let him burn in peace. Long live King Hamlet!

HORATIO [*anxious*]

> Farewell, Lady Truth, farewell illusion!
> My gracious lords, I tremble for you all.
> And for the people, too. If they but knew.

HAMLET

> Have I not told you time and time again,
> Though truth delights us when she naked shows,
> Before the public eye she cloaks herself.
> For the people's eye we shall bedeck her charms.
> They may then strip her to their heart's content.
> All will say: I have found her, she is mine.
> Look here, how hideous her beauty is.
> All good go with her! Still, th' authentic truth,
> The absolute and abominable truth,
> Whose outer bounds we have just barely glimpsed,
> And whose mere sight gives us our sovereign strength,
> Would be for common folk a cause of death.
> Long live the people of Denmark!

FORTINBRAS

And long live
The people of Norway! We shall dress truth
In garb of such enticing nudity
That her offspring will double within the year.
The phantom's lies are still to be revealed—
Since falsehood is fraught and oppressed with guilt,
While truth endures light, fruitful, and untainted.
It's time to find our own truths. Have courage,
Horatio. We rely on your wisdom.

HORATIO

My mind is slow. At last I understand.
Our truths derive from the bungles of the ghost.
Adverse to his son, he sold the Union
To Norway. Why? you'll ask. The wise will know:
To hide his shame over unlawful gains.
Others, better advised, say other things:
The Queen and Claudius conspired to slay
The traitor King. The inner circle delights
In bedroom scenes: Polonius, ready
To rape the Queen, was surprised by Hamlet,
Who killed him. Those in the know will rejoin. . . .
Must I go on?

HAMLET

It's enough. But tell us, Horatio, what should the Chamberlain
know?

HORATIO

Do not worry, my gracious lord, the next Chamberlain will be I,
Horatio.

HAMLET

To Horatio: the King's Chamberlain!
Long live Denmark!

FORTINBRAS

The Kingdom of Hamlet!

HAMLET

On this day when we both lose a father,
Let us, brothers of ill hap, seal a pact.
These lands of the Union we ought to share
As we spoke the truth about our forebears.
And for having waged an unequal war

Against the Poles, I insist that we purge
The evil which can come from former crimes.
We shall return the corpse of Polonius,
Traitor for us, but hero in his land.
Faithful Horatio, it is your charge,
As gardener of past events, to grow
Within the tract of time the grain of truth
Upward through the depths of eternity.

FORTINBRAS *and* HORATIO [*together*]
Long live King Hamlet!

HAMLET
Long live Denmark!

[*The Cups are brought.*]

ALL TOGETHER
Let us drink.

[*Curtain*]

Part VI

Psychoanalysis of Theoretical Discourse

Editor's Note The essays in this section come from different time periods and are grouped here because of their common preoccupation with the issues and methods involved in studying aspects of both clinical and theoretical psychoanalytic discourse. Of the three essays only Abraham's "Psychoanalysis Lithographica" (1973) appears in the French editions of this work. Torok's articles, "Unpublished by Freud to Fliess: Restoring an Oscillation" (1984) and "A Remembrance of Things Deleted: Between Sigmund Freud and Emmy von N" (written in 1982, published in 1986; condensed and reworked by the author and the editor for this translation), represent the general orientation of her more recent work and—along with "Theoretra" (1982) and her early, unpublished "Fantasy" (1959)—constitute additions.

Abraham's "Psychoanalysis Lithographica," initially intended as a review of Conrad Stein's *L'enfant imaginaire* (Paris: Denoël, 1971)—a book dealing with the "psychoanalytic situation" and the concepts of classical psychoanalysis—posits the possibility and fruitfulness of psychoanalyzing theoretical discourse. Abraham converts Stein's reflections on psychoanalysis into an unwitting attempt at self-analysis. The approach was suggested to Abraham by Stein's mixing theory with accounts of his dreams and his numerous references to the problem of self-analysis. The central premise of Abraham's essay extends his conception of patients—described in "Introducing the 'Filial Instinct'" (1972; will appear in volume 2 of this collection) as either "poems" or the "poets" of their own existence—to psychoanalysts. This implicitly raises the question of people's unconscious motivation in their choice of profession, in particular the question of the psychological origins of the desire to practice clinical psychoanalysis. The essay's conceptual focus advances Abraham and Torok's evolving theory of introjection (see Editor's Note to Part IV, "Cryptic Mourning and Secret Love," as well as the General Introduction), especially the issue of people's introjection of their own emerging sexuality. In this sense, "Psychoanalysis Lithographica" can be considered a sequel to Abraham's *The Case of Jonah* (written in 1972, published 1981; to appear in volume 2 of this collection), an interpretation of the biblical story in terms of the prophet's gradual detachment from God and his concurrent acquisition of both emotional and sexual autonomy. The method of textual analysis in "Psychoanalysis Lithographica" parallels the approach Abraham and Torok developed to the problem of psychic and linguistic concealment in contemporaneous essays, such as "The Lost Object—Me" (in this volume) and their concurrently drafted book, *The Wolf Man's Magic Word* (1976; English translation 1986).

After the French publication of *The Shell and the Kernel* in 1978, Torok enlarged on the methodological base of Abraham's "Psychoanalysis Lithographica," raising the possibility that Freud's unwittingly endured childhood traumas had a role to play in the genesis of his psychological theories. Torok's recent investigations are foreshadowed in the "Story of Fear" (1975) and *The Wolf Man's Magic Word*, both of which reassess major case studies by Freud, hinting that, in Abraham and Torok's view, internal rather than external factors might have kept Freud from understanding the Wolf Man and little Hans on their own terms. In her postscript to the English translation of *The Wolf Man's Magic Word* ("What is Occult in Occultism: Between Sergei Pankeiev–Wolf Man and Sigmund Freud," 1983) Torok outlined an approach to studying the ways in which Freud's family traumas may have shaped some of his clinical and theoretical endeavors. With myself as collaborator, Torok has expanded the scope of her research to include the history of the psychoanalytic movement, Freud's interpretations of literature, and the contradictions inherent in Freud's basic theories, such as dream interpretation.[1] This project constitutes a logical sequel to Abraham's and Torok's previous work. Accumulating a new body of clinical discoveries, the essays in *The Shell and the Kernel* delineate a transformation of Freudianism. Our more recent study of Freud and his theories seeks to specify the nature of the internal methodological obstacles which serve to undermine the interpretive freedom of Freud's investigations; furthermore, we attempt to identify the root of the contrarieties of Freudian thought in Freud himself. The unprejudiced use of new clinical evidence and the study of the internal discrepancies in Freud's work, as well as the hope of understanding why Freud himself sometimes forced his discoveries into predetermined directions, can be combined today to explain Abraham's and Torok's need to refashion psychoanalytic theory.

1. N. Rand and M. Torok, "Questions à la psychanalyse freudienne: Le rêve, la réalité, et le fantasme," *Les temps modernes* 48, no. 549 (April 1992); in English as "Questions to Freudian Psychoanalysis: Dream Interpretation, Reality, Fantasy," *Critical Inquiry* 19, no. 3 (Spring 1993): 567–94; "The Secret of Psychoanalysis: History Reads Theory," *Critical Inquiry* 13, no. 2 (Winter 1987): 278–86; "*The Sandman* Looks at *The Uncanny:* The Return of the Repressed or of the Secret, Hoffmann's Question to Freud," in M. Münchow and S. Shamdasani (eds.), *Speculations after Freud: Psychoanalysis, Philosophy, and Culture* (London: Routledge, 1994). Our book-length study of Freud, titled *Questions to Freud*, is forthcoming in English and French.

TWELVE

Psychoanalysis Lithographica

N. Abraham, 1973

> Seal up those things which the seven
> thunders uttered and write them not.
>> Revelation 10.4; quoted by Conrad Stein

The imaginary child. The child: the fruit of conception, the beneficial objectivation of an instant's delight, a promise and a project,
a fulfillment reaching toward this very delight as recreated in a
being made of our own stuff and yet already an other . . . , a child, yes,
of the imaginary, of nostalgia, of unsatiated desire; a child out of coitus,
born of the sole power of the mind, a child bereft of reality, excluded
from the coherent world of symbols. An excluded child, relegated into
the realm of the imaginary! But why? The Freudian response is unambigu-
ous: the child is imaginary so as never to be born completely, so it can
endure in endless gestation, in order to perpetuate the analysis whose
undesirable, final product it would constitute, were it to come alive in the
"real" world.

More than results, what counts for Conrad Stein is the very act of
assisting birth, the forever unfinished maieutic gesture, the indefinitely
renewed delight of preparing a "birth." . . . To prepare it merely because
if the birth were actually to take place, something other than a child would
be born. What exactly would that be? We do not know yet but we are
likely to catch a glimpse of it by the end of this road.

I should say at the outset that Conrad Stein's book bears very little resemblance to an imaginary child: it is definitely real, endowed with an elegance
of presentation, bordering on coyness, a style of divine fearlessness, and
lastly equipped with the theoretical scope of its cleverly disguised controls.
By now the book has had a life of its own for more than two years. *Habent*

Previously published as "Psychoanalysis Lithographica," *Critique* 319 (1973): 1102–17;
and in *L'Écorce et le noyau* (Paris: Flammarion, 1987), pp. 276–94.

sua faţa libelli (books have their destiny), notes Imre Hermann, echoing the Roman adage, in the postscript to his long-neglected book, *Filial Instinct*. If we discount the general climate of opinion and the workings of chance, we can safely say that *The Imaginary Child*'s destiny is already well underway. And even those who, owing to ideology or snobbery, have tended to disregard it will in time not escape its influence. A question lingers then: how could a work of such quality have failed to make its mark or be recognized within the author's circle at the very least? Why has there been no need or desire to share the experience, to start a dialogue; why has there not even been attacks attempted against this disconcerting book, no formulation of the irritation, the objections, the criticisms? Perhaps what follows will provide an implicit answer.

It would be impossible to forgo mentioning the various incarnations this book has assumed for me in the course of several rereadings, motivated by its inherent interest as well as by the fact that I had promised the author to write a review essay expressing my regard. But as this project ran aground on repeated attempts, I was driven to ask whether Stein's undertaking was not in fact intended to neutralize and disarm commentaries, at least with respect to the theoretical contents of his book.

Let me recount first the history of my failures. In my initial attempt, I said, not without some frustration, that this book was worthy of Kant, and might better have been titled "The Critique of Pure and a priori Psychoanalytic Reason." If the author had confronted me with this title, I would immediately have understood the fruitlessness of my efforts and could have spared myself the scores of marginal annotations I had made on points of agreement, disagreement, or discussion, with a view to writing the article. Based on my erstwhile readings of Kant, I would have known better than to engage in dialogue with a priori principles, which one expects to have to accept without argument. Still, I could not disguise the fact that, in contrast to my Kantian yawns, reading this book was undeniably enjoyable. Watching the book's elaborate gymnastics was quite interesting since it invariably resulted in a novel exercise, new findings, and also unexpected forms of logic. An air of spontaneity definitely permeated every page. In fact, I said to myself in a thin fit of renewed courage, the author simply intends that we participate in his way of thinking; he is moving us gradually closer to the instruments of his search. Inspired, I quickly drew up the outlines of my paper.

"VISITING A LABORATORY"

The visitors are welcomed. Everything is neatly arranged to facilitate their task. There are labels, impeccable traditional order prevails: *The Psycho-*

analytic Situation, The Oedipus Complex, The Castration Complex. At the end comes the author's own research interest: *Psychoanalytic Space.* About all these tidily arranged devices we are told that their functioning is exceedingly smooth. Apart from being shown these patent truths, the visitors are given their fair share of the gropings that led to the results, the investigative process, the searchings, and the perseverance of our researcher. But in the end, everything has its proper place. Next comes the list of the machines: incest, the foundational words, dual identification before the advent of the word, the acceptance of castration, the difference between the sexes. . . . Care is taken to remind us that these machines are for the most part produced in the laboratory itself, and at all times explanations are given as to why the machines were purchased, invented, used, and to what end.

We may note a measure of complacency with regard to the visitors, who are assumed to be important people. Indeed they will never be subjected to persuasion or any attempts to win them over for the laboratory's cause. The book has to speak for itself. And whenever a new machine is introduced, its functioning is illustrated with minutely detailed examples. Well-disposed visitors will have no choice but to accept the obvious value of the machines. Now, the visitors must be well disposed indeed not to find fault with the presentation of obvious facts, the fault of a masked penchant for eliciting recognition for the laboratory even as the laboratory is being heralded as the very instrument of recognition.

Thoughts of self-analysis follow. Self-analysis is not meant to be an application of the branch of knowledge the author presents, but rather its enlargement with the help of the analysands. Consequently, there is to be no separation between self-analysis and "hetero-analysis." Patients are presented as the team of collaborators who assist the author's forever unfinished self-analysis. The patients' privileged encounter with the author would seem to constitute psychoanalysis.

I ended my paper on the following note: Full of admiration and frustrations, the important visitors take their leave. They step over the threshold without uttering a single comment on what they have just experienced, quite certain they will soon write the director requesting the singular favor of being admitted as a member of the team so that one day they may in turn become directors of a laboratory capable of accommodating their own teams of self-analysis.

Clearly, I can do no better than make a display of cheap wit, I concluded on rereading my draft. I was taken by my own trap. Wanting to remain aloof, to remain outside the moving forces of the author's thought, I was content to be a reporter of essentially trivial details. What writing as compact and multifarious as Stein's requires first and foremost is that we investigate the author's deeper aims. Of course, an undertaking of this sort runs a great risk of failure. My visitors to the lab had every reason to remain silent. I must admit that this book leaves me speechless or pushes me into the unenviable role of the village idiot. Unless . . . , yes, unless I can get past the difficulty by speaking of the author himself, not the person I know so well, but the person who emerges from his book, as a direct result of his relationship to it. Let us see where that would lead us.

TOWARD A THEOLOGY, OR HOW TO BECOME GOD
BY SPEAKING

Stein is a conscientious writer. He scrupulously describes the difficulties he encountered in writing his book and points out all that this should teach us. He is certainly qualified to do so since, with respect to his own inhibitions, he knows he is hardly at fault. The inhibitions are the inescapable and pervasive result of something that is beyond us all—original sin. The author wants us to know this, just as we need to consider that original sin itself results from the original word, inasmuch as it proclaims a prohibition, albeit too late, after the prohibition had been transgressed. So we are all innocent of being guilty but yet all guilty for wanting to prove ourselves innocent. There is no way around it ever, we are all sinners. Only an eccentric would ask: is it our fault that we desire our mother? We would have to respond: yes, after all, we are ordered to be at fault— provided that the circumstances are favorable—the fault of desiring her. . . . Guilty of a desire, that is what is called *being*, no less. Saying that I am not guilty is simply a tautology. It would be enough to say: "I am not." . . . But that is simply absurd. What we need to say instead is the following: "I am not guilty of being guilty, just as I am not innocent of all innocence." Conclusion: to be able to say all that, there is no need for me to be either "innocent" or "guilty"—all I have to do is be an analysand-analyst. I will accept my anthropological guilt and this will remove the slightest suspicion of any real sin. I can then say with genuine innocence: everything in my book is good for me and everybody else should recognize that the same thing applies to all of us. Any objections? None. Good, you are quite right not to contradict me. I can assure you of this as a result of my thorough and impartial study of the question. Since I opted for impartiality, I have the privilege—and you alone may decide whether or not you want to share this privilege with me—of having one leg on this side and the other leg on the far side of the "fence" of incest. Straddling the thing that divides me, I forge ahead, cleaving through the in-between of illusions, in the immortality of death, en route to eternal life.

Not so bad this time around, really, I reassure myself with a pang of anxiety. At any rate, I do seem less of a half-wit than earlier, don't I? And then I see Conrad turning to me and humoring me as people would simpletons: "But Nicolas . . . ," I hear him say with an infinite series of ellipses. Clearly I have failed once again to grasp the drift of his book and there is not much chance that I ever will. "But Conrad, what is it? A book is a book," I say, reciprocating with an ellipsis to match his own. Conrad falls silent. I sense, however, that he is holding back a sentence. I am not much good at riddles, but I am catching on this time. It is a sentence he is not saying because it is unspeakable: *"The book is me!"* There. What a relief. That is what I call a "propitious dialogue." I did intimate that he and the book were one but I was unable to draw the appropriate conclusions. Properly understood, he proposes: the book is a work of art and this work of art is me. Quite clear. I can start all over again.

THE BOOK WRITING A BOOK

A lithographer. The stone (Stein) is the one writing. But it is merely a block and can only replicate. It duplicated the impressions made by the person who gave it its name and functions. The block has the power and the duty to replicate its own design. But the design is not directly visible; it has to be unearthed first then cleaned and restored just like a paleontological imprint. Only after this is completed can the block function. Then it will print what was drawn on it at the Beginning of Time: the creation of the word. All you need to do is read the designs and you will find obvious anthropological truths. The stone's initial task is to display these truths in minute detail, one by one. Above all, the book needs to be meticulous, carefully laid out, moving ahead step by step, so that the precious inscriptions are not altered in any way. (The next subject in my article: a review of all that we are learning, the actual "book" being simply the journal of the process of "restoring" the design.)

A distinction needs to be made between the Book with a capital B and the book that is writing a book. When the journal of obvious truths and of the illustrative accounts has exhausted its resources and the block's reconstruction is complete, a highly unusual phenomenon occurs. The journal that has been recording truths about the art of printing "books," rules about their content and typography, this same journal is now registering an incredible fact: *The Book has had a dream.* And the Book is desperately trying to inscribe the dream onto itself, into its stone, attempting to treat the dream just like all the other obvious truths that are written on it. But there is no reason to believe that the attempt is at all successful. Is the dream of the "archeopteryx" just another copy of the age-old impressions or rather, was it surreptitiously added in longhand directly on the paper? The author is still a lithographer of course, at least in spirit, but has he run out of printing blocks? Or has the dream itself become the author of a potential book, though only in manuscript form, so that the corresponding stone is still quite virginal? Now, if the stone is untouched . . . , then the paper must be intact too. But over all of this hovers a presence: the manuscript of the dream, that is, the writer himself. His is an awkward flight, reminiscent of the flight of these prehistoric animals, half reptiles, half birds, whose full scientific name is archeopteryx *lithographica.*

Handed down from father to son, the lithographer's vocation is to impress stone. It was a vocation waiting to be discovered. That is now done. It was to be enacted as well. Also done. Conrad Stein has become an engraver of stones just like his father. How does Stein incise his stone? How does Stein make a printing block out of stone, a lithogram, a STEINDRUCK [literally: stone impression—*Trans.*]? He does it by dint of words. Because to be a stone is in itself nothing. But to be a printing block, that is *being* itself, being engraved by the inaugural word. . . . Do look for that word in the recesses of memory. . . . Going back in time will pull us ahead. The prehistoric bird, impressed into stone, is coming to life again, though it is a mere archeopteryx and is a bit cowardly because it chooses X, the unknown. Still it is ready to take off. This is what Conrad Stein's book is like; it is a prelude to new originary words. Look unceasingly, but never, never find what is nevertheless engraved in you: the TOUCHSTONE. From now on, nobody is going to be untouched by . . . Stein.

Conrad was right to alert me: his book is himself. Not only as regards the letters engraved in his stone block by his father but also as concerns his journals of paleontology, dream interpretation, and self-analysis. These are all going to be good themes for me to develop without looking like a greenhorn. I keep repeating all this strenuously to myself as though I needed to convince myself. It is clear, I am trying to dissemble my own discomfort. But I had better overcome it before plunging ahead. To tell the truth, I pretty much know what it is that bothers me about this auto-biographical endeavor. It is not so much that the author is conducting his own analysis in public but that I as reader am made to feel condemned to utter passivity; I am merely admitted to help the self-analysand after the fact, when things have cooled off, so to speak; I am an observer who has no choice but to admit his own uselessness. This of course runs counter to one of the book's main arguments, one I especially like, the thesis that psychoanalysis is the joint work of two participants. Under these circumstances, why should my reading be reduced to being a mere reflection, a reflection adapted to my own tastes of course, but nonetheless no more than a reflection of somebody else's work. And then I am re-minded of my painstaking attempts to review this book. No matter what angle I adopted—submission to a priori assumptions, a syncretic account of my personal understanding, a philosophical and theological elaboration on the author's hidden intentions, or finally, an allusive, metaphorical, and highly condensed description, a kind of paraphrase—none of these efforts ever culminated in the joint and enviable work of art that should be the sole privilege reaped by the partners occupying the analytic chair and couch, the very privilege the author keeps denying me on every page. The reasons for this are quite clear to me now and I have reached a decision. I will not allow myself to be shunted aside to play the role of chronicler, stylist, or journalist. If it takes two to have an imaginary child, I am to be counted. Is it not true that Conrad actually invites his public to serve as his analyst? He literally says: "Notice the role my imaginary public, my future readers will play in my continuing analysis" (p. 252). Surely this is a mischievous statement, punctuating as it does the author's commentary on a very brief dream of his: "Somebody is being shaved." There! I can finally hear my ears popping open. *Rasieren* [to shave— *Trans.*] or, better yet, *barbieren* means in German "to cod someone" [*couillonner:* to diddle or screw someone—*Trans.*] But perhaps, and espe-cially for the dreamer, it means "to be given cods." Come what may, the decisive move has now been made. From now on, I will let him try to lead me up the garden path. Let him have fun at the TV producer's expense, making his interview impossible to edit. I am certainly not ready to have the same bad luck. Consider, for example, the mysterious word "archeopteryx," taken from one of the author's dreams. He claims, doesn't he, that this word seemed to him to be a neologism as he woke up? Of course, he very kindly omits the word's origin and its referential signified. Yet there is no need to feel beaten for all that. To his neologism I can respond with my own. As a matter of fact, I am tempted to do just that, but watch out, because my neologism is going to provide the missing referent for archeopteryx. Sometimes two obsolete words revive suddenly, emerging in all of their forgotten freshness as they eject the undesirable and deceitful newcomer. Linguists call this phenomenon "neologism through recurrence," and psychoanalysts sometimes refer to it as an *archeonym*. I am still trying to soothe my doubts. I keep repeating to myself that anybody who provides a rich display of his dreams and associations lays himself open to wild analysis. But my word arrived regardless; it came to me with the compelling force of the obvious. No, I definitely do not have the impression that it is the fleeting result of a transitory state of mind. On the contrary, I am absolutely convinced that the word emerged as the logical coronation of my many readings. It came providentially and, judging from its looks, it is truly a sacred word, a hieronym. Like the divine Word, it has marvelous density and I can already foresee that it will accommodate an endless series of commentaries. Well, this word, at once new and old, *saying "archeopteryx" differently,* is nothing more than a medical term, designating the fact of having at least one "hidden testicle," undescended into the scrotum because of being trapped in the inguinal passage: *cryptorchia.* This word is just as rare as the "archeopteryx" it is meant to supplant. To be sure, French terminology prefers the term "crypotorchidism" [English offers the variant "cryptorchism"—*Trans.*]. No matter. In Latin, the term is most likely *cryptorchia.* A useful hint that directly orients my work of exegesis: this word was not spoken by a French doctor. But first, let us examine the "genotypical" correspondences between the two "grammatosomes":

```
1 2   3  4  5  6  7  8  9  10 11 12
A R  CH  E  O  P  T  E  R  Y  C  S


11 2 10 6  7  5  9    3  ?  1
C  R  Y  P  T  O  R  CH  I  A
```

I must note that the second word, my archeonym, contains two phonemes fewer than the first. Counting them up, I find this: The "I" of the second word does not correspond to anything in the first; conversely, the two E's and the "X" of the first word are missing in the second. But if you pronounce the E's of the first word in English, you get the [French] "I". That bolsters my hypothesis and so, without much ado, I draw a second conclusion: the fateful original word was said by an English-speaking doctor. All right. What about the remainder, the final X? Happily the author's associations are available: the word "narthex" appears right after the "neologism" and of all languages, it is interpreted in English by the self-analyst as *not rex:* not King. For my part, I would be inclined to reach for another English variant: not the X, to which—laterally and playfully, but why not?—I associate naughty eggs. The dreamer says quite clearly that we do not need to take the X at face value but only consider the K-like sound in it. If there were any more lingering doubts as to whether the dream, or even the waking subject, really did create the cryptogram mentioned above, his next association would dispel them. We are told about a recent feat of *deciphering* carried out by the author on another very long word: Nabuchodonosor.

Let us assume that, barring some extraordinary coincidence, a crypt-orchism was diagnosed in the young boy during his stay in England. Establishing this fact is of interest only to the extent that it allows us to determine the guiding forces that prevail in the psychoanalytic realm. Then the relevant question to ask is: why cloak this rather banal meaning—especially as its effects have by now undoubtedly disappeared—in a rebus coyly paraded as being utterly undecipherable? The outlines of an answer will emerge as we continue the exegesis and consider that, at the time, at the beginning of the 1930s, once a cryptorchism was diagnosed, it was customary to prescribe a regimen of massage and exercise to help release the trapped testicle(s). Here is the answer then: this regimen most likely brought about sensations that were both too intense and too shameful to speak about.

Those sensations have probably remained unspoken to this day, the wild analyst said preemptorily. Wild or not, he was undisputably solicited for the task. Perhaps one of the author's secret aims in publishing the fragments of his self-analysis was precisely the desire to be heard in this way, for want of another. The dream of the "archeopteryx" does look like one of these "bottles thrown into the sea" and I feel privileged to have been given the opportunity of fishing it out. Nonetheless, I insist that it would be discourteous for anyone, myself included, to ask the interested party either to confirm or deny the validity of my construction on the level of actual reality. I certainly hope that, on this point, he will leave me great latitude for the development of a hypothesis that has definitely proved quite productive. *The aim of my construction is not to guess a hidden "reality"*—though at times we can succeed in making the construction coincide with reality—but to discover *what it is in the analysand's discourse that makes it into a work of art.*[1] And I have done that, it seems to me.

___

1. "In our view, elements comprising the perception of 'genuine nothings' do not refer to a timeless figure, inscribed like a platonic form in the intelligible sky of the subject's history, where all other figures would be mere copies; these very elements are reworked, rearranged, and reorganized in the psychoanalytic space which is not limited to repeating

What is left for me to do now is provide the justification for all of this and listen to some dreams so that we can observe their transformation into poetry.

Let us start with the main dream about the archeopteryx (p. 246).

"An archeopteryx and its young [literally, little one: *petit—Trans.*]. It had the little one after having revived, after having been exhumed at the excavation site. A pity they didn't find yet another archeopteryx: it would also have had a child and the two young ones would have procreated, saving the entire species from extinction."

> "An archeopteryx and its young"; Archeopteryx (= cryptorchia) is at once the child's and his testicle's name. The name was given by the English doctor's initial "sermon."
> "the little one": the testicle
> "It had the little one after having revived": after being born, it revived
> "after having been exhumed at the excavation site": when it was released from the belly
> "A pity they didn't find yet another archeopteryx": another cryptorchism
> "It would also have had a child [a little one]": that would have led to more massage
> "the two young ones would have procreated, saving the entire species from extinction": these two phrases are the result of secondary revision.
> The dream thoughts are: I am going to finish my book just as I finally gave birth to my testicle.

"The archeopteryx and the young one are lying side by side in some kind of box made of transparent material, their wings folded next to their bodies": probably an allusion to the exploratory x-rays. It is also an allusion to the mother with its newborn and, finally, to the author and his book.

"It is really rather curious that my patients should pay so little atten-

---

forms but may cause them to exist in a way that is also a beginning. Reading the subject's unconscious past does not merely entail deciphering the sediments of memory and rearranging the broken sequence of historical traces in order to read the oblique meanings; it would not suffice to return them to their original position to have them coincide with a truth always true to itself; reading entails work on two sides: the analyst [works] by interpretation, the analysand by interpreting the interpretation in order for truths to emerge, in the course of treatment and the space defining it, that had not existed anywhere else prior to their being discovered in the psychoanalytic situation through the work that constitutes them." Serge Viderman, *La construction de l'espace analytique* (Paris: Denoël, 1970), p. 163.

This bracketing of the "truth" transforms the psychoanalytic process into "poetry" and an account of it into "poetic truth," not unlike the phenomenological reduction that transforms the verb "to be" into the verb "to signify." This "constructivist" orientation has the merit of freeing the psychoanalytic methodology from a major and paradoxical restraint: the impossible "reconstruction" with all the legalism, predicationism, and veridism this ideal implies.

tion to my archeopteryxes (the implication is: they were visible). I awakened with this thought at dawn."

"It is really curious that my patients": my parents
"should pay so little attention to my archeopteryxes": to my cryptorchism
"the implication is that they were visible": the condition was visible
In sum, the dreamer, like the doctor, is surprised at his parents' negligence.
Also: will people pay attention to his book?

"I dreamed next that I was alone in a dark and ugly apartment (probably where my archeopteryxes had been visible) and that great advantages accrued to me as a result, but I couldn't say what kind. . . . This dream belonged to the category of my geographical or topographical dreams, most of which have to do with my father's absence during my childhood; it was similar to a previous night's dream in which I was exploring an urban site, grouped around a medieval edifice that was both a cathedral or a crypt, depending on which side you approached it from; I finally set up a museum there and had visitors [literally: had it visited, i.e., inspected—*Trans.*]."

"I was alone": I = testicle
"in a dark and ugly apartment (probably the one where my archeopteryxes were visible)": the dreamer speaks of his scrotum containing a single testicle
"great advantages accrued to me as a result, but I couldn't say what kind":
what kind? No difficulty in guessing . . .
"This dream belonged to the category of my geographical or topographical dreams, most of which have to do with my father's absence during my childhood": (father: testicle)
"during my childhood; it was similar to a previous night's dream," with the only difference, the commentator might add, that the previous dream alluded to the treatment of cryptorchism, while this one speaks of the preliminary medical examination.
"I was exploring an urban site": the English doctor's words are coming back: "I shall explore it, sit down" (urban—town—down [the French *site*, same meaning as its English cognate, is pronounced "sit"—*Trans.*]).
"grouped around a medieval edifice [French word order is "edifice medieval"—*Trans.*]: a disease . . . medically
"that was at once like a cathedral or a crypt": (called) crypt-or-chia (chia, an incomprehensible sound for the child)
"depending on which side you approached it from" secondary elaboration on the theme of *or*, crypt or . . . .
"I finally set up a museum there and had it visited: in the end I had a good time having it examined [museum—*musée: m'amuser:* having a good time; *visiter* in the now obsolete English sense of "examination"—*Trans.*].

The medical verdict was engraved in the child's mind: "I shall explore it, sit down. (It is) a disease, medically (called) cryptorchia." The verdict was anxiety-producing but in the end I enjoyed having the thing examined: a reference to both the massage that was recommended and the writing of the book.

Quite remarkable, the exact preservation of snippets of English, reproducing the doctor's words along with their homophonic and cryptonymic translation into French: *édifice:* a disease; *ville: urbain:* down: town. The author's interest in a ship, hauled out next to a headland is in the same class. An etching by Jacques Callot shows a wrecked ship with a group of people swarming about (ship: [in English] she; we will see the importance of this pronoun; *fourmillement:* swarming and, figuratively, pricking bodily sensation). The same is true of the dream about the "underwater father," that is, about the "testicle" that remained under the reservoir of urine (= water). The author concludes aptly: "My father made of coral and pearls (= my testicle which risked being lignified if it remained in the inguinal passage much longer) was made to be exhibited as an archeopteryx" (to be released into the scrotum; also: my book is made to be read).

The long dream about the bookseller is more difficult to interpret. Let us sample its highlights. "The bookseller is giving me one of my father's books whose title is condensed from two of his real books." This has to do with the father's two testicles, condensed into the boy's one testicle, to which the "bookseller," the specialist, is referring in order to compare it with the hidden testicle about which the dreamer says that "it had been left too long and by negligence in a trunk," in the canal. "I examine it with the bookseller and we conclude that the damage can be repaired."

Associations follow. . . . Hidden things are being revealed, the apocalypse is near. Another association: "the angel of the Anunciation lets out a yell like a lion's roar." We may guess that the cry takes the shape of the Latin word bearing the well-known witness: *habet.*

To conclude this passage, the author says: "My father's book that I carried in my entrails is like a child, but a child that I would give birth to, being at once its father and mother." Surely it could not be any better put.

Finally, here is the last dream in this long self-analysis conveyed by *The Imaginary Child,* a dream that completes the series of memories conjuring up the medical examination and the massages. "The dream takes place in Algiers. A pier in Algiers. The crossing to Marseille should take two hours. Then follows a burlesque scene as I get on board. I arrived late, just at the appointed time of departure. To cross the bridge, you had to go through a small building that had a small door facing the town. The door was obstructed by Americans dressed in white who, oblivious to the fact that the ship was being rigged up to get underway, formed a chain, passing from shoulder to shoulder big, soft, light-beige colored leather suitcases, stuffed up like big balls. With a similar bag over my shoulders, I passed the custom agent without stopping." The dream and the associations go on but, for reasons that will become clear in a moment, I gave up pursuing my interpretation beyond this point.

"The dream takes place in Algiers": In English Algiers is pronounced much like *algia:* [Greek for] pain. Was there a period of pain before the doctor was consulted?

"The crossing to Marseille": the massage (Marseille-Massilia) "should take two hours": probably a reference not only to the two testicles but also the length of the massages that were prescribed. In sum: To get the pain to go away, the painful testicle has to cross the canal. The massages must take as long as is necessary for me to have "the two of them" [my two: *mes deux—Trans.*].

"I arrived late, just at the appointed time of departure": It is late but not too late to do it. Also: this is the last chance to finish my book.

"To cross the bridge, you had to go through a small building that had a small door facing the town." To effect the passage of the testicle, the little foundation [building: *bâtiment:* basement] and the tight opening, the inguinal canal, needs to be opened downward [facing the town: *côté ville:* downward].

"The door was obstructed": The opening was obstructed.

"by Americans dressed in white"—Mary can, says the doctor, and this leads to a remark by the young [German speaking] neophyte in English: *can* does not mean *kann* in German but *weiss* [knows how]. Now *weiss* also means "white"; hence perhaps the phrase should read "Americans dressed in white." It is easy to guess that *Mary* is the name of the physician's attending nurse.

"oblivious to the fact that the ship was rigging up to get underway": Don't worry, she'll get you underway [*t'appareiller:* rig you up, tool you up] she'll get your instruments back in place.

"formed a chain, passing from shoulder to shoulder": shoulder to shoulder = together, probably a fragment of the physician's words.

"big and soft light-beige colored leather suitcases [*valises*]": in the present context, calls up both "vaseline" (or some other cream) used in the massage and the word "release"; "balloon" and "light-beige colored leather" lead us to the scrotum and ball.

"With a similar bag over my shoulders": is this a description of the testicle's release?

"I passed the custom agent without stopping": "custom agent" probably refers to Mary: "she's accustomed" to do this kind of thing. This final part of the dream seems to conjure up the crucial hours of massage and also describes the author's apprehensions as to his book's reception.

From this point on, the interpreter is uneasy; he no longer knows which way to turn. For a good reason too, it seems, since the author himself is reminded just then of his exploits on television when he thwarted the producer's plans. Well, the same thing must be in store for me, I said, somewhat resigned, but happy about my results so far. Yet can I be content to stop there? Why not turn my abrupt and untimely deafness to advantage? Aha, I see: the misleading tactics are meant to conceal something. And what is closest to the author's consciousness if not the sensations he felt at Mary's touch, sensations that were highly inappropriate in the situation and an unscheduled part of the show. We suspected as much but without having concrete evidence, gleaned live from a "session."

At this nearly final stage we need to make clear that the quality of the sensation is of little consequence to the analysis. The same is not true of its significance and especially its effect, the improperly called feeling of "omnipotence" that I would much rather simply call the self's sense of its own powers. This feeling is the most prized and most desired possession. Surely, it was this narcissistic exaltation that needed to be concealed, even more than the unexpected orgasm, its cause. "To have been climaxed," in the words of a patient, is to have acquired one's right to life. How to conceal, or else, have this right acknowledged? That is the aim of much human activity as well as the stakes of quite a few psychoanalytic cures. Independently of the question of whether or not the prescribed regimen of massages resulted in the birth of a healthy testicle, that is, whether it resulted in this or that representation, the certainty of something felt for the first time endured: the capacity to be the equal of the gods. To outlaw "almightiness" is to deny the "all-delight"; to advocate castration as a means of coming to be amounts to renouncing the privilege of sensual pleasure by dint of which we awaken to ourselves, albeit in the child's mind often unduly so. Such a coming to (be) oneself could not occur without its having to be kept a secret. Its disavowal is perfectly understandable in a child who is precociously propelled into "adulthood," whereas in an adult such a disavowal would no longer be valid for want of purpose. The memory's disclosure no longer involves any sort of narcissistic loss.

Strangely paradoxical in the case before us is that theoretical discourse founded on a disavowal should be suitable, if not to understand oneself, at least to analyze others in whom such an inaugural experience could or should have taken place, but who in reality experienced only its painful absence. I mean the suffering of hysterics. Arriving at this idea, I am reminded of my first assessment of *The Imaginary Child*. "Here is a manual for analyzing hysterics." Stein himself is of course no more a hysteric than Freud was.

Should we conclude that the fact and the substance of a disavowal imply a positive element in the psychoanalytic understanding of others? Thinking about it, I find that the reverse would be surprising. Is not disavowal based on the idea that the admission would have disastrous consequences for the other party? We can go so far as to say that in the present case the partner to be kept from knowledge is a hysteric par excellence. Nonetheless, no psychoanalytic theory or practice can be based on concealment. For Conrad Stein to be the authentic analyst that we sense on every page of his book, he must have a keen desire—putting himself alternately in the doctor's shoes who prescribed his salvation or Mary's, the wet nurse of his testicle—a desire as profound as it is genuine to have his patients symbolically share the unavowed experience that gave him his riches. In some ways, psychoanalysis does entail giving birth to one's own sexuality. The unconscious processing of a real-life cure of cryptorchism, in the form of imaginary child-bearing, acquires an exemplary and genuinely poetic value through psychoanalysis.

We sense in Conrad Stein that his theories are not a hollow intellectual exercise, as some of his detractors sometimes suggest, but are authenticated by the active and productive unconscious that is their source. I am happy to have had the opportunity to raise the veil ever so slightly and to have discovered—for me personally but perhaps for you as well—in a technical work of great value, a work of art that, far from diminishing the former, enriches it with a poetry only psychoanalysis can bring to light.

THIRTEEN

Unpublished by Freud to Fliess: Restoring an Oscillation

M. Torok, 1984

The etiology of the neuroses haunts me wherever I go like the Briton who is haunted, when traveling, by the song of Marlborough. The daughter of the innkeeper from Rax came to see me recently. Hers was a beautiful case for me.[1]

Sigmund Freud, Letter to Fliess, 8 August 1893

I hope this girl, whose sensual sensibility had been injured at such an early age, derived some benefit from our conversation. I have not seen her since.

Freud, Standard Edition 2:133

T he aim of the following lines is to reinstate some unpublished fragments into two letters written by Freud to Fliess on 12 and 22 December 1897, respectively. These dates refer to a period traditionally considered subsequent to Freud's renunciation of the seduction theory. As is well known, the standard interpretation of an earlier letter to Fliess, written by Freud on 21 September 1897, makes his revocation into the first stage of what has since become Freudian psychoanalysis. This "turning point" has allowed many an interpreter to grasp Freudian psychoanalysis as a theory of instinctual fantasies. Yet, the conventional ellipsis, frequently used in *The Origins of Psychoanalysis: Letters to Wilhelm Fliess* to indicate editorial omissions, raises the issue: Do hitherto

---

Previously published as "Des inédits de Freud à Fliess: La restitution d'une oscillation," *Cahiers confrontation* 12 (1984): 123–30; "Unpublished by Freud to Fliess: Restoring an Oscillation," trans. N. Rand, *Critical Inquiry* 12, no. 2 (1986): 391–98.

1. This fragment, printed here with the permission of Editions Aubier, authenticates Katarina's case and permits the reader to date it. See Sigmund Freud, *Studies on Hysteria*, vol. 2, *The Standard Edition of the Complete Psychological Works of Sigmund Freud*, ed. and trans. James Strachey, 24 vols. (London, 1953–74). [No complete edition of the Freud-Fliess letters was available when Torok wrote her essay. Torok and I together substantially expanded this paper in "Les Cryptes de la psychanalyse: Autour des notions freudiennes de séduction et de fantasme," in J. Nadal et al., *Emprise et liberté* (Paris: L'Harmattan, 1990), pp. 37–66.—Ed.]

unknown quantities mar our understanding of what the precise nature of this "turning point" might be?

In the English and subsequent German editions of the Freud-Fliess correspondence there are indeed some indications of uncertainty as regards Freud's definitive repeal of his seduction theory. Consider, for example, the statement from a letter dated 31 August 1898: "The secret of this restlessness is hysteria."[2] Freud cannot rest on his new hypothesis about the nature of neurosis, since the etiology of hysteria continues to be a secret. A particularly dense passage of the same letter seems to elaborate on the causes of Freud's agitation: "True, I have a good record of successes, but perhaps they have been only indirect, as if I had applied the lever in the right direction for the line of cleavage of the substance; but the line of cleavage itself remains unknown to me" (O, p. 262).

This passage connects, though not in an obvious manner, with yet another sentence in the letter about direction or orientation. "My work seems to me now to be far less valuable, my disorientation is complete" (O, p. 262). Is Freud experiencing restlessness, or a lack of orientation regarding the nature of hysteria? Is hysteria produced by memories of sexual traumas or by memories of fantasies arising from inveterate instincts? It appears impossible to decide the issue after reading the letter of 31 August 1898. The only certainty is the tension brought on by an unresolved question: "Die Erfolge sind zwar gut, aber vielleicht nur indirekt, als hätte ich den Hebel in eine Richtung angesetzt, die allerdings eine brauchbare Komponente für die Spaltrichtung des Zeugs abgibt; letztere bliebe mir aber selbst unbekannt."[3] A modified translation of this passage will perhaps help clarify what is at stake in Freud's disorientation of orientation:[4] "My successes have certainly been satisfactory, but they have perhaps been merely indirect as if I had applied the lever in a direction that would no doubt furnish some useful component for obtaining the line [direction] of cleavage [of hysteria]; it is as if the direction of the line of cleavage itself had remained quite unknown to me."

It is well known that Freud returns periodically to seduction as an etiology of neurosis (see the footnotes he added to the case of Katarina and his essay "Sexuality in the Aetiology of the Neuroses" [1898], among

---

2. Freud, *The Origins of Psychoanalysis: Letters to Wilhelm Fliess, Drafts and Notes, 1887–1902*, ed. Marie Bonaparte, Anna Freud, and Ernst Kris; trans. Eric Mosbacher and James Strachey (London, 1954), p. 262. All further references to this work, abbreviated O, will be included in the text.

3. Freud, *Aus den Anfängen der Psychoanalyse: Briefe an Wilhelm Fliess, Abhandlungen und Notizen aus den Jahren 1887–1902* (Frankfurt am Main, 1962), p. 225.

4. [This statement applies to the published French translation of Freud's letter, considered unclear by Maria Torok and omitted here.—Ed.]

others), Quite recently, in the spring of 1984, a systematic attempt to resuscitate the seduction theory took place. Jeffrey Masson's book *The Assault on Truth* gathers a large number of partially unpublished documents in support of the seduction theory. Without wishing to enter into a discussion of the book itself or of its principal thesis—that Freud's theory of fantasy is an assault on truth which resides in an etiology of the neuroses based on seduction and sexual abuse—I would like to use a few of its documents to perform a restoration of texts.

The clue of uncertainty already noted in the letter of 31 August 1898 grows into a certainty of disorientation when we examine the documents published by Masson. The letters are numbers 78 and 79, as printed in *The Origins of Psychoanalysis*. For letter 78 the fragments to be reinstated are as follows:

> My confidence in the father-etiology has risen greatly. [Emma] Eckstein treated her patient deliberately in such a manner as not to give her the slightest hint of what would emerge from the unconscious, and in the process obtained, among other things, the identical scenes with the father. By the way, the young girl is doing beautifully.[5]

For letter 79 the omitted fragments are:

> The following little scene which the patient claims to have observed as a three-year-old child speaks for the intrinsic genuineness of infantile trauma. She goes into a dark room where her mother is sorting out her feelings and eavesdrops. She has good reason to identify with that mother. The father belongs to the category of deflowerers for whom bloody injuries are an erotic need. When she was two he brutally deflowered her and infected her with gonorrhea, so that her life was in danger as a result of the loss of blood and vaginitis. The mother now stands in the room and screams: "Rotten criminal, what do you want from me? I will have no part of that. Just whom do you think you have in front of you?" Then with one hand she tears off her clothes while with the other hand she presses them against her body, making a funny impression. Then, with her features distorted with rage, she stares at a spot in the room, covers her stomach with one hand and pushes something away with the other. Then she raises up both hands, claws at the air and bites the air. While screaming and cursing she bends over backward, again covers her stomach with one hand, then falls forward so that her head almost touches the floor, finally falls over backward quietly

---

5. Jeffrey Moussaieff Masson, *The Assault on Truth: Freud's Suppression of the Seduction Theory* (New York: Farrar, Straus and Giroux, 1984), p. 114. All further references to this work, abbreviated A, will be included in the text.

to the floor. Afterward, she wrings her hands, sits down in a corner with her features distorted with pain, and weeps.

Most notable to the child is the scene where the mother is standing bent forward. She sees that the toes are strongly pointed inward. When the girl is six to seven months old(!!) the mother is in bed almost bleeding to death as a result of an injury inflicted by the father. At the age of sixteen she again sees the mother bleeding from the uterus (carcinoma), which brings about the beginning of her neurosis. The neurosis breaks out one year later when she hears of an operation for hemorrhoids. Can it be doubted that the father forces the wife into anal intercourse? Can one not recognize in the fit of the mother the separate phases of this assault, first the effort to get at her from the front, then the pressing down from behind and the penetration between her legs, which forces her to turn her feet inward? Finally, how does the patient know that in fits one usually performs the part of both persons (self-mutilation, self-murder), as in this case where the woman tears off her clothes with one hand, like the assailant, and with the other holds on to them, as she did then? A new motto: "What have they done to you, poor child?"

If this is madness, there is system in it.[6] However whimsical the editorial omission of these fragments may seem, they are certainly not deprived of method or reason. In both cases, references to sexual traumas, occasioned by violent fathers, are omitted. In the letter of 12 December 1897 (no. 78) the specific name given to the type of trauma had been left out: *Vaterätiologie,* etiology of/by the father. In addition, the editors omitted Freud's statement of renewed confidence in this etiology after his earlier renunciation of it in September. As for the letter of 22 December, the editors omitted the description of a clinical case of sexual abuse by the father, illustrating the renewed confidence Freud had expressed on 12 December; the new motto, authenticating this confidence, was also deleted. (The motto "What have they done to you, poor child?" is quoted from Mignon's song in Goethe's *Wilhelm Meister's Years of Apprenticeship*: Mignon appears to have been an abused child.) Who could see in this series of fragments (Emma Eckstein's authenticating discoveries, the case of sexual violence, and the motto) anything but a revival of the seduction theory?

Why obscure the progress of Freud's thoughts on the etiology of hysteria? Ernst Kris and the editorial team of *The Origins of Psychoanalysis* would probably respond that they did so in order to safeguard theoretical coherence. After all, in September 1897, Freud had already rejected the etiology of sexual violence inflicted upon children. Why confuse the

6. [In English in French text.—Ed.]

reader with the oscillations of the master when his vacillations are minute and useless if compared with the vast system that later came to be and which was not centered around early sexual traumas? For the sake of the Freudian canon, the editors consolidated a system they wanted to present as stalwart and invulnerable.

Let me print the complete text of letter 79 to Fliess with the restored fragments in italics. Let us take by surprise and admire at the same time the passage on Russian censorship, an unwarned companion, yet somehow privy to the fate that was to befall Freud's letter.

Vienna, 22.12.97

My dear Wilhelm,

I am in good spirits again, and keenly looking forward to Breslau—that is, to you and the fine new things you will have to tell me about life and its dependence on the world-process. I have always been curious about it, but hitherto I have never found anyone who could give me an answer. If there are now two people, one of whom can say what life is, and the other can say (nearly) what mind is, it is only right that they should see and talk to each other more often. I shall now jot down a few novelties for you, so that I shall not have to talk and shall be able to listen undisturbed.

It has dawned on me that masturbation is the one major habit, the "primal addiction" and that it is only as a substitute and replacement for it that the other addictions—for alcohol, morphine, tobacco, etc.—come into existence. The part played by this addiction in hysteria is quite enormous; and it is perhaps there that my great, still outstanding, obstacle is to be found, wholly or in part. And here, of course, the doubt arises of whether an addiction of this kind is curable, or whether analysis and therapy are brought to a case of hysteria into one of neurasthenia.

As regards obsessional neurosis the fact is confirmed that the locality at which the repressed breaks through is the word-presentation and not the concept attached to it. (More precisely, the word-memory.) Hence the most disparate things are readily united as an obsessional idea under a single word with more than one meaning. The trend toward breaking through makes use of an ambiguous word of this kind [with its several meanings] as though it were killing several flies at a blow. Take, for instance, the following case. A girl who was attending a school of needlework and was near the end of her course was plagued by this obsessional idea: "No, you mustn't go off, you haven't finished yet, you must make [*machen*] some more, you must learn a lot more." Behind this lay a memory of childhood scenes in which she was put on the pot but wanted to get away and was subjected to the same compulsion: "You mustn't go off, you haven't finished yet, you must do [machen] some more." The word "machen" [meaning both "make" and "do"] made it possible to bring together the later situation and the infantile one. Obsessional ideas are often clothed in a remarkable verbal vagueness in order to permit of this multiple employment. If we take a closer (conscious) look at this example, we find alongside of it the expression "You must learn more," which later became the fixed obsessional idea, and arose through a mistaken interpretation of this kind on the part of the conscious.

This is not entirely arbitrary. The word "machen" has itself passed through an analogous transformation in its meaning. An old fantasy of mine, which I should like to recommend to your linguistic penetration, deals with the derivation of our verbs from originally coproerotic terms like this.

I can scarcely enumerate for you all the things that I (a modern Midas) turn into—excrement. This fits in perfectly with the theory in internal stinking. Above all, money itself. I think the association is through the word "dirty" as a synonym for "miserly." In the same way everything to do with birth, miscarriage, menstruation, goes back to the lavatory via the word "Abort" ["lavatory"] ("Abortus") ["abortion"]. This is quite crazy, but it is entirely analogous to the process by which words take on a transferred meaning as soon as new concepts appear which call for denotation . . .

The following little scene which the patient claims to have observed as a three-year-old child speaks for the intrinsic genuineness of infantile trauma. She goes into a dark room where her mother is sorting out her feelings and eavesdrops. She has good reason to identify with that mother. The father belongs to the category of deflowerers for whom bloody injuries are an erotic need. When she was two he brutally deflowered her and infected her with gonorrhea, so that her life was in danger as a result of the loss of blood and vaginitis. The mother now stands in the room and screams: "Rotten criminal, what do you want from me? I will have no part of that. Just whom do you think you have in front of you?" Then with one hand she tears off her clothes while with the other hand she presses them against her body, making a funny impression. Then, with her features distorted with rage, she stares at a spot in the room, covers her stomach with one hand and pushes something away with the other. Then she raises up both hands, claws at the air and bites the air. While screaming and cursing she bends over backward, again covers her stomach with one hand, then falls forward so that her head almost touches the floor, finally falls over backward quietly to the floor. Afterward, she wrings her hands, sits down in a corner with her features distorted with pain, and weeps.

Most notable to the child is the scene where the mother is standing bent forward. She sees that the toes are strongly pointed inward. When the girl is six to seven months old(!!) the mother is in bed almost bleeding to death as a result of an injury inflicted by the father. At the age of sixteen she again sees the mother bleeding from the uterus (carcinoma), which brings about the beginning of her neurosis. The neurosis breaks out one year later when she hears of an operation for hemorrhoids. Can it be doubted that the father forces the wife into anal intercourse? Can one not recognize in the fit of the mother the separate phases of this assault, first the effort to get at her from the front, then the pressing down from behind and the penetration between her legs, which forces her to turn her feet inward? Finally, how does the patient know that in fits one usually performs the part of both persons (self-mutilation, self-murder), as in this case where the woman tears off her clothes with one hand, like the assailant, and with the other holds on to them, as she did then?

Have you ever seen a foreign newspaper which went through Russian censorship at the border? Words, entire phrases and sentences obliterated in black, so that the rest becomes unintelligible. Such Russian censorship occurs in psychoses and produces the apparently meaningless deliria.

A new motto: "What have they done to you, poor child?"

But now, enough of my filthy stories. [A, pp. 116–17] Au revoir,

Your

Sigm.

I shall take the eight o'clock train on Saturday as arranged. [O, pp. 238–40]

Reading this somewhat lengthy letter is useful in that it is restored here in its entirety for the first time. While the editors of the Freud-Fliess correspondence wished to uphold an unshaken system, this restoration (and others which can now follow) points to a reconsideration of the system of instinctual fantasies by Freud himself.

I consider the period of oscillation, extending from September 1897 to August 1898, significant. Restoring fragments omitted from the Freud-Fliess letter may, however, create the impression (as is the case in Masson's book) that I wish to replace the theory of individual fantasy life with a theory of infantile sexual traumas or seductions. This would mean trading one exclusive theory for another, substituting one dogma for another. The suggestion that we should replace one by the other would force us into a circuit of alternatives. No matter where we turn our gaze, we are imprisoned in the following alternative: either sexual fantasy or sexual trauma through the father.

A possibility for breaking out of this constrained alternative arises from a consideration of the importance of the alternatives for Freud himself. Is there no resting point between two sides? Let me formulate the hypothesis that beyond this particular pair of choices there is for Freud a trauma of alternatives, bearing on the reality or the mythologized fiction of an event. At this point, a response can be given to the editorial committee of *The Origins of Psychoanalysis* as well as to the canonical aspects of Freudian psychoanalysis. Throughout Freud's oeuvre, the distant messengers of a restlessness have left their mark. Consider Dora, Schreber, Little Hans, the Wolf Man, Emmy von N., cases whose interpretation entails a critical reading of Freud's texts. This type of reading, at once disjunctive and reconstructive, owes it to itself to pluck the veil from a semblance of serenity attributed to a letter of Freud to Fliess (no. 79), in which even the possibility of an alternative has been obscured.

Once Freud's oscillation between sexual trauma and fantasy is recognized, reflection can begin. That is: if a critical eye were to examine the fact of this alternative (and not merely its specific content) as a problem for analysis and as an analyzable entity, then the introjection of psychoanalytic history could take place as well as the introjection of "Freud" by Freud.

Have you ever seen a foreign newspaper which has been censored by the Russians at the border? Words, whole clauses and sentences are blacked out so that what is left becomes unintelligible. A *Russian* censorship of this kind comes about in psychoses and produces the apparently meaningless deliria. [My emphasis]

In Freud's letter, fallen prey to just such a "Russian" deletion, a comparison has been left intact—by some chance hard to believe— between a text that has been rendered unintelligible and the senseless speech of delirium. And even if the intelligibility of the Freud-Fliess letters will be a long time in coming, the procedure of their "censorship" points up the type of ambiguity hinted at in Freud's letter. To black out parts of a text means the reader is being deprived of a text that is, nevertheless, obviously displayed by dint of its being crossed out.

Circulating Freud's letters with fragments happening to pass "Russian" censorship is enough to throw the reader and psychoanalysis into a kind of *historical neurosis* in which deletions impede us from attempting to read the fact of oscillation as a symptom-symbol. Once this road is open, it will be easier to read the deletion itself, rendering it intelligible. Behind the manifest blacking out of the letter, there is the "Russian censorship" of an encrypted text to be found in Freud. There the specificity of *Russian* censorship will surely have something to say.

FOURTEEN

A Remembrance of
Things Deleted:
Between Sigmund Freud
and Emmy von N.

M. Torok, 1986

W e will embark on a journey through time that will land us in turn before and after 26 August 1898, the date of a letter Freud wrote to Wilhelm Fliess, in which he recounts how he forgot and then recalled the name of a poet.

Aussee 26.8.98

You know how one can forget a name and substitute part of another one for it; you could swear it was correct, although invariably it turns out to be incorrect. That happened to me recently with the name of the poet who wrote *Andreas Hofer* ["Zu Mantua in Banden"].[1] It must be something with an *au*—Lindau, Feldau. Of course, the man's name is Julius *Mosen;* the "Julius" had not slipped my memory. Now, I was able to prove (1) that I had repressed the name Mosen because of certain connections; (2) that infantile material played a part in this repression; (3) that the substitute names that were pushed into the foreground were formed, like symptoms, from both groups of material. The analysis of it turned out to be complete, with no gaps left; unfortunately, I cannot expose it to the public any more than my big dream.[2]

This letter is incomplete; it includes the ellipsis of censorship.[3] Let me draw attention to the significance of a sound cluster, especially since

Previously published as "Restes d'effacement: Emmy von N," *Cahiers confrontation* 15 (1986): 121–36.

1. [In Mantua in fetters]

2. J. M. Masson (ed.) *The Complete Letters of Sigmund Freud to Wilhelm Fliess* (Cambridge: Harvard University Press, 1985), p. 324. Further references from this edition, abbreviated *C*, will appear in the text.

3. [When Torok wrote the original version of her essay in 1982, no complete edition of the Freud-Fliess letters was available. For additional discussion see Torok's "Unpublished by Freud to Fliess" in this volume.]

Freud is speaking here of a poet whose business it is to find rhymes and assonances. The sound cluster, appearing in Feld*au*, Land*au*, and *Au*ssee, is most frequently used as a geographical suffix, but its independent substantive form, meaning meadow (*Au*), is richer. *Au!* provides the German equivalent for the English exclamation ouch! indicating pain. I am in pain, something is painful to me. Freud's letter hovers between a "meadow" (*Au*) and an "ouch" (*Au!*) of pain.

Freud's next letter to Fliess (31 August 1898) speaks of a trip.

> At noon today I leave with Martha for the Adriatic . . . "To gain riches," according to an apparently eccentric but wise saying, "is to sell your last shirt." The secret of this restlessness is hysteria. In the inactivity here and in the absence of any fascinating novelty, the whole business has come to weigh heavily on my soul. My work now appears to me to have far less value, and my disorientation is complete. (*C* 325)

The secret of the restlessness that made Freud leave Aussee was hysteria. We should recall that a year earlier, in September 1897, Freud had revoked, as it is usually called, his seduction theory of hysteria to replace it gradually with the idea of universally found endopsychic fantasies, arising in the progress of infantile sexuality. The circumstances of Freud's agitation over hysteria may be clarified somewhat since we now possess additional information through the documents published in J. M. Masson's book *The Assault on Truth* (1981). How indeed could Freud revoke this theory of sexual traumas "calmly" when two months after his initial rejection, Emma Eckstein, a crucial person in his life, was confirming the theory's continuing vitality?[4] We have known Emma Eckstein, alias Irma of the specimen "Dream of Irma's Injection" in the *Interpretation of Dreams,* since 1966 when Max Schur demonstrated her identity with Irma, revealing for the first time the fact and the extent of her illness after Fliess had operated on her nose at Freud's behest, inadvertently leaving a long piece of gauze in the cavity.[5] Eckstein, Freud's first patient in a "training analysis," reaffirmed the existence of seduction in one of her patients.

We have also learned recently that Freud was planning a new motto

---

4. [The reference is to Freud's letter to Fliess, dated 12 December 1897. The relevant passage is: "My confidence in paternal aetiology has risen greatly. Eckstein deliberately treated her patient in such a manner as not to give her the slightest hint of what would emerge from the unconscious and in the process obtained from her, among other things, the identical scenes with the father." *C,* p. 286.—Ed.]

5. Max Schur, "Some Additional Day Residues of the Specimen Dream of Psychoanalysis," in Rudolf M. Loewenstein et al., *Psychoanalysis, A General Psychology* (New York: International Universities Press, 1966), pp. 45–85. [Masson's book provides additional information about the circumstances of Eckstein's surgery; Freud's letters related to the incident, omitted from earlier editions, are now available in *The Complete Letters.*—Ed.]

for his research at the time: "What have they done to you, poor child?" (*Was hat man Dir, Du armes Kind getan?*), to be understood in the sense of, what suffering have they inflicted upon you.[6] The motto seems to return Freud to his early theory of real (as opposed to fantasized) traumas. It also refers us implicitly to the pain, subtly filtering through Freud's letter of 26 August 1898. Of course, the motto also gives valuable insight into Freud's way of listening to his patients as well as to himself, this being the period of his self-analysis. In addition, *Was hat man Dir, Du armes Kind getan?* is an example of Freud's constant use of quotation from Goethe. The sentence immediately brings to mind the fate of a "poor child" as recounted in Goethe's novel *Wilhelm Meister's Years of Apprenticeship*. The child, Mignon, born of a shameful and therefore secret sexual union, is stolen by gypsies, to be sacrificed ultimately on the altar of a longing and impossible love; her mother, in a climax of trauma, is unable to find her daughter's remains so as to honor them with the rite of burial. Freud's motto shows me Mignon, dancing, jumping, climbing, and prostrating herself by turns throughout Goethe's novel. Identifying Goethe as the source of Freud's projected motto has the advantage of leading us to *Faust,* which may be linked to an early case of hysteria. Freud's patient Emmy von N. appears before my eyes in the company of Mephistopheles.

Three years before his letter to Fliess (26 August 1898), Freud had noted in his case study of Emmy von N.:

> She was a hysteric and could be put into a state of somnambulism with the greatest of ease; and when I became aware of this I decided that I would make use of Breuer's technique of investigation under hypnosis, which I had come to know from the account he had given me of the successful treatment of his first patient. This was my first attempt at handling that therapeutic method.[7]

When reading the final sentence we should recall that Henri Ellenberger, a historian of psychoanalysis, has raised doubts about Freud's assertion. The method applied seemed closer to Pierre Janet's than to Joseph Breuer's.[8] Freud himself stated further on that he was under the pervasive

---

6. [The letter containing this motto is quoted in full in Torok's "Unpublished by Freud to Fliess," in this volume.—Ed.]

7. Joseph Breuer and Sigmund Freud, *Studies on Hysteria: Standard Edition,* vol. 2, p. 48. All references to this edition, abbreviated *S,* will appear in the text.

8. Henri Ellenberger, *The Discovery of the Unconscious* (New York: Basic Books, 1970), p. 484.

influence of Hippolyte Bernheim at the time (*S*, 77). The year Freud began his treatment of Emmy von N., 1889, was also marked by his translation of Bernheim's book on suggestion, for which he also wrote a preface. Faced with a measure of uncertainty, we need to emphasize the question: what therapeutic method did Freud use with his first hysterical patient?

If we consider technique alone—such as the uplifted finger inducing hypnotic sleep, the request to recount every detail related to the emergence of a symptom—we can see aspects of the cathartic method introduced by Breuer in 1881. Looking further, we will also find elements borrowed from Janet, for example the transformation and/or weakening of the emotional charge of traumatic memories. Didactic suggestions, made under hypnosis and intended in part to prohibit the reappearance of symptoms, are equally present, no doubt inspired by Freud's familiarity with Bernheim. Several complementary therapeutic methods seem to coexist in the case. Freud confirms this assessment in a brief review of his work with Emmy von N.

> As is the usual practice in hypnotic psychotherapy, I fought against the patient's pathological ideas by means of assurances and prohibition, and by putting forward opposing ideas of every sort. . . . I investigated the genesis of the individual symptoms so as to be able to combat the premises on which the pathological ideas were erected. . . . I cannot say how much of the therapeutic success each time was due to my suggesting the symptom away in *statu nascendi* and how much to my resolving the affect by abreaction, since I combined both these therapeutic factors. (*S*, 101)

Yet Freud's statement does not resolve the uncertainty about the precise role catharsis played in his treatment.

Upon closer examination of the case study we will see that the essence of Breuer's therapeutic procedure is missing in Freud's application. Paradoxically, catharsis is rarely to be found in Freud's first use of the cathartic method. Had Freud been working with the complete idea of catharsis, his treatment of Emmy von N. would have (1) led to the purgative release of her strangulated affects, (2) ended the amnesia that had cut off the pathogenic ideas from associative communication with the rest of the patient's mental life, (3) thereby bringing the traumatic memories to consciousness, (4) with the ultimate result of dissipating the symptoms deriving from emotions connected with forgotten traumatic events. The successive stages of recall under hypnosis, release of tension, the restoration of the free-flowing continuity of mental life, and finally the disappearance of the symptom characterize Breuer's cathartic method, set forth repeatedly in the *Studies on Hysteria,* for example at the end of the "Preliminary Communication":

> It will now be understood how it is that the psychotherapeutic procedure which we have described in these pages has a curative effect.
>
> *It brings an end to the operative force of the idea which was not abre- acted in the first instance, by allowing its strangulated affect to find a way through speech; and it subjects it to associative correction by introducing it into normal consciousness. (S, 17)*

Freud stresses this last point again at the end of case number 3: "The therapeutic process in this case consisted in compelling the psychic group that had been split off to unite once more with ego-consciousness" (*S,* 124). Moreover, in an 1888 encyclopedic article on "Hysteria" (a year prior to his treatment of Emmy von N.) Freud singles out this very aspect to illustrate the chief characteristic of Breuer's method of treatment: "[Hypnosis] is even more effective if we adopt a method first practiced by Joseph Breuer in Vienna and lead the patient under hypnosis to the psychical prehistory of the ailment and compel him to acknowledge the psychical occasion on which the disorder in question originated" (*S.E.* I:56).

In reading Emmy von N.'s case we discover that Freud encouraged the release of pent-up emotions in accordance with Breuer's theory of abreaction. However, he did not restore forgotten traumatic memories to his patient's consciousness; he did exactly the opposite. In addition, Freud did not simply suggest away the symptoms, as might be expected given his acquaintance with the work of Bernheim or Janet. Freud used a tech- nique of his own invention. He deleted his patient's traumatic memories under hypnosis. Freud did not stop at purging the affects or the symptoms deriving from them; he erased the traumatic memories themselves.

> I requested her, under hypnosis, to talk, which, after some effort, she suc- ceeded in doing. . . . This series of traumatic precipitating causes which she produced in answer to my question . . . was clearly ready to hand in her memory. . . . At the end of each separate story she twitched all over and took on a look of fear and horror. At the end of the last one she opened her mouth wide and panted for breath. . . . In reply to a question she told me that while she was describing these scenes she saw them before her, in a plastic form and their natural colors. She said that in general she thought of these experiences very often and had done so in the last few days. When- ever this happened she saw these scenes with all the vividness of reality. . . . My therapy consists in wiping away these pictures, so that she is no longer able to see them before her. To give support to my suggestion I stroked her several times over the eyes. (S, 52–53)

I had asked her the origin of her stammering. . . . I further learnt from her that the stammer had begun immediately after the first of these two occasions. . . . I extinguished her plastic memory of these scenes. . . . (*S*, 57–58)

Finding her disposed to be communicative, I asked her what further events in her life had frightened her so much that they left her with plastic memories. She replied by giving me a collection of such experiences: . . . How she had nursed her sick brother and he had such fearful attacks as a result of the morphine and had terrified her and seized hold of her. I remembered that she had already mentioned this experience this morning, and, as an experiment, I asked her on what other occasions this "seizing hold" had happened. To my agreeable surprise she made a long pause this time before answering and then asked doubtfully "My little girl?" She was quite unable to recall the other two occasions (see above). My prohibition—my expunging of her memories—had therefore been effective. (*S*, 58–59)

I saw that I had come to the root of her constant fear of surprises and I asked further instances of this. She went on: how they had a friend staying at her home . . . ; how she had been so ill after her mother's death . . . ; and lastly, how, on the journey . . . . I wiped out all these memories, woke her up and assured her she would sleep well tonight. (*S*, 59)

Under hypnosis I asked her what event in her life had produced the most lasting effect on her and came up most often in her memory. Her husband's death, she said. I got her to describe this event in full detail, and this she did with every sign of the deepest emotion. . . . I made it impossible for her to see any of these melancholy things again, not only by wiping out her memories of them in their *plastic* form but by removing her whole recollection of them, as though they had never been present in her mind. (*S*, 60–61)

My therapeutic procedure was based on the course of this activity of her memory and endeavored day by day to resolve and get rid of whatever that particular day had brought to the surface till the accessible stock of her pathological memories seemed to be exhausted. (*S*, 90)

Breuer's cathartic method provided Anna O. with diverse means—speech, convulsion, tears, rage—of coming into contact with herself and her traumatic recollections. Freud's therapy of Emmy von N. consisted of deletion. The result was the exact opposite of Breuer's, it involved the removal of the possibility of coming into contact with one's own forgotten and even consciously remembered past. Freud knew that the richest store of Emmy von N.'s memories was to be found in the somnambulistic state. Since he eradicated her recollections under hypnosis, they never managed to reach her consciousness. Freud indicated that he had hoped to master

Breuer's cathartic method through his analysis of Emmy von N. and even noted some dissatisfaction with not having been able to pursue Breuer's method systematically enough (S, 48). Yet his constantly recurring metaphors described a mechanism of extinction rather than the cathartic procedure of enhancing contact with oneself: I wiped out all these memories; I made it impossible for her to see these melancholy things again . . . by removing her whole recollection of them; my prohibition—my expunging of her memories; I extinguished her plastic memory; I took this memory-picture away; in a few weeks we were able to dispose of these memories too, etc. The effect of this very uncathartic method was that Emmy von N. forgot the most important events of her life.

> When as much as eighteen months later, I saw Frau Emmy von N. again in a relatively good state of health, she complained that there were a number of most important moments in her life of which she had only the vaguest memory. She regarded this as evidence of a weakening of her memory, and I had to be careful not to tell her the cause of this particular instance of amnesia. (S, 61) It was during these days, too, that she made her complaints about gaps from her memory, "especially the most important events," from which I concluded that the work I had done two years previously had been thoroughly effective and lasting. (S, 84)

It would be fruitless to question Freud's ability to apply Breuer's method or doubt his sincerity. My intention is to focus on the significance of Freud's procedure of deletion, bearing in mind that Freud used it exclusively with Emmy von N. The other patients he reviewed in the *Studies on Hysteria* (Elizabeth von R., Lucy R., Katarina) did not receive this type of treatment. Freud's procedure of deleting his patient's recollections under hypnosis is unique. It has neither precedent nor sequel in his own works or in the theories of his contemporaries. The therapy of memory extinction is inseparably linked to Emmy von N. What is the significance of this link? What does it tell us about Freud?[9]

Emmy von N. represents a fundamental disparity in the sequence of cases presented in the *Studies on Hysteria*. The break can hardly be defined any better than by Emmy von N. herself when, some two years after her treatment, she called to Freud's attention her forgetting of the most important events of her life. No better confirmation of the therapeutic discrepancy can be provided than Freud's own statement when he thought to himself that this "unusual case of forgetting" was a mark of

9. [Torok's 1982 version of this essay carries a section after this paragraph on the repeated omission of Breuer's two contributions to the *Studies on Hysteria* from Freud's collected works (in 1925 and 1946) and on the reinstatement of these contributions in James Strachey's edition of *The Complete Psychological Works of Sigmund Freud.*]

the "overwhelming success of [his] treatment" (*S*, 61) by deletion. Freud's Emmy von N. cannot be placed in the same class with the other cases in the collection, each of which combines clear examples of cathartic treatment with technical innovations pointing toward the methodology of psychoanalysis Freud would later develop. The reason for this discrepancy may well be worth wondering about. Regardless of the fact that Freud was applying Breuer's method for the first time, it seems to me that his treatment through memory extinction derived from a source deeper than any initial hesitation he might have had about the nature of cathartic psychotherapy. Memory extinction constituted a distinct innovation and yet was used only once. This form of therapy cannot be found in the theories of the men who influenced Freud's thought (Bernheim, Breuer, Charcot, or Janet) any more than in his own intellectual growth that within a decade would culminate in *The Interpretation of Dreams* (1900) and *The Psychopathology of Everyday Life* (1901). The reasons behind his singular invention of the therapy of deletion may lie in Freud's own personality. This leads me to ask as well whether any connection can be established between aspects of Emmy von N.'s life and Freud's own. If such connections exist, they may explain why, after having released the emotional tension, Freud chose to suppress his patient's recollections.

What follows is conjecture and a result of my growing conviction that some of Freud's theoretical hesitation and reversals (such as his rejection of the seduction theory), and even some of his concepts are traceable in part to personal traumatic factors. By this I mean that, quite apart from their objective value or therapeutic usefulness, a number of Freud's theoretical constructions are intimately linked to his own inner life and unresolved suffering. This is a broad claim whose validity and fruitfulness need to be tested on specific examples. Here I am merely broaching the subject and will deliberately refrain from providing decisive arguments in its favor.

I will gather some fragments to help explain why Freud chose to extinguish Emmy von N.'s traumatic memories as she recounted and relived them under hypnosis. This work will afford us with additional insight into the causes of Emmy von N.'s suffering as well. The complete title of the case study is: "Frau Emmy von N. . . . , Age 40, from Livonia." Freud is fond of titles. This is not the appropriate place to pursue the issue further but it is worth noting that at times Freud concealed crucial information in a name by using anagrams, for example. A case in point is the pineapple liqueur (*Ananas*) about which Freud says in his interpretation of the specimen dream of Irma's Injection that it bore a remarkable resemblance to his patient's real name.[10] We know that Irma was Emma

---

10. [*The Standard Edition*, vol. 4, p. 115.]

Eckstein. What does pineapple or *Ananas* in German have to do with her name? Nothing, yet the connection to this patient becomes obvious if we think of Emma's nose operation. *Ananas* is quite similar to the drawling Viennese pronunciation of *eine Nase* (a nose). Fliess's ill-fated surgery on her nose denoted Emma Eckstein, alias Irma, in Freud's mind. As for the title "Frau Emmy von N. . . . , Age 40, from Livonia," it also contains an anagram. We can now reconstruct it since, thanks to Ola Andersson, the patient's real name is known.[11] Emmy von N. = Von-Ny-Em(m) = Vonny M = Fanny M. Emmy von N. covers up Fanny M. The anagram stops there, but not the concealment. Livonia (a province of Russia on the Baltic sea) was known as "Livonian Switzerland." Fanny M. (née Fanny von Sulzer-Warth) lived in Switzerland on Lake Zurich in the town of Au. (The letter to Fliess, sent from Aussee and featuring the sound cluster *au*, was written nine years after Freud's treatment of Emmy von N.)

This series of concealments is clearly not intended for the readers of the case, since they have no way of seeing through it. The cryptogram seems to serve only the writer, Freud, who is thereby reminded of his patient's name and place of residence. But what justifies this type of secret mnemotechnic writing when Freud obviously knew and presumably continued to remember his patient's name? There seems to be a paradox here. Freud is concealing his patient's name in a cryptogram he alone can read, yet does so needlessly as he knows the name already. Cryptography is used for communicating a secret message to someone. In the case of Emma Eckstein, for example, I can see the concealment of her nose operation in a name (*Ananas*, pineapple) as being a veiled reproach addressed to Fliess. If, in Emmy von N.'s case, nobody apart from Freud understands the concealment, is there someone *in* Freud who can appreciate its significance? I cannot answer yet, but am inclined to suggest a link between this instance of private secrecy and Freud's deletion of his patient's memories, resulting in their being transferred for safekeeping to his own mind. Does this mean that Freud is intimating to someone (whoever this may be) that he has seen and heard something, that he knows it, but has either concealed or erased it?

I return to 26 August 1898. Freud's letter to Fliess, written from Aussee and dominated by the sound cluster *au*, is undoubtedly connected with Fanny M., residing in nearby Au. Is it the relationship between Fanny M.'s case and Freud's forgetting of the poet Mosen's name (a forgetting recounted in the letter) that prevented him from including the latter as an example in his *Psychopathology of Everyday Life?* The poet's

11. Ola Andersson, "A Supplement to Freud's Case History 'Frau Emmy von N.'" *Scandinavian Psychoanalytic Review* (1979): 15 *sequ.*

name, *Mosen,* in *Au*ssee must have resonated in Freud's mind with *Au,* Fanny's residence, and with her full married name, Fanny *Moser.* Surely, this is what Freud alluded to when he said "unfortunately I cannot expose it to the public any more than my big dream." Was there more to his silence than professional discretion?

Freud's patient, Fanny Louise von Sulzer-Warth, alias Emmy von N., had married Heinrich Moser, a very successful industrial entrepreneur and forty-three years older than she, with whom she had two daughters, Fanny and Mentona. (Mentona recalls the first verse of Mosen's poem *Andreas Hofer,* which Freud quoted in his letter to Fliess: "In Mantua. . . .") Mentona, the younger of the two girls, was so named because she had been conceived in the city of Menton, France, where Fanny and Heinrich Moser were having a "second honeymoon." Mentona carried her parents' happy memories in her name. Later she became associated with a tragic event. She was just a few weeks old when her father died of a heart attack while reading his newspaper at breakfast. Heinrich Moser's sudden passing prompted his side of the family to accuse Fanny Moser publicly of having poisoned her husband for his money. The name Moser eventually became so distressingly shameful to her that at one point she asked her daughters not to use it. The shame did not derive from the alleged murder, since Fanny Moser was cleared of all charges following two autopsies performed on her late husband. Fanny Moser's shame was due to her having been slandered in public, to having been at the center of an ugly scandal. At the time, her name appeared all too frequently in the local press. Even though she had been born into the nobility and was cleared of any wrongdoing, her scandal-tainted name made her an outcast. (For further biographical information see Ola Andersson's article.) It is understandable why Freud felt that he could not divulge the sad circumstances of the scandal that besmirched Fanny Moser's name after her exceedingly rich husband's death.

Based on this biographical sketch, it is possible to interpret at least one of Emmy von N.'s major symptoms, her violent fear of animals. Freud recounts a hallucination of hers about an apprentice who tied up a young boy and put a white mouse in his mouth. The boy died of fright. (The patient claimed to have read this in the newspaper but, Freud tells us, the article in fact contained no reference to mice.) On another occasion Freud says: "I unfortunately failed to enquire into the significance of Frau Emmy's animal visions" (*S,* 62). It is not impossible to repair this oversight now and it may be helpful to speculate at the same time about Freud's reasons for not inquiring further. Fanny Moser's animal hallucinations, which sometimes were followed by pictures of corpses (cf. *S,* 53), have a double bearing on her husband's death. On one occasion, Fanny Moser made the following statement (as recorded by Freud):

She; had had some fearful dreams. The legs and arms of the chairs were all turned into snakes; a monster with a vulture's beak was tearing and eating at her all over her body; other wild animals leapt upon her, etc. She then passed on to other animal-deliria, which, however, she qualified with the addition "That was real" (not a dream): how (on an earlier occasion) she was going to pick up a ball of wool, and it was a mouse and ran away; how she had been on a walk, and a big toad suddenly jumped out at her, and so on. I saw that my general prohibition had been ineffective and that I should have taken her frightening impressions away from her one by one. I took an opportunity of asking her, too, why she had gastric pains and what they came from. (I believe that all her attacks of zoopsia [animal hallucinations] are accompanied by gastric pains.) Her answer, which she gave rather grudgingly, was that she did not know. I requested her to remember by tomorrow. She then said in a definitely grumbling tone that I was not to keep on asking her where this and that came from, but let her tell me what she had to say. I fell in with this, and she went on without preface: "When they carried him out, I could not believe he was dead." (So she was talking of her husband again, and I saw now the cause of her ill-humor was that she had been suffering from the residues of this story which had been kept back.) After this, she said, she had hated her child for three years, because she always told herself that she might have been able to nurse her husband back to health if she had not been in bed on account of the child. And then after her husband's death there had been nothing but insults and agitations. His relatives, who had always been against the marriage and had then been angry because they had been so happy together, had spread a rumor that she had poisoned him so that she had wanted to demand an enquiry. Her relatives had involved her in all kinds of legal proceedings with the help of a shady journalist. The wretch had sent around agents to stir people up against her. He got the local papers to print libelous articles about her, and then sent her the cuttings. (S, 62–63)

The vultures and wild animals tearing at her and her past happiness were her husband's relatives. Her hallucinations about mice provide the decisive clue, since *Maus* (mouse) and *Mäuse* (mice) much resemble the German pronunciation (tending to drop the final r) of her husband's name, Moser. The setting for her first hallucination about mice was a newspaper. There can be no doubt that Fanny Moser's life trauma had been the mistreatment and public opprobrium she had had to endure. Her hallucinations and fear of animals derived form the terrible stories the Moser (*Mäuse:* mice) family circulated on her account. Here is where Freud's passing mention of Mephisto as the master of animals (S, 87) can be made more significant. In Scene 3 of Goethe's *Faust,* Mephisto is shown surrounded by wild animals in the witches' kitchen. As a well-educated

German-speaker, Fanny Moser certainly knew the scene and it must have played on her imagination. In sum, Fanny Moser's animal phobias seem to me to have sprung from three separate sources, each denoting a different aspect of her situation: (1) her persecutors behaved like wild beasts and she had cause to fear them; (2) she was being slandered and persecuted on account of her husband by his relatives, so she included a resonance of her married name in her hallucinations; (3) she took in the accusation and saw herself as a witch, basing her idea of witches on her readings in school, for example *Faust*. Her unpleasant tics (such as her spastic stammer and the clacking of her tongue) indicate that her illness was due in part to her unwitting identification with the image others had painted of her as a repulsive witch.

Let me return now to Freud. The restlessness about hysteria in his letter to Fliess (31 August 1898) concerned the question of childhood traumas versus fantasies. Emma Eckstein (or *Ananas*-Irma of the nose) had resolved this question for herself in December 1897, but Freud continued to remain uncertain for some time to come. The year 1897 witnessed a series of important events in Freud's personal and professional life. On 5 March 1897, there was the death of Joseph Freud, an uncle who had been imprisoned in 1866 for four years in the Austrian prison at Stein. (He had been arrested and tried on charges of selling counterfeit rubles and being connected to an international network of counterfeiters.)[12] A few months after his uncle's death Freud made his first decisive break with the traumatic aetiology of hysteria. I do not want to jump to conclusions but I have every reason to believe that Freud could not help but recall his family's trauma on some level (he was ten years old in 1866) when his uncle died and on the occasion of his uncle's funeral. Joseph Freud died in March 1897; in September of the same year Freud revoked his theory of the traumatic origins of hysteria. Yet his letters to Fliess continued to indicate that he could not do so unequivocally or with complete peace of mind. Did he hope that by rejecting his (and Breuer's) theory of trauma, he could avoid feeling the pain of his own family's traumas? Did his technique of deleting Emmy von N.'s traumatic memories foreshadow his subsequent rejection of trauma in the aetiology of hysteria? Let me note for the moment that Fanny Moser's "scandal" received full coverage in the newspapers in the 1880s just as Joseph Freud's trial had in 1866. Both families were shamed, their names publicly

12. [For factual information and documents drawn from the criminal investigation of Joseph Freud, see Marianne Krüll's biography (1979), now available in English in *Freud and His Father* (New York: W. W. Norton, 1986), pp. 164–66. Torok verified the authenticity of the relevant documents, visiting the *Oesterreichisches Staatsarchiv*, Vienna, in 1977 with her colleague Barbro Sylwan.]

sullied. A connection (whether conscious or unconscious) must have emerged in Freud's mind between his own family's and Fanny Moser's suffering. His uncle's death in 1897 would have reawakened the connection. Freud's letter to Fliess (26 August 1898) seems to corroborate the relationship: (1) Joseph Freud had been chained in his prison cell (his sentence included the phrase *schwerer Kerker*, heavy imprisonment, which in those days implied chains tied to the ankle); (2) Andreas Hofer in the poem quoted by Freud is in chains; (3) Julius Mosen, whose name was obstructed in Freud's mind by the sound cluster *au*, most likely reminded him of Au where Fanny Moser lived.

I ask once more: why did Freud wipe out Fanny Moser's traumatic recollections? Why did he not suspect some connection between her frightful hallucinations about mice and her own name (*Mäuse:* Moser)? We know very well that Freud was far from lacking the ability to make such links, since shortly thereafter he went on to champion their use in the study of psychopathology. We cannot even claim that his ear for verbal subtleties developed long after his treatment of Fanny Moser, since as early as 1895 he had published her case history with a title showing Freud's skill in utilizing anagrams. In fact, taking my reading of the German title a step further, I can demonstrate that the key word *Maus* did not really escape Freud's notice. "Emmy von N. . . , aus Livland": Vonny M-aus: Fanny MAUS. Freud concealed Fanny Moser's identity by way of referring to her distinctive symptom of hallucinating an article in the newspaper about mice. Does this mean that Freud did indeed hear the connection *Mäuse:* Moser and that he could have localized the source of his patient's animal phobias in the public slurs the Moser family had inflicted on her? My answer is definitely yes. But if Freud did not actually communicate his inner intuition, either to himself or to his patient, it was because for him the combination of hearing and deleting proved more compelling. At one point in the case study Freud noted that his technique of extinction remained ineffectual unless he had listened to every single detail of Emmy von N.'s account. "When three days ago, she had first complained about her fear of animals, I had interrupted her after her first story. . . . I now saw that I had gained nothing by this interruption and that I cannot avoid listening to her stories in every detail to the very end" (S, 61). Freud listened to everything, then extinguished it all. Listening here is invariably followed by deletion. Freud listens to everything, sometimes even twice, in order to make sure he has deleted it all permanently.

> I observed that she had in mind the same story during the hypnosis and which I thought I had wiped out (S, 79) . . . in the end these symptoms had come to be attached not solely to the initial traumas but to a long

chain of memories associated with them, which I had omitted to wipe out. (*S, 75*)

What memory did Freud try to expunge in himself as he was disposing of Fanny Moser's recollections? The indications collected so far point me in three directions: the poet Julius Mosen's name, Fanny Moser's name, and her residence in Au (since this was the sound cluster Freud was reminded of when speaking of Mosen in his letter to Fliess). Checking the various meanings of the word *Au* in German surprisingly permits us to link this word directly to both Mosen or Moser through one of its synonyms, namely *Moos*, meaning swamp. The word *Moos* also has the slang meaning of money. Fanny Moser, Julius Mosen, and his poem ("In Mantua the faithful Andreas Hofer was put in chains") converge to suggest an occurrence having to do with money. Is this related to the counterfeit rubles that landed Joseph Freud in the prison where he was chained, like the hero of Julius Mosen's poem? No one can prove this, but I can offer it as a hypothesis, especially since Fanny's husband, Heinrich Moser, amassed his immense fortune through business ventures in Russia. In deleting Fanny Moser's memories, Freud is attempting perhaps to erase the residues of the counterfeiting trial that disrupted his family in 1865–66. This idea is sustained by the common meaning of *Moser* in Yiddish (a language Freud already knew as a child), imported into German thieves' cant, namely betrayer, informer, snitch.[13] (The variant forms of this word are *Moisser, Mosserer, Mauser;* the verbal form is *mosern* or *mossern.*) Did the therapy of erasure mean that Freud need not betray his family, need not ever reveal the counterfeit story, expunging to the last detail all of his painful memories? This is also what Fanny Moser must have meant for Freud. Her name (*Moser:* money; betrayer) and her life circumstances (a widely publicized scandal about her inheritance of the fortune her husband had earned in Russia) surely reminded Freud of his own family's past traumas and prompted him to depart significantly from Breuer's therapeutic procedure. He could not help but wipe out, expunge, remove all the memories he could elicit, promising his patient (and no doubt himself) that this would lead to "her being freed from the expectation of misfortune which perpetually tormented her" (*S,* 61). In my view, Freud's account of Fanny Moser's case is the memorial of this accomplishment.

The examples which follow throw light on the behavior of her memory in somnambulism. In conversation one day she expressed her delight at the

---

13. Siegmund A. Wolf, *Wörterbuch des Rotwelschen* (Mannheim: Bibliographisches Institut, 1956).

beauty of a plant in a pot which decorated the entrance hall of the nursing home. "But what is its name, doctor? Do you know? I used to know its German and its Latin names, but I've forgotten them both." She had a wide knowledge of plants, while I was obliged on this occasion to admit my lack of botanical education. A few minutes later I asked her under hypnosis if she now knew the name of the plant in the hall. Without any hesitation she replied: "The German name is 'Türkenlilie' [Turks'-cap lily]; I really have forgotten the Latin one." Another time, when she was feeling in good health, she told me of a visit she had paid to the Roman Catacombs, but could not recall two technical terms; nor could I help her with them. Immediately afterward I asked her under hypnosis which words she had in mind. But she did not know them in hypnosis either. So I said to her: "Don't bother about them any more now, but when you are in the garden tomorrow between five and six in the afternoon—nearer six than five—they will suddenly occur to you." Next evening, while we were talking about something which had no connection with catacombs, she suddenly burst out: "'Crypt,' doctor, and 'Columbarium.'"

Crypt and columbarium denote Roman burial places, but they also evoke the silence of the grave. Once erased, the traumatic memory will never again speak. "'Crypt,' doctor, and 'columbarium.'" I will be silent like you.

When you visit Schaffhausen, the town in Switzerland which still bears the powerful imprint of Heinrich Moser's industrious hand, when you visit the municipal museum, you can see Fanny Moser's guest book bound in richly grained red leather. A picture of her castle at Au decorates the frontispiece. Inside you will find the names of her guests, Bleuler, Wetterstrand, poets, intellectuals, many of whom improvised little poems or inscriptions playing with the name Au. A line dated 18 July 1889 seizes my attention. It says simply, without flourish: Dr. Sigm. Freud, Wien. Around it you can still see the trace of a strip of paper that had covered it and was carefully removed. Is this a vestige of Fanny Moser's unwitting response to Freud's therapy of deletion?

Part VII

Psychoanalytic Communion

Editor's Note Maria Torok delivered "Theoretra" orally in 1981 at Brunel University in England as an introduction to a panel discussion about Melanie Klein, based on research initiated by Torok with the participation of two colleagues, Adèle Covello and Barbro Sylwan. (Torok's contribution "Melanie Klein or Melanie Mell? The Vicissitudes of a Traumatic Name," 1982, will appear in volume 2 of this work.) "Theoretra" (published in 1982) is part of Torok's effort, ongoing since 1976, to demonstrate the possibility and usefulness of analyzing the psychological roots of psychoanalytic theories (see Torok's "Remembrance of Things Deleted: Between Sigmund Freud and Emmy von N." in this volume). This project had led Torok and myself as collaborator to study the history of the psychoanalytic movement as well as the emotional milieu of its early participants.[1] The almost poetic tone of "Theoretra" allows a great

1. Representative examples of this work include Torok's "L'os de la fin: Quelques jalons pour l'étude du verbarium freudien," *Cahiers Confrontation* 1, no. 1 (Spring 1979): 163–88; "What Is Occult in Occultism: Between Sigmund Freud and Sergei Pankeiev Wolf Man," in *The Wolf Man's Magic Word*

variety of themes to be compressed into a few pages. The historical focus of the piece is Freud's mysterious mistrust of Sandor Ferenczi's clinical discoveries after 1931. Ferenczi was Freud's most intimate friend and trusted lieutenant between 1910 and 1933, a period during which the two men exchanged more than three thousand letters. Torok immersed herself in the unpublished Freud-Ferenczi correspondence, made available to her in typescript by Judith Dupont (heir and executor of Ferenczi's intellectual estate), as she composed "Theoretra." Torok later wrote a full account of the impression the letters made on her in "The Freud-Ferenczi Correspondence: The Life of the Letter in the History of Psychoanalysis" (1983; to appear in volume 2 of this work).

"Theoretra" questions the notion that theories can be applied to the psychotherapy of people. Torok seems to call for a psychoanalytic art of giving up theory, when theory entails a separation from the actual life experience of patients. Theory can become a form of rigidly cold observation, even the instrument of manipulative terror, as opposed to being the reflective by-product of a free-flowing and continuously open-ended process of sympathetic understanding. Probing the Greek word *theoretra*, Torok provides an allegory of psychoanalysis as the exchange of gifts between patient and analyst. Patients reveal the inmost recesses of their minds and hearts; the analyst gives the gift of listening. For Torok, listening means to summon and welcome the voices patients cannot hear in themselves. The psychoanalytic dialogue then is a joint conjuring of dead voices, either the voices of dead relatives or the faint voice of dead secrets, nameless hurts, and stifled sufferings. This description of psychoanalysis as the invocation and revival of unlaid ghosts, with the purpose of finally giving them their deserved psychic rest, condenses the substance of Abraham and Torok's discoveries concerning obstacles in the path of our ability to transcend trauma or accept loss (see Part IV of this volume) as well as Abraham's theory of the transgenerational phantom, the poster-

---

(Minneapolis: University of Minnesota Press, 1986); Rand and Torok's "La psychanalyse de Freud devant son secret," in Nicholas Rand's *Le cryptage et la vie des oeuvres: Du secret dans les textes de Flaubert, Stendhal, Benjamin, Baudelaire, Stefan George, Francis Ponge, Edgar Poe, Heidegger et Freud* (Paris: Aubier, 1989), pp. 147–62; Rand and Torok's "Les cryptes de la psychanalyse," in Jean Nadal et al., *Emprise et liberté* (Paris: L'Harmattan, 1990), pp. 37–66.

ity of family secrets (see Part V). The allusive but sharp rejection of the concept of the death drive suggests Torok's dissatisfaction with Freud's idea of destruction as an a priori and irreducible psychic force rather than as the result of dramas that are in principle open to analysis and understanding, if not resolution.

FIFTEEN

Theoretra: An Alternative to Theory

M. Torok, 1982

M any people think that the psychoanalytic voyage entails our putting into practice a number of theories previously put into practice by others. This supposes that theorizing and practice belong to two disparate realms. Some people also think that the best thing that could happen to an idea is for it to be applied to malleable and compliant objects.

From the couch or the analyst's chair, a word may sweep you off to unknown shores in a whole host of ways. In such cases, an etymological or cryptological plunge into the word shatters our segregating manner of conceiving things. A consideration of the word "theory" (as in the title of our colloquium *Theory in Practice*) should serve as proof. The meanings of this word provide many paths: brilliance, voyage, spectacle or theater; consulting the oracle; the place of the consultation; speculation, the place of speculation or contemplation; coherence of thought, etc.; finally, the word comes to abolish the distinction between theory and practice through one of its related forms, namely *theoretra*.

Theoretra occurs between the bride and the bridegroom. Both are expecting presents from each other: she will lift her veil, he will hand her gifts. This moment of *theoretra*, I will call *theoretric*. The theoretric moment clinches the pact of a long journey to come, a journey that the brilliance (*theo*) filtering through the uplifted veil serves to announce discreetly, confidently, theoretical-practically, theoretrically.

This gift of the Greeks I have no reason to fear. Because the word is crucial to me. I look for the advent of its obvious illumination, especially during the "preliminary sessions" and at the close of analyses, but the word gives me genuine sustenance throughout the entire analytic adventure; it greets me, it bolsters my confidence. Every time I experience its approach, the full depth of its complexity, I say to myself: there it is, there! It is,

Previously published as "Théorêtra," *Cahiers confrontation* 8 (1982): 129–32. (The subtitle was provided by Nicholas Rand for the purposes of this translation.)

after all, possible. Promise. Hope. Promise of what? Hope of what? As these questions rise up in me, once again theoretra gives a "push" to the "what." Promise of promise. Hope of hope. Seed of seed. Life of life. Love of love.

He or she is dead. Yet a tiny something survives, emerges from its hiding place. From under the veil, he or she lets me catch a glimpse, hear a whisper of some continuing faint movement or noise. There is a murmur, a ventriloquy, rising from the tomb in which he or she or someone else, either a contemporary or an ancestor, was buried alive, sequestered, with their desires cut out, deprived of both life and death; and above all, something has been left *unsettled.*

No, I do not really look for it. But it does happen, it is coming, already in our midst, even now present in a common "yes." Theoretra. Is it a form of reciprocal introjection? Do we thereby receive a house to abide in each other? Is theoretra a welcoming acceptance, an entrance? Words come, sit down, speak to each other. Is this perhaps what Ferenczi, in his last years, called trance, the moment he would never set into a theory? As a result, we cannot use this idea as an instrument of terror, as anxiety, panic, or institution. At the most, we can shape it into a hypothetical stretch of the imagination. We cannot say with theoretra that we need to apply the theories of yesterday, today, tomorrow: (1) in order to transform persecutory anxiety into depressive anxiety; (2) to make the depressive withstand the assaults of the death instinct, retaliation, vengeance, and the persecutive effects of the Breast, the Penis, Feces, or the total Object; (3) we cannot say that envy must yield to gratitude and hate to love; finally, (4) we cannot be expected to produce the Oedipus complex, its dissolution, the parricide, or the incestuous, blinding, and fateful marriage.

No, in the *theoretric* moment there is *trance.* Right there, the two partners will on occasion fall asleep together, dream the same word, the same image, for an instant, and for once have a real session, a seance, to summon the specter, the spirit of the spirit of Spirit itself, assassinated by some ghost. The theoretric moment is always preceded by a long series of seances. The absent spirits arrive not so much through invocation as through a convoking summons. For them to rap, for them to want to rap, the spirits need to understand that their absence has always already been a presence in the form of unrecognized knowledge, a *nescience.* They must understand that we were able to surmise this.

An arm plunges to the bottom of a well, retrieving a wet angel. Is it still breathing? Enough perhaps for its unacknowledged murder [*ange:* a murdered baby from *faiseuse d'anges:* killer of unwanted babies] to have caused an entire generation of descendants to suffer from asthma, lung ailments, bronchitis, stifling diseases, be haunted by obsession or anxieties.

And certainly "reparation" will not answer the question: how to bury the unburied, how to settle in and for ourselves the lot of the unburied dead? Here is matter for a seance. Sandor Ferenczi had tended to withdraw in his final years into these seance-like sessions. Ernest Jones believed he was mad. Mad for wanting to stay close to his patients? Ferenczi gave up everything, the presidency of the International Psychoanalytic Association, political ambition, and even a passionate and bruising love affair; he gave up all that to understand the seance, the trance, the essence of traumas in the greatest detail. As for traumas, he dreamed of a complete and scar-free recovery. Was he giving lessons to Freud? Certainly, the facts declare it, though Ferenczi himself suspected nothing. He set an example for Freud, whose illness could not, in Ferenczi's eyes, excuse him when in a letter Freud wrote that he was "fed up," that "I have had it to here with therapy." Fed up, enough of that! All right, Freud was really ill, but so was Ferenczi, though Freud did not really know that. The *theoretical* Freud could not understand the *practical* Ferenczi, who, as Freud put it, merely wanted to cure people. And since Freud rejected all those who, even at a great remove, might have attempted to come near his own traumas, the only path left to Ferenczi, and all others like him, was to withdraw, to retreat into the seance. I can hear a voice calling to Vienna in 1931: "You won't accept my essay 'Child-Analysis in the Analysis of Adults'? All right, I'll stay on in Budapest. I know I am about to die, my blood is getting thinner, I am being sucked dry by a vampire, stifling in my chest." It is called *Atemnot*, need of air in German, dyspnoea. Jones had written about this phenomenon in 1911 that it constituted the essence of nightmares: a feeling of oppression in the chest, *Alp* [*Alptraum,* German for nightmare], vampire, devil, horse, possession, incubus. Is this Ferenczi dreaming through Jones? Or is Jones dreaming Ferenczi dreaming Freud's nightmare? Dreaming the nightmare Freud could never dream for himself? In any case, Ferenczi, the "madman" of Budapest, unrelentingly implored Freud in 1933 to leave Vienna for a more secure country. Ferenczi knew that every breath was also an inspiration. And if he wants to continue the session, he will need a lot of breath. . . .[1] Because Ferenczi expected that the slab sealing the crypt of his *theoretra* would be thick indeed.

The Sultan's sky predicted the great Vizir's death (see Freud's 1933 necrology for Ferenczi). Five years after his passing, the Sultan, with a disease gnawing at his bones, was raising the paladin's question, not knowing that it had been Ferenczi's question all along (see Freud's "The Splitting of the Ego in the Process of Defense," 1938). Freud is wondering:

---

1. [This is an oblique reference to Freud's famous phrase "La séance continue" after his daughter Sophie's sudden and traumatic death in 1920.—Ed.]

is it new or have I always known it . . . , the self-sectioning (autotomy), described by Ferenczi as a potential consequence of traumas.[2] Yet the hand forming these lines in 1938 stopped in midcourse as it had ceased to be extended to his friend. And most certainly, it was not a writer's cramp that forever interrupted the two friends' theoretric encounter.

Why so much effort, all these gravediggers, morticians; and why all the laurels and honors heaped upon the survivors, so that they may stifle, ridicule, and pronounce mad the vitals of a thought which asks only to live? Why? Unless it is that the dead within the dead force the living to perform a *danse macabre*. How to warn the brides and the bridegrooms and make them see that this work of death being wrought in them, is a death which is definitely *not a drive*.

2. [Ferenczi's 1933 article, "Confusion of Tongues between Adults and the Child" deals with the atomization and fragmentation or splitting of the personality due to trauma.—Ed.]

Selected Bibliography

WRITINGS FOCUSING ON ABRAHAM AND TOROK'S WORKS OR INSPIRED BY THEM

Derrida, Jacques. *"Fors:* The Anglish Words of Nicolas Abraham and Maria Torok,"* Foreword, trans. Barbara Johnson, to *The Wolf Man's Magic Word: A Cryptonymy,* by Nicolas Abraham and Maria Torok, trans. Nicholas T. Rand, pp. xi–xlviii. Minneapolis: University of Minnesota Press, 1986.

———. "Me-Psychoanalysis: An Introduction to the Translation of 'The Shell and the Kernel' by Nicolas Abraham," trans. Richard Klein, *Diacritics* 9, no. 1 (1979): 4–16.

Dumas, Didier. *L'ange et le fantôme.* Paris: Minuit, 1985.

———. *Hantise et clinique de l'autre.* Paris: Aubier, 1989.

Kamuf, Peggy. "Abraham's Wake." *Diacritics* 9, no. 1 (1979): 32–45.

Lukacher, Ned. *Primal Scenes: Literature, Philosophy, and Psychoanalysis.* Ithaca: Cornell University Press, 1986.

Nachin, Claude. *Le deuil d'amour.* Paris: Editions Universitaires, 1989.

———. *Fantômes de l'âme: Des héritages psychiques.* Paris: L'Harmattan, 1993.

Rand, Nicholas. "Translator's Introduction: Toward a Cryptonymy of Literature." In *The Wolf Man's Magic Word: A Cryptonymy,* by Nicolas Abraham and Maria Torok, pp. li–lxix. Minneapolis: University of Minnesota Press, 1986.

———. "Family Romance or Family History? Psychoanalysis and Dramatic Invention in Nicolas Abraham's *The Phantom of Hamlet.*" *Diacritics* 18, no. 4 (1988): 20–30.

———. *Le cryptage et la vie des oeuvres: Du secret dans les textes de Flaubert, Stendhal, Benjamin, Baudelaire, Stefan George, Edgar Poe, Francis Ponge, Heidegger, et Freud.* Paris: Aubier, 1989.

———. "The Red and the Black, Author of *Stendhal.*" *Romanic Review* 80, no. 3 (1989): 391–403.

————. "The Truth of Heidegger's 'Logos': Hiding in Translation." *PMLA* 105 (1990): 436–47.

Rand, Nicholas, and Maria Torok. "Paradeictic: Translation, Psychoanalysis, and the Work of Art in the Writings of Nicolas Abraham." *Diacritics* 16, no. 3 (1986): 16–25.

Rashkin, Esther. *Family Secrets and the Psychoanalysis of Narrative.* Princeton: Princeton University Press, 1992.

Ronell, Avital. *Dictations: On Haunted Writing.* Bloomington: Indiana University Press, 1986.

Royle, Nicholas. *Telepathy and Literature.* London: Blackwell, 1991.

Tisseron, Serge. *Tintin chez le psychanalyste.* Paris: Aubier-Archimbaud, 1985.

————. *Tintin et les secrets de famille.* Paris: Librairie Séguier, 1990.

————. *La honte: Psychanalyse d'un lien social.* Paris: Dunod, 1992.

Index

Abraham, Karl, 80, 103n1; and introjection and incorporation, 102,
110, 111, 111n3; and melancholia,
134–35; sexual activity and mourning of interest to, 102–3, 107,
108, 109, 110, 115
Abraham, Nicolas, 103n1; distillation
of ideas of, 5–6; emigration from
Hungary to France of, 1–2, 15;
theoretical forebears of, 7, 7n5, 8,
15, 16, 17; writings of, 2, 2n1, 3,
4, 23–24
Abreaction, 8–9, 179–80
Affect, 76, 82, 91, 92
Anasemia, 3, 7n5, 75 (see also Language, and psychoanalysis); defined, 85–86, 105; and myths, 94;
and the Oedipus complex, 95; and
the paradoxes of psychoanalytic interpretation, 77, 78; of sex, 88–89;
and symbol, 86–87
Andersson, Ola, 242, 243
Andreas Hofer (Mosen), 243
Antisemantics, 75, 84–86
Archaic heritage, 168–69
Assault on Truth (Masson), 228, 235
"At Sea" (Maupassant), 12, 13, 19

Behaviorism, 81, 82
Bernheim, Hippolyte, 237, 238, 241
Brentano, 93
Breuer, Joseph, 8, 117, 240n9, 245;
cathartic psychotherapy of, 236,
237–38, 239–40, 241, 247

Camus, Albert, 19
Case of Jonah (Abraham), 101, 208

Castration, 10, 33, 53n4, 88, 135; de-
fined, 152; and the Oedipus com-
plex, 96, 97; and penis envy, 44,
69, 70; and phobia, 177, 178, 181,
182; and repression, 177, 178
Charcot, Jean Martin, 241
Complex: defined, 95
"Confusion of Tongues between
Adults and the Child" (Ferenczi),
256n2
Conscious the, 83, 84, 91; nucleic
roots of, 93–94; and the Unconscious of, 5–6, 91, 93
Contes de la Bécasse (Maupassant),
12
Coprophagy, 132, 133
Covello, Adèle, 249
Cryptonymie: Le Verbier de l'Homme
aux Loups. See Wolf Man's Magic
Word
Cryptonymy, 7, 16, 21, 168, 176; de-
fined, 17, 18n12, 104, 105; and
Freud, 18, 18n12; and multilin-
gualism, 18n12; and preservative
repression, 18n13; and the Wolf
Man, 106
Cryptophoria, 146, 152, 158, 159,
160; defined, 131; and hysteria,
134

Death drive, 16; and Freud, 13n8,
15, 175, 251; rejected by Abraham
and Torok, 5, 13n8, 251
Deconstruction, 16–17
De l'art à la mort (M'Uzan), 124n5
Demetaphorization, 126
Derrida, Jacques, 2